THE MAN NEXT DOOR DANCES
the art of Peter Bingham

THE MAN NEXT DOOR DANCES
the art of Peter Bingham

by Kaija Pepper

Toronto, 2007

Published by Dance Collection Danse Press/Presse
145 George Street, Toronto, Ontario Canada M5A 2M6
www.dcd.ca

Library and Archives Canada Cataloguing in Publication

Pepper, Kaija
The man next door dances : the art of Peter Bingham / Kaija Pepper.

Includes bibliographical references and index.
ISBN 978-0-929003-63-4

1. Bingham, Peter, 1951- 2. Dancers--Canada--Biography.
3. Improvisation in dance--Canada. I. Title.

GV1785.B52P46 2007 792.02'8092 C2007-904955-9

Dance Collection Danse gratefully acknowledges the support of the Metcalf Foundation, Charles H. Ivey Foundation, F.K. Morrow Foundation, Woodlawn Arts Foundation, Linda Stearns Estate, and all the individual donors.

 Canada Council   Conseil des Arts
for the Arts   du Canada

ONTARIO ARTS COUNCIL
CONSEIL DES ARTS DE L'ONTARIO

torontoartscouncil
An arm's length body of the City of Toronto

Table of Contents

Acknowledgements | vii

Foreword | ix

Author's Note | xiii

Waltzing With Grandma | 1

A Radical Time and Place | 11

First Contact | 25

Making EDAM | 37

Coming and Going in the Garden of EDAM | 51

And Then There Were Four | 69

Gift of a Lifetime | 79

Dreamtigers | 91

Just People Dancing | 103

A Case for Improvisation | 115

Remember Me From Then | 125

Born Naked, Died Blonde | 133

A Simple Act of Balance | 143

Vuelta | 151

Deserving Isadora | 157

This Particular Place | 167

A Man Dancing | 173

List of Works by Peter Bingham | 177

Source Notes | 181

Index | 193

Acknowledgments

One of the highlights of researching this book was the chance to talk with many of the people involved in Peter Bingham's story. These included in-person and telephone interviews with Bingham's colleagues from the creative and management sides, as well as with those who were close observers of the scene. Sincere thanks to John Alleyne, Sheenah Andrews, Serge Bennathan, Marc Boivin, Barbara Clausen, Daniel Collins, Coat Cooke, Anne Cooper, Mary Craig, Daelik, Susan Elliott, Jane Ellison, Bruce Fraser, Mona Hamill, Andrew de Lotbinière Harwood, Karen Jamieson, Ziyian Kwan, Mark Lavelle, Monique Léger, Michael Linehan, Lola MacLaughlin, Jennifer Mascall, Lee Masters, Kathleen McDonagh, Jaci Metivier, Crystal Pite, Chris Randle, Linda Rubin, Peter Ryan, Sylvain Senez, Paris Simons, Nancy Stark Smith, Chick Snipper, Tom Stroud, Gina Sufrin, Wen Wei Wang, Brian Webb and Elizabeth Zimmer. Jay Hirabayashi made himself available for more than one conversation, and also gave me free access to his extensive archival material.

Phone interviews with Sarah Baumert and Jennifer McLeish-Lewis, who were training with Bingham at the time, as well as email exchanges with Dena Davida, Peggy Florin, Helen Clarke Lapin and Savannah Walling, supplied helpful background information. My conversations with Montague Bingham and the late Father Jim Roberts are deeply appreciated.

I am grateful to Maureen Riches of *Dance International* magazine and Megan Andrews of *The Dance Current*, who over the years have published my reviews of Peter Bingham's work. Since the performances themselves are not, of course, available for viewing, these records were key to recreating my particular understanding of the past. Stimulating conversations with Miriam Adams, involved from the first draft of the manuscript, and with Mary Kelly, who read a later draft, helped to develop and articulate my ideas.

Much appreciated financial support from the Canada Council for the Arts allowed for some of the time needed to research this project. Also deeply appreciated is the support of Dance Collection Danse, whose archives and design team contributed expertise and enthusiasm.

Finally, thanks must go to Peter Bingham, whose substantial body of work provided multi-faceted and challenging material that was rewarding to explore through the process of writing this book.

Kaija Pepper

Foreword

By Max Wyman

I arrived in Vancouver in the spring that preceded the Summer of Love: April 1967. The city's first Easter Be-In had just been held in Stanley Park. Kitsilano was wreathed in a mellow vibe. Much of the rest of the upright citizenry was aghast; merchants organized to have the hippies ousted.

Forty years on, it's a very different city. The uptight Outpost of Empire has become a welcoming, polyglot Pacific Rim metropolis. And the protest movement of the late 1960s and early 1970s has been diluted to a fashion statement: tie-dyed cottons and bare feet, the costume of choice on Fourth Avenue in those days, have been replaced by Lululemon gear (inspired by yogawear and originating in, of course, Kitsilano), and Kitsilano itself has become a trendy, up-market residential enclave.

What has endured – indeed, what has become to many a permanent identifier for the city – is the spirit of Lotusland that those days generated: laid-back, hedonistic, characterized by a kind of languid, meditative searching, vaguely spiritual in nature, vaguely related to the abundant natural beauty of the city's surroundings, deeply introspective. It is a city where connection with one's feelings sometimes seems to take precedence over hard-edged intellectual inquiry … a place where the spontaneous, personalized response is invited.

All of which, of course, makes Vancouver an ideal home for the kind of dance research that has been undertaken by Peter Bingham: a lifelong inquiry into the nature and possibilities of contact improvisation, itself a form of (in Elizabeth Zimmer's happy phrase, quoted here) "moving meditation".

As can be seen from Kaija Pepper's perceptive and illuminating biography, it is possible to trace some of Bingham's formative roots to that early Vancouver hippie movement, which makes a nicely convenient contextual bridge for the work he has done and continues to do. But other characteristics of Vancouver also play into his work, and underline its unique role and seminal importance in the city's evolving arts story.

It is often remarked, for instance, that made-in-Vancouver art is out of step with trends on the wider arts scene. There is more than a grain of truth in the assertion. The city is so far from anywhere that much of what happens in the rest of Canada – in the rest of the *world* – passes the city by. Its creators can exercise their imaginations with perhaps more freedom than those in a more "connected" place, in the sense that they are not forever being forced to measure up to someone else's expectations.

At the same time, the city's proximity to the wilderness – it is encircled by ocean and forest and mountains and sky – encourages an intimacy with the natural that sometimes seems at odds with the intellectual and technological trends in other metropolitan centres.

A third reality that contributes to Vancouver's particularity is its richly threaded pattern of demographic diversity. Over 100 languages are heard daily in the city's streets, businesses, schools and homes. This interplay and overlay of cultural influences inevitably affects the flavour, look and content of the art the city's artists make, and at a far more subtle and complex level than a simple superimposition of overt cultural signifiers.

These factors help to explain why the art of Vancouver artists has so often been out of alignment with what has gone on elsewhere. They also illuminate the phenomenon of Bingham and his evolving exploration of contact improvisation as a creative tool (that is, seeing what happens when bodies move together in an unplanned way), as well as the dance audience's willingness to follow him in his explorations.

While many of us understand choreography to consist of finished works of movement art, there has always been an audience – sometimes, admittedly, a painfully small one – for the process by which movement art is made. With EDAM (Experimental Dance and Music) – the group Bingham and his colleagues founded in 1982 and which he now directs – we have watched creation happen through the process of contact improvisation, and at the same time been able to monitor the exposed artistic maturing of creative individuals ... a generous sharing that has its own distinct pleasures. Movement of the specific moment and probably no other ... its exposure in real time of an individual's physical, mental, imaginative, psychic resources through the medium of the unchoreographed body ... in such a context, its appeal was undeniable. How could this not resonate with the Westcoast post-hippie, post-counter-culture ethos of individual freedoms, self-perfection and the defiance of the accepted way?

Although not always, of course. From the viewer's side of things, it sometimes seemed as if performances in the early EDAM years were of more value to the performers than to us in the audience. Everyone who attends contact shows has probably experienced the occasional desire to throw a shoe at the performing space in frustration. On the other hand, I've been at contact presentations where the inspiration has been running so freely that the audience has responded to the spontaneous finesses with murmurs of approval, the way a crowd shows its admiration for the skills of a bullfighter.

Something else, though, has had to be present to hold the audience's interest for all these years. And that has been the way that Bingham and his EDAM collaborators of dancers and musicians have pioneered in the exploration of what improvised movement and music might be able to do. Experiment, after all, was built into the company's name, and this story of his artistic life makes it clear that, very early on, he chose to steer clear of the easy option and commit to that principle as his basic *raison d'être* – as performer, as choreographer, as mentor/presenter … and, in no small measure, as an access point and ongoing reference for a whole generation of audience members.

Luckily for his audiences, that meant taking the kaleidoscope that is contact improvisation and shaking it hard to see what new pictures it might produce. We have travelled with him from contact improvisation at its purest – two bodies (it's usually two) interacting without any pre-set plan – to a form of choreographed dance theatre in which the spirit of improvisation persists but the structure has more definition.

Slowly, over time, the work began to take on new textures and nuances, to carry colourations of emotion or intent: a kind of abstracted imagism, even an abstracted drama. Though some might say it always had this – even at its most deliberately non-significant – the interplay of human bodies carries overtones of trust, support, shared balance and flow, countervailing strengths. Layered into the flood of fresh abstraction were tiny elements of what we might recognize as theatre – a facial gesture, sometimes the use of fingers and hands, sometimes the manner in which Bingham moved and carried himself, sometimes the dancers' willingness to pick up on a movement event – a turn, say, or a lift – and give it a continuing life.

The contact improvisation purists that I talk to in other places scoff at this kind of almost-theatricality. It is a distortion of the original intent, they say, it blunts the edge of pure movement inquiry. Perhaps that is so. But the work is Bingham's. And it is interesting. And it is very much a product of where he works and why he does the work he does. It is indissolubly linked to his lifelong "passionate commitment to the investigation of movement itself" … an early and enduring EDAM mantra. And he offers it to us with freshness, curiosity and generosity, confident that those of us who have chosen to make our lives in this unique and mysterious part of the world – and not only those who have survived from the Summer of Love – will remain willing to join him on the journey.

Author's Note

The Man Next Door Dances begins with Peter Bingham's formative years growing up in the 1950s and 1960s. Then, as his life begins to be driven by a passion for and commitment to dance, the focus is on the art and on the all-consuming creative act.

Studying Bingham's work so closely and gaining access to the choreographic process from behind the scenes – through video records, archival material and interviews with the artistic team – has been a great adventure. The result is an investigation of the "why" and the "how" of making dance from Bingham's perspective: Why choose this particular movement? Why make this dance at all? How to begin and how to keep going?

This might seem a bit like peeking under the magician's cape, but there was never any fear the magic would be revealed and the work would lose its luster. The art of dance is such a strange and wonderful thing … surely, that it exists in this world at all will always continue to amaze.

To Lawrence Adams, who set this book in motion

And to Miriam Adams, who continues the dance

Peter Bingham, 1961.

Waltzing With Grandma

I used to catch bees with my bare hand, then let them go. I did that a number of times. One day my mum saw me and said, "Don't do that – it'll sting you." And it did. It's funny the things you remember.
— Peter Bingham

On the day that Peter Alan Bingham was born, life was bright with promise. A feeling of optimism naturally surrounds a healthy newborn baby but, in a larger sense, promise and progress were part of the spirit of the times. Belief in the future was strong and people were eager to look forward, not back to a past in which the horror of World War II had ended only a few years earlier. Families with a handful of children, like the one Peter would grow up in, were common in the post-war baby boom. What shows more faith in the future than bringing a new life into the world?

Etelka Bingham gave birth to Peter, her third son, on May 31, 1951, at St. Paul's Hospital in the west coast city of Vancouver, British Columbia. Etelka Stewart, of Scottish descent, and her husband, Montague Bingham, of English ancestry, were a hardworking, Prairie-born couple who had married in 1946, after knowing each other for just seven weeks. Etelka, often called Telka, was thirty-three years old, though she was willing to claim only thirty, and Montague, or Monty, was twenty-six. Their new baby joined three-year-old Dan and two-year-old Bruce in the family's large, wood-shingled home on York Avenue, across the street from Kitsilano Beach. Etelka, who had been a primary school teacher and then a public health nurse before her first baby, was busy looking after the children and the housekeeping, while Montague went to school.

As a returning serviceman – he had been the navigator on bomber planes during the war – Montague was eligible for subsidized education for veterans, and was studying to become a minister at the Anglican Theological College (now the Vancouver School of Theology) on the University of British Columbia campus. By the time Peter was born, Montague's studies were almost complete, and he had just been made a deacon, serving at St. Christopher's Anglican Church in West Vancouver.

Before enrolling in college, Montague had spent an intense six months finishing high school, having quit in grade eight to work in his father's lumber mill. He remained a practical man throughout his life, and even while completing his studies was able to supplement the family's finances with a small business venture running two dump trucks, one of which he drove himself during the summer. The Binghams also rented out a couple of suites in their house, keeping the large centre apartment, with its upper-floor view of the ocean and the north shore mountains, for themselves.

It was a wonderful part of the city to live in, with the beach just a few steps away. In addition to its natural beauty, the city also had a lively arts and entertainment scene, but Etelka and Montague were too busy to get out much. Raising a family took all their time. "We were fascinated by our kids," Montague recalls. "After each one, we'd say, 'Let's have another.'"

<hr />

However seldom the Binghams took advantage of what the city had to offer in terms of culture, Vancouver was a great place to be. A shipping centre whose economy had benefited from the war, the city was prospering, and the arts scene was rapidly growing. During the 1950s, the Maritime Museum, the main branch of the Vancouver Public Library and the Queen Elizabeth Theatre were all built. The Canadian Broadcasting Corporation opened local television studios in 1953 and, a year later, the locally produced, three-part music and dance series, *Bamboula*, starring the Leonard Gibson Dancers in Afro-Cuban-styled modern choreography, was a national hit.

The Vancouver Symphony Orchestra was well-established and professional theatre flourished. Everyman Theatre's sixth season in 1951 included T. S. Eliot's *Murder in the Cathedral*, as well as plays by Shakespeare, Molière and Chekhov. At Stanley Park's outdoor Malkin Bowl, Theatre Under the Stars showed hit Broadway musicals like *Oklahoma!* and *Kiss Me, Kate*, providing summer employment for local dancers. There was a proliferation of ballet schools, and, the year Peter was born, *Étude*, a sleek, neo-classic quartet by one of Vancouver's high-profile teachers, Kay Armstrong, was the first Canadian choreography taken into the repertoire of the new National Ballet of Canada.

Dance from around the globe was an important part of the cultural scene, with visits from Spanish dancer José Greco, African-American modern dancer Katherine Dunham, and companies from Ceylon, Japan and Israel. Among the international ballet companies making regular west coast stops were the Sadler's Wells Ballet, London's Festival Ballet, American Ballet Theatre and the Ballets Russes de Monte Carlo. *Giselle*, *Swan Lake* and *Coppélia* were regular offerings, as were works by George Balanchine, Léonide Massine, Frederick Ashton, Kenneth MacMillan and Antony Tudor. Michel Fokine was one of the most popular choreographers, and his *Les Sylphides* was featured in numerous company repertoires.

Closer to home were visits from The National Ballet of Canada, whose 1952 mixed bill included Armstrong's *Étude*. When the Royal Winnipeg

Peter Bingham in school photo, 1962.

Ballet toured to Vancouver, works by artistic director Gweneth Lloyd, such as *The Shooting of Dan McGrew* and *Shadow on the Prairie* figured largely in its repertoire.

The demands of work led to the family leaving the city when, in 1954, Montague accepted the post of parish priest in the small northern Cariboo town of Quesnel, a busy centre for the forest industry. That year, Etelka gave birth to her last child, John. Nora Bingham, Montague's recently widowed mother, joined the family to help out with the four boys.

It was tough looking after a family of seven on the salary of a small town priest, so Montague decided to re-enter the air force, resulting in a decade of constant relocation. Montague's first assignment as an air force chaplain was in another small town, Claresholm, Alberta, south of Calgary. Peter started kindergarten there, with a teacher called Auntie Alice, who gave him a toy helicopter for his sixth birthday. The family bought their first black-and-white television, a large set with two antennae called "rabbit ears" perched on top to improve reception. The boys enjoyed watching *The Mickey Mouse Club*, a children's show from the United States with friendly young hosts called "Mouseketeers".

Money was still tight. "I spent carefully," Montague says. "The boys all had the same jackets. I bought a set, and when they outgrew them, they would just hand them down. I always bought one that was bigger than Danny [the eldest] for him to grow into." When it was too cold or wet for the children to play outdoors, he set up inexpensive indoor play. "In the wintertime when the boys were wondering what to do, I gave them a bunch of paper and a bucket. They built trains and other things out of paper, using paste made from flour and water."

After three years, Montague was posted to Calgary, where they lived for another three years before spending a short time in Clinton, Ontario. Despite constantly moving, life had a familiar rhythm comprised of the ordinary acts of childhood. Peter recalls of these years:

I shared a room with at least one brother, if not two. And I remember I had a crystal radio. I'd attach a clip to the radiator heating our bedroom, which acted as an aerial, and then listen through a little earplug. Lots of kids had them.

Montague was away at work during the day, and often went out after supper to attend to his parish, while Peter's mother and grandmother were at home taking care of endless domestic details. Etelka's domain was the kitchen, where she was kept busy baking and cooking. Although the boys preferred evenly sliced, store-bought Wonder Bread over Etelka's homemade baking, an exception was the small loaves she sometimes made for an after-school treat. Peter recalls:

> I loved coming home and getting a loaf baked in a tobacco tin. It looked like a chef's hat, and I'd crack it open and pile in the butter. I also remember the desserts my mom made: butterscotch pudding, bread pudding, banana cream pie. And lemon meringue pie — that was probably my favourite.

On their birthdays, the boys could forgo the family supper. Instead, "the birthday boy" was allowed to choose whatever dessert he wanted and gorge on that as a special treat. Peter usually asked for rice pudding.

Etelka, who disliked being disturbed when she was busy in the kitchen, was occasionally driven to spank one of her energetic sons. A hug would follow and the incident was soon forgotten. If their behaviour got really out of hand, she reported to her husband when he returned from work. Montague, instead of further punishment, would sit down with the son who had misbehaved to discuss the situation.

More than his mother's spankings, which were not unusual at that time, Peter remembers how every now and then Etelka would giggle and dance around the kitchen. This deeply embarrassed her children, who could not comprehend their normally sensible mother's silly behaviour, and they would beg her to stop. If Peter's friends were visiting, he quickly ushered them downstairs to the basement to play. Every house the family lived in had an unfinished basement, where the boys were free to make forts and set up a dartboard.

Nora, in charge of the cleaning, began each day by putting her hair up in two tidy rolls. Before she started the housework, she tied an apron neatly over her skirt. Of the adults, Nora was the most effective disciplinarian, and the boys would not dare say anything rude or behave badly when she was present. Though their grandmother was a traditionalist who insisted on the virtues of hard work and proper behaviour, she had a playful side and, like Etelka, would break out into occasional bouts of dancing. She loved waltzing, and would put Strauss' *Blue Danube* on the record player and whirl Peter around the living room.

When he was twelve years old, Peter signed up for square dance lessons at a community centre with younger brother John in tow. Before walking over together, Peter made sure they were both properly dressed because he considered the lessons a good opportunity to meet girls: "It's formal, and you have to hold hands or put your hands around each other's waist." Having already learned to waltz, Peter confidently worked his way through the interweaving patterns of a square dance.

Etelka's piano followed the family from town to town, and Peter also had a few music lessons at home. Although he wanted formal piano lessons, which his two older brothers had taken, this was not allowed. Perhaps his parents were discouraged after Dan and Bruce asked to stop, unhappy with the way the teacher rapped their knuckles whenever they made a mistake, or maybe the cost had become prohibitive. Dan had actually taken ballet classes for a short time through a community centre program, but nothing came of it and dance lessons were not offered to his siblings.

Sports, not creative pursuits, were central to the boys' upbringing. Peter swam from the age of four, later competitively; he began skating at five, and for a couple of years was a competitive speed skater. He was a minor league hockey player until the age of fifteen. At high school, Peter trained in track and field, and played basketball and volleyball. Montague attended athletic events to cheer his sons on – but never too vigorously, feeling it inappropriate as a chaplain to show excessive zeal over winning.

The four Bingham boys also competed against each other, with Bruce offering stiff competition the younger Peter was determined to equal, if not surpass. But, Montague explains:

> Bruce was a tough one to beat because he was very athletic, and academically strong, too. Peter would struggle to keep up. One day he came home from school and said, "Well, dad, I got news today. I got ninety-eight in math." I think it was the only day Bruce got a hundred.

The boys also learned practical skills. Montague was a competent carpenter and handyman who once built an outdoor playground for the children, and all his sons eventually wielded a hammer and used a saw with ease. John became a skilled carpenter and Bruce, after studying psychology and theology at university, went into construction. Montague also taught the oldest boys how to fix their bicycles, and made sure they passed the skill on to the two younger ones.

Wherever they moved, the church was central to their lives. Spirituality was a Christian, family affair, with their father's deeply held beliefs about the innate worth of the individual and the need for God's unconditional love at the heart of how he lived, worked and brought up his children. Nora and Etelka supported him both emotionally and practically. Sometimes Nora did duty as church secretary, usually when the official secretary was assisting the Roman Catholic priest for whom she also worked. Etelka helped out by replacing the regular organist during services whenever needed.

The children attended Sunday School every week until they were old enough to join the choir. Peter had to sing solos on special occasions, which, he admits, "was pretty earth-shattering at first. But when your dad's the minister, you just do it." A greater hardship came at Christmas, when they were not permitted to open presents until after church. "The year I was thirteen, we complained so much we were allowed to open one present on Christmas Eve."

Whenever they did attend the full church service, the four boys sat in a row at the front, jostling and restless, trying to restrain themselves from fighting. "Sometimes, when they were little," Montague recalls, "they'd put their hand up when I was preaching and say, 'I have to go to the bathroom, dad.'" After church, there was an early supper – roast beef and mashed potatoes, or something similarly substantial. Typically, grace would be a quick "Thank you, Lord, for supper" from one of the boys.

Peter felt so comfortable in church that, back in Claresholm, he had sometimes played there. The church was never locked and it was, after all, his dad's place. With two girls who were good friends, he remembers playing house in the hollow space at the back of the altar, sometimes exploring physical differences in the age-old game of "doctor".

It was during their brief stay in Clinton that Montague made yet another career move. He had become interested in the social work side of his pastoral role, and decided to leave the ministry to become a social worker. This led to momentous changes in the Bingham family's life as Montague left Ontario to return to British Columbia for retraining. The family, as always, was supportive and, in fact, Nora went with him to keep house so he could devote himself to studying. Etelka and the children remained behind, moving into a small farmhouse next to the air force base, with three boys in one bedroom and Dan on the couch. Etelka managed to find work as a public health nurse in a local school to help ease the financial situation.

In 1964, the air force sent the family to the prairie city of Winnipeg for two years. Montague was no longer in charge of a parish; instead, he provided counselling to individuals from all denominations, happy he could now devote himself to one-on-one care. The prospect of starting anew in yet another city was less daunting for Peter than it was for his brothers: like his father, Peter was good with people and made friends easily, relating to them with genuine interest and empathy. The constant moves did not bother him, and Montague recalls his son explaining: "It's like being able to walk away from all my debts to start over."

Dan, Nora (Gran), Bruce, Montague, Peter, Etelka and John in front with Nipper, 1963.

Not that everything went smoothly. When the family arrived in Winnipeg, Peter was in grade eight, a year marked by a dramatic drop in his marks. He had always done better in mathematics than in English, but now this split intensified: though math continued to come easily, he read at a snail's pace.

As well, for the first time Peter was not accepted on the school's basketball team. Part of the problem was dealing with a sudden growth spurt when he shot up from five foot two inches to five foot ten and a half inches, almost his full adult height of six feet, which took him from being one of the smallest kids in his age group to one of the tallest. It was around this time that Peter injured his left knee playing football, resulting in chronic knee problems. Some good news came when Peter was elected president of his junior high school student council, though his success did not last long – he was removed from office after throwing bottles of ink at the school building with a group of friends.

Yet Peter remained a popular student, and there were always a few girls with crushes on him. His grandmother disapproved of them calling Pip, her nickname for Peter, at home, and would ask, "What do you want him for?" At fourteen, he entered into a relationship with a seventeen-year-old. It did not last long – after some older boys ganged up on Peter in front of her, she stopped seeing him. The worst part about being beaten up was that he told his dad about it and when Montague talked to the father of one of the boys, word got out that Peter had squealed. In fact, Peter was used to talking things over with his dad and had not expected Montague to take any action.

As for Winnipeg itself, for Peter and his fellow teenagers, it was a great place to be. The post-Beatles musical explosion happened there with a vengeance, and in community clubs, church basements, schools and teen nightclubs, rock and roll music thrived. Portable transistor radios were tuned to Winnipeg stations CKY and CKRC, which promoted teen dances and local bands like Chad Allan and the Reflections, who later became the internationally successful Guess Who. Everybody wanted to join a band, and Peter played his brother Bruce's Harmony acoustic guitar so often that Bruce got fed up and bought him his own guitar for Christmas.

The music of the day thrived on television, too. *Shindig*, on American prime time TV, was one of Peter's favourite shows. Guests included The Beatles, The Rolling Stones, The Beach Boys, Chuck Berry and Petula Clark, who sang her hit single, *Downtown*. Another favourite show was *American Bandstand*, an afternoon dance party hosted by Dick Clark. Viewers could watch fellow teenagers perform the latest dances like the Slop, the Hand Jive and the Bop. Peter began attending Saturday afternoon recording sessions for Winnipeg's version of *Bandstand*, CJAY-TV's *Teen Dance Party*, which featured popular guest bands The Chord U Roys, and Mickey Brown and The Velvetones.

⸻

The Binghams moved back to British Columbia when Peter was ready to enter grade ten, settling in Deep Cove, a small, oceanside community a half hour's drive from Vancouver. Their comfortable corner lot was a stone's throw from a cliff leading down to the water.

Since the family had been away, Vancouver had changed considerably. During the 1960s, the city became known as the "Hippie Capital of Canada". Hordes of young men and women with long hair, faded jeans and handmade leather sandals rolled marijuana joints and smoked hash in pipes, greeting each other with a casual "Peace, man." In 1967, shortly after the family returned to the west coast, Canada's first "be-in", a peaceful gathering meant to spread love and hope, took place in Stanley Park, on the same day as a large anti-Vietnam War protest. The same year, peace and environmental activists founded the Don't Make a Wave Committee, which would be renamed Greenpeace, today a worldwide environmental organization.

Once again, Montague initiated changes in the family's life when he left the secure financial situation of the air force to work in Vancouver's alcohol- and drug-ridden Downtown Eastside. This meant Etelka needed to go back to nursing to supplement the family's income, leaving Nora to run the home.

Montague was in charge of Central City Mission, turning what he describes as "little more than a flophouse" into a treatment unit for the homeless. He was often at the Mission on Sunday and the family's regular church attendance fell off, although they always went to the local Anglican church, St. Simon's, whenever Montague was asked to preach.

The Bingham brothers kept connected to the church on their own through a folk singing group called the Deep Cove Singers, which a couple from St. Simon's had helped to launch. Bruce led the group of about a dozen young people, which included Peter and his oldest brother Dan. The Deep Cove Singers, accompanied by acoustic guitars, performed songs by popular artists of the day, including The Beatles' *Norwegian Wood* and *Michelle*, two of the "Fab Four's" gentler songs. These and more traditional folk numbers were performed at church coffee houses and during lunch-hour concerts at their school, Windsor High in North Vancouver, with the proceeds going to charity. One Christmas, they performed at Montague's Central City Mission.

Socially, Peter continued to do well, enjoying high school dances, practicing funky moves to rhythm and blues music at home until he had mastered them. In grade eleven, he began to travel downtown to a club called the Pink Elephant, where he danced to soul music by Smokey Robinson, Aretha Franklin and Otis Redding and, though still under the legal drinking age of nineteen, usually managed to buy a few drinks. The same year, he began a relationship with a Chinese Canadian who lived above a corner store – another older girl, this time by only one year, whose mother disapproved of inter-racial relationships. When her parents discovered the teenagers on their couch with their daughter's bra in Peter's hand, they demanded she leave home. Montague and Etelka allowed Peter's girlfriend to stay in their downstairs recreation room until she graduated from high school a few months later. "I was pretty much in love," Peter says. "After we split up, I kind of thought we'd get back together, but this didn't happen."

Academically, Peter was plummeting. He was unable to concentrate in class or deal with the tedium of homework. Depressingly, he had to study French at summer school. His parents never punished him, or even nagged, and Peter was too bored to motivate himself. Perhaps, after a lifetime of competing with his brother Bruce, who continued to excel at sports and was naturally studious, Peter was tired of trying to keep up. In any case, in grade twelve he made an arrangement with the principal to simply phone and inform the school whenever he was not going to be in attendance.

A few months into his final academic year, while his parents were in Saskatchewan for the funeral of Etelka's brother, Peter quit school altogether. He found a job at Vancouver Shipyards, where he repaired barges, swinging a sledgehammer as he removed and installed decking. He made a half-hearted attempt to finish grade twelve at night school, but enjoying a few glasses of beer at the end of the day with his co-workers was more compelling.

His parents said little. Montague had finished high school as an adult, motivated by his ambition to become a minister, and perhaps he thought Peter would also find his way when the time was right. But first Peter had to find his calling and, at this stage, nobody knew what that was. There were no particular moments or events signalling the creative journey ahead. Soon, there would be.

Bruce, Peter, John and Dan, circa 1966.

A Radical Time and Place

HERE WE ARE/ HERE & NOW/ THAT'S ALL THERE IS/ AND IF IT ISN'T BEAUTIFUL, MAN/ THERE'S NOTHING
 — BABA RAM DASS

It was a time of drifting. Eighteen-year-old Peter Bingham was happy to get a regular pay cheque as a labourer, though he was laid off after working less than a year at Vancouver Shipyards. Through his uncle, he quickly landed a job at Bingham Equipment, a small business in the False Creek industrial area that sold heavy-duty logging and road building supplies. Peter worked in the parts department, driving a truck for deliveries and pickups, and helping with ordering and shipping.

Bingham moved out of his parents' home when an opportunity arose to share a two-bedroom apartment in North Vancouver with a couple of young women. Much of his free time was now spent fixing up the vintage Chevrolet he purchased with the boyfriend of one of his roommates. "The 57 Chevy had a fibreglass front end and engine mounts in the front seat, so we had to sit in the back," Bingham recalls. "We were going to rebuild it for drag racing but we never did."

Once the manager of the apartment building discovered Bingham's presence, he put an end to the living arrangements. "He was a minister," Bingham says, "and couldn't abide me living with the women, even though we were just friends." He found another place with a young man who had the distinction of owning a nifty 1968 Firebird convertible.

Bingham's next job was in the galley of a cruise ship called the Prince George, which travelled up the British Columbia coast to Alaska. During his second season in September 1970, he met Chris Randle, one of the waiters, and they became immediate friends. In order to take photographs of the stunning scenery, which included regular whale sightings, Randle bought his first camera and built a small darkroom in the ship's hold. Both men enjoyed the seasonal employment, with six months on the ship and six months off, especially since they qualified for Unemployment Insurance during the winter off-season. For the most part, Bingham did not handle unemployment well – he slept late and drank heavily.

When he was in Vancouver, Bingham often spent the night dancing at Rohans, a popular showcase for local bands. Rohans, with tie-dyed tablecloths and blue and orange walls, was on 4th Avenue across from the Naam, one of Vancouver's many new natural food restaurants. This was in the heart of the hippie enclave of Kitsilano, not far from where Bingham now lived.

Chris Randle and Peter Bingham, 1970s .

Bingham also enjoyed attending rock concerts, held either at Queen's Park Arena a few miles out of town in New Westminster or at the Pacific Coliseum, a massive arena in the east end of Vancouver, built for the Canucks hockey team. At his first Coliseum concert, he saw the British rock group, Led Zeppelin. That's also where Bingham saw a local band called Chilliwack, the opening act for a popular U.S. rock group, Ten Years After, whose music featured the shrieking guitar of Alvin Lee. "I was really into guitar players," Bingham says, "and Alvin Lee was my hero." Like many concert-goers, Bingham would smoke a bit of marijuana or hash, the scent of which filled the air; others in the audience would be stoned on the magic mushrooms that grew out by the Vancouver airport, or were hallucinating on the much harder drug LSD, commonly called acid.

When he and Randle started talking about going to college together, Bingham knew he needed to tackle the unfinished business of high school graduation. In January 1971, he enrolled at Kitsilano High School and, despite the awkward situation of being the oldest kid in every class, completed his grade twelve education by June. The following January, he entered the Bachelor of Arts stream at Vancouver City College's Langara campus (now called Langara College). Randle began the photography program.

Bingham enjoyed the small, friendly campus, and was happy to be able to bring his girlfriend's daughter to the college daycare. Two favourite courses were Human Functional Anatomy and Applied Physiology, and Comparative Religion. The latter was taught by Jim Roberts, a charismatic teacher and independently minded Catholic priest who presented world religion at a time when Eastern philosophies were gaining popularity. Father Roberts treated his students with the same respect he gave the religions presented in his course, and he appreciated Bingham's "reassuring, hopeful presence". From the anatomy and physiology course, Bingham received a good grounding in how the body's skeletal and muscular systems function.

In order to pay his school fees, Bingham sold his treasured Harley Davidson motorcycle and also took substantial time off to work on the ship, so it took three years to complete the two years of degree work available at Langara. He then transferred to Simon Fraser University, a ten-year-old institution with a reputation for being radical, situated on top of Burnaby Mountain just outside Vancouver. In 1975, he signed up for a range of courses in psychology and philosophy. Bingham recalls:

> *At first, in philosophy, when someone said something I disagreed with, I'd think, "You can't say that!" I'd been brought up to believe there was one right answer to things — you might not know it, but there is in existence the right answer to everything, not a bunch of thoughtful answers that could all be right.*

A friend, Bruce Fraser, suggested Bingham join him in a movement workshop. Fraser was one of a growing number of young people searching for a more spiritual meaning to life, drawn to vegetarianism and to the gentle movement form of Tai Chi. Fraser had also discovered a holistic form of creative movement taught at a friendly place called Synergy. "I thought Peter would enjoy Synergy," Fraser explains. "He's a people person and a natural mover. Back then he had a strong interest in music, and we had jazz musicians in class sometimes."

Fraser was persuasive and Bingham was eager for a study break, so he agreed to give Synergy a go. The innovative dance studio was run by Linda Rubin, a key figure in the city's creative life and part of a whole network of dance and dancers Bingham as yet knew nothing about.

Linda Rubin Via Norbert Vesak

Linda Rubin had moved to Vancouver from the small community of Foam Lake, Saskatchewan at age eleven. Soon after, she took her first ballet classes at the Kay Armstrong Vancouver Ballet School. By age thirteen, she also took folk dance at the Jewish Community Centre.

In 1964, Rubin enrolled at the Emily Carr Institute of Art and Design, studying art history, commercial art, sculpture, painting and multimedia performance. Dance continued to exert a pull, and in the same year she founded the Nirkoda Folk Dance Company, directing the group until 1968. The company performed suites of dances, many of which Rubin choreographed, around the Lower Mainland. After visiting New York in June 1966 for her first intensive course at the Martha Graham school, Rubin craved more modern dance. Back at art school, she heard about Norbert Vesak.

Vesak, who trained first in modern dance with Laine Metz in Edmonton and then in ballet with Josephine Slater in New Westminster, British Columbia, was in the forefront of Vancouver's growing modern dance scene. Also active were two sisters, the Czechoslovakian-born Gertrud and Magda Hanova, who had offered a unique blend of Mary Wigman-styled modern dance, East Indian dance and yoga since the late 1950s. Vancouver-born Paula Ross, who had studied ballet with Mara McBirney and was a showgirl for some years, began teaching modern dance in 1964. Ross was a guest teacher of modern jazz at Joy Camden's West Vancouver school in 1967 when Anna Wyman, newly arrived from Austria via England, introduced Laban-styled modern movement there.

At about the same time, the two universities began to be active in dance. From the mid-sixties, Helen Goodwin organized creative dance classes at the University of British Columbia and Iris Garland offered modern dance workshops at Simon Fraser University's Physical Development Centre. Garland would go on to found the Dance Program at SFU's Centre for the Arts.

Throughout the 1960s, Norbert Vesak worked hard to establish himself as the city's leading contemporary dancemaker. His one-man concerts at the Vancouver Playhouse and at Simon Fraser University were popular, and he was in demand as a choreographer for the city's opera and symphony. In 1963, Vesak was the sole west coast participant at the Canadian Modern Dance Festival in Toronto, premiering his work, *Parenthesis*, set to Beethoven's *Romance for Violin and Orchestra in F Major*, Opus 50. The following year, Joy Camden brought him in to help with her short-lived Pacific Dance Theatre, a ballet/modern dance crossover company. Vesak contributed a number of dramatic, contemporary works, which often featured an intense, dark-eyed Paula Ross.

Rubin found Vesak's classes technically challenging, and she enjoyed the creative movement he set to a range of music. Soon, she was performing in his choreography. She had the lead role of the gypsy, Candelas, in *El Amor Brujo* for a 1967 Dance and the Symphony pop concert. In 1968, she was cast as The Woman, opposite Vesak as The Man, in his *Once for the Birth of…*. Rubin continued to make extended visits to New York to study and perform – notably, she was a demonstrator for classes at the Martha Graham School and danced with Deborah Hay's company – but returned often to perform with Vesak.

Western Dance Theatre

When Rubin flew back to Vancouver for the official May 1970 launch of Vesak's professional modern dance troupe, Western Dance Theatre, it was to perform as well as to present one of her own choreographies. In a substantial interview in *The Province* newspaper to mark the occasion, writer Terry French described the twenty-five-year-old Rubin's appearance: "In her jeans and sandals, leotard and bolero, flowing woven belt and Indian medallian [sic] and wristlet, she looks much like other very pretty girls enjoying youthful style, long hair and a braid or two." What makes Rubin stand out from the crowd, he explains, is her dedication to dance.

The interview quotes Rubin extensively. "I'm interested in getting through to more people," she says. "I want the dance to be interesting but less complicated than the highly intricate and structured things seen in classical ballet." About her style of movement, Rubin says:

> It's not ballet, it's not modern, it's not jazz. It's just moving in a different way with no hang-ups about doing things exactly the same or perfectly. Some areas are left to chance, not choreographed, within a changing structure. I've just used jogging. Everyone's jogging. You see them everywhere.

The launch of Western Dance Theatre, described as a "modern ballet company", took place at the Queen Elizabeth Theatre, with an appearance by guest artist Lynn Seymour adding prestige to the event. Born Berta Lynn Springbett in Wainwright, Alberta, and raised in Vancouver, Seymour was a star with England's Royal Ballet. Partnered by Vesak, she danced a pas de deux from Kenneth MacMillan's *Solitaire* that two newspaper reports suggest did not show off the high profile guest at her best. Max Wyman in *The Vancouver Sun* blamed Vesak's partnering, which he considered "barely adequate for the job – this is not, after all, his sort of dance, and his attempts to carry it off, while gallant and well-intentioned, were misplaced." James Barber, a reporter for *The Province* who attended the afternoon preview, found Seymour's "edges were ragged, and instead of the youthful, graceful purity of her Juliet we saw a heavier, slightly wilted rose."

Little was said about Vesak's two choreographic contributions, which Rubin's *Movement Piece No. 1* quite upstaged. Barber wrote:

> … Movement Piece No. 1 *[was] a gently humorous, quite delightful piece of loose, uncomplicated, explicit exploration of the sense outside the garbage and clutter of words.*
>
> *Seven dancers, buried in newspaper, emerge like chickens from the shell, dance, move, paint the senses on the stage, and go back to their beginning – all very easy, all very free.*

And Linda Rubin emerges as something more than a local girl who used to try things out with not too much confidence. She is a very confident choreographer, big enough and old enough to say what she thinks the way she thinks it.

At the *Sun*, Max Wyman also came in thumbs up, saying of Rubin:

Watch her; she has a fine knack of sugaring the pill of very direct social comment with a liberal coating of sweet ridiculousness — on top of which there is, in this at least, an openness and a spirit about her movement style that is strongly reminiscent of the choreography of Hair.

For Western Dance Theatre's second mainstage show, at North Vancouver's Centennial Theatre in November 1970, Rubin was credited as Artistic Affiliate. She also choreographed a work for eight dancers to music by The Who from their recent album, *Tommy*. Wyman described Rubin's choreography, called S*ee Me, Feel Me, Touch Me*, as having "cheeky, bouncy eagerness and … pithy bite…."

Vesak engaged Rubin to teach at his West Vancouver Studio of Dance and the Allied Arts, where she offered classes in creative dance for children and contemporary dance for adults. According to a school brochure, Rubin was one of a "selected staff of experienced instructors" hired to "assist Mr. Vesak with the program of the school", which was "built entirely on his approach to dance, his principles and technical beliefs." In reality, Rubin recalls that she offered her own approach, working with expressive movement and story-building in the creative classes, and with a Graham base in the contemporary ones.

Shortly after Rubin became a company dancer, things took a downturn. Serious financial difficulties and poor press were hounding Western Dance Theatre. After their February 1971 appearance with the Vancouver Symphony Orchestra, Wyman described Vesak's choreography to Stravinsky's *The Soldier's Tale* as "a lumpy, uneven presentation" with "some of the most graceless dancing we have seen from this company."

It was their final performance. Bitterly discouraged, Vesak sold his studio and left Vancouver for the Royal Winnipeg Ballet. Although he had failed to sustain his dream of having his own company, in Winnipeg Vesak choreographed two memorable works: *The Ecstasy of Rita Joe* in 1971 and *What to do Till the Messiah Comes*, with its award-winning *Belong* pas de deux, in 1973. He eventually settled in the United States, where he directed the San Francisco Opera Ballet and then New York's Metropolitan Opera Ballet. Vesak died in October 1990 from a brain aneurysm.

Two women took his place at the forefront of the Vancouver dance scene: Paula Ross and Anna Wyman, artistic directors of what became the city's major modern dance companies. Anna Wyman (then married to newspaperman Max Wyman) bought Vesak's studio. Like Vesak, both strong-willed choreographers were dedicated to personal visions of what dance should be. Ross and Wyman were also known for demanding complete loyalty from their company dancers, who were discouraged from studying or performing elsewhere – or even attending performances by other groups. In a competitive funding climate, with Vancouver's small dance audience, there was no room to be generous to rivals. It was a legacy passed on from the great teacher/choreographers of the 1940s and 1950s, when each school had its own group of dancers and followers, and were suspicious of the rest.

The time had come, however, for another tradition to be launched, one more in keeping with the free spirit of the 1970s. From communes to cooperative housing, from free love to open relationships, men and women were experimenting with alternative life-styles. Freedom, power sharing and the rights of the individual, particularly women's rights, were important contemporary issues. Vancouver, with its mild climate and numerous parks and beaches, was a magnet for young idealists. It was the perfect setting for the alternative dance community Linda Rubin was about to develop.

Synergy

When Vesak folded Western Dance Theatre and sold his studio without a word of warning to the dancers, Rubin was devastated. But not for long: that summer, she opened her own school. It was situated at the southwest corner of Robson and Granville Streets, an ideal

Entrance to Synergy (Arcadian Hall), Main St., Vancouver.
Photo: Daniel Collins

location right in the centre of a busy downtown shopping area. Synergy Movement Workshops was a new and holistic initiative, advertised as "based on the premise that the mutual cooperation of the arts will produce a greater effect than their separate components." Artists from the worlds of dance, music, theatre and filmmaking were encouraged to make use of the third-floor space. Contemporary dance, contemporary choreography, stretching, jazz and ballet were offered at all levels, taught by Rubin and former Vesak company members Gisa Cole and Jamie Zagoudakis, among others. There were also more unusual offerings like belly dancing, Tai Chi, yoga, experimental theatre and communications. The latter was a class in improvisation meant to focus attention on what it is that artists do, i.e., communicate, when they improvise together.

A description of the studio was published in a five-year-old, free newspaper called *The Georgia Straight*:

> *The first room you enter is a warm, carpeted lobby/lounge replete with rocking chair, sofas, coffee-maker, plants, and people, many comfortably barefoot … someone cross-legged on the floor strumming a guitar, some others just slowly sipping coffee … No one will object if you continue through into either of the two large studios. There, at just about any time, you can watch a theatre group rehearsing, a ballet class doing its first pliés, or Israeli folkdancing.*

In the same article, Rubin describes her intention "to break down the isolated dance scene or art scene where you belong to one group and you have to be faithful to them. If you talk to someone else from another group you've crossed over the line."

Besides teaching, Rubin was keen to continue choreographing; not only did she feel she had something important to say, but her contributions to Western Dance Theatre had received encouraging press. In January 1972, Rubin and seven students performed in her work, *Software*, for a noon-hour show at the Vancouver Art Gallery. The performers were barefoot, with the three women in black dance tights and tunics, and the five men in jeans and t-shirts. In *The Georgia Straight* article, Rubin explained that *Software* treats "a very serious problem very lightly – the whole impact of advertising on us, on our culture." The title came from American media art theorist Gene Youngblood's idea that "Television is the software of the earth."

This time, the critical response to Rubin's choreography was not as positive. In a review in *The Vancouver Sun*, Max Wyman was "depressed and disappointed" by the work's "distracting looseness and roughness of edge." On the plus side, James Barber of *The Province* found the mixture of film, sound and dance "fun", enjoying Rubin's "nice sense of humour", as when someone dances a love story with a dead chicken.

Barber opened with the facetious remark that *Software*, with a little bit of work, "could easily become one of the minor contemporary classics, with mentions in *Time* magazine, reviews in *Rolling Stone* and raves in *Women's Wear Daily*." This remark was misinterpreted by the newspaper's headline writer, who took it seriously, headlining the review: "A minor classic at gallery." In his review of a later remount at the Burnaby Art Gallery, Barber announces that he regrets his use of satire as being too subtle. This time, he is far less "kind", calling *Software* "very sloshy, very obvious, not overly inspired choreography" though it is, he admits, "still, occasionally, a lot of fun." He is more enthusiastic about the workshop that followed, which attracted between thirty and forty "fairly young and hairy" participants.

In 1973, Rubin scaled down the school – she was now the sole teacher, aside from guests – and focussed her creative energies more tightly. She relocated to the Western Front, a recently established artist-run centre in a quiet, low-rent residential district just east of Main Street. It had an ideal dance space in a ground floor hall that boasted a smooth maple wood floor.

At the Western Front studio, most sessions began with bodywork. Dancers stretched in pairs, using each other's weight to increase flexibility, and often taking turns massaging their partner. Synchronization of breath and movement was fundamental. Technical exercises like pliés were done to African drums, as were Graham-based combinations.

In improvisation classes, students did exercises in mirroring and shadowing, and tried out balances on various parts of a partner's body. When it was time to move across the floor, this might begin with individuals crossing one at a time and trying out their own movement ideas. The class finished with a more formal improvisation to music, usually to popular recordings or to live drums. Here, it was important that participants remain aware of the overall impact of their improvisation, and that they enter the space with a clear intention to either support the predominant energy or shape, or to change it.

Rubin, who teaches today in the Drama Department of the University of Alberta in Edmonton, explains:

My teaching is about designing improvisationally. If you have ten performers, they're all choreographers. Their duty is to see and feel and create.

I usually start with ideas about how to manage your own weight and how to understand what you bring to the dance. Is it a nervous energy, a heavy energy or a light energy that can't support anything? Then I bring people together and teach skills of connecting, lifting, leverage, following through, momentum, gravity and duration.

One of Rubin's students from the 1970s, photographer Daniel Collins, describes Rubin's classes as "touchy-feely and very modern." He remembers how the keener students – "and any man!" – would be asked to join the Synergy Performing Association, or SPA, a loose-knit group of committed students who performed in Rubin's socially aware choreography and improvisations. Collins recalls one performance at the Western Front studio, which was the first time his father saw him dance: "The piece was about the medical profession and we were wearing trusses and other medical things. At the end, we were all naked against the back wall, and I heard my father say, 'Oh, my God!'"

Rubin learned some of her innovative practices when, in 1973, she travelled to San Francisco to experience the ritual and healing movement work of Anna Halprin. Though Rubin insisted her own work was not therapy, people could nonetheless have very emotional experiences during the intense classes. Indeed, many of her students came from the medical and other healing professions, impressed with the body-mind-spirit connection. Others were rebels from the dance world, eager for self-expression. Amazingly, Rubin attracted almost as many men as women. In the egalitarian atmosphere of the times, changing rooms were co-ed, and Synergy regulars sometimes relaxed together at the Hastings Street steam baths after weekend workshops.

Peter Bingham at Synergy

It was in 1975, with Linda Rubin, that Peter Bingham took his first dance class. Comfortably dressed in drawstring pants and an East Indian-styled cotton shirt, the twenty-four-year-old felt very much at home: "I got turned onto it completely and immediately signed up for classes four nights a week." Here was the physical excitement he craved, and a dance space where there was room to move. As well, unlike the clubs where he normally danced, there was a strong health-conscious atmosphere and he managed to cut back his cigarette habit, which had reached between one and two packs a day. Soon, he was not smoking at all.

Bingham's attraction to Rubin's classes went deeper than the physical, and he also connected to her affinity with the era's intense social conscience, which made for a radically different kind of dance studio. At Synergy, dance was about cooperation, not competition, and the way an individual dancer felt about what they were doing was crucial. The deep relationship between body, mind and spirit appealed to Bingham; here, dance expressed the individual as a whole human being, in an atmosphere that was calm, stressing inner serenity and strength. Synergy brought together the various strands of Bingham's life in a way he had never before experienced: his religious upbringing and his love of athletics were transformed into a dance practice that reflected the holistic social and spiritual philosophies of his generation.

After studying with Rubin for about five months, Bingham began helping with administrative chores, as well as assisting during classes. He absorbed the more abstract concepts that were part of Rubin's teaching, such as awareness of shape and line, and fostering a central focus during group improvisations.

Soon, Bingham joined the Synergy Performing Association. In addition to Daniel Collins, other members were Bingham's friend Bruce Fraser, and English teacher and tutor Peter Ryan. Also in the group was dancer Mary Craig; Michael Seamus Linehan, who had been "into" yoga before discovering dance; Andrew Harwood, who came to Vancouver from Montreal to work for his brother at Lifestream, a popular natural foods store; and Helen Clarke, an Australian who travelled west after taking a workshop with Rubin in Halifax.

Another SPA member, Jane Ellison, had studied modern dance with Paula Ross while in high school. "The bodywork was significant for me," she says of Synergy. "It really changed my idea of working in dance. It was so experiential – you breathed, you felt, you used your senses, your own experience." Later, Ellison coordinated the dance program and managed the studio rentals for the Western Front until a dance company called EDAM took over.

When Rubin left the Western Front to move into her own space

Linda Rubin, circa 1975.

on the upper floor of the Arcadian Hall, a simple wooden building built in 1905 by the Independent Order of Odd Fellows, Bingham joined the eager work crew. Situated on Main Street next to an auto wrecking operation and just a few blocks northwest of the Western Front, the large studio had lots of windows, a high ceiling and a sprung wood floor. The crew painted the walls and ceiling white, added some plants and mirrors, and installed a good sound system.

It was in this warm and welcoming space, where he felt very much at home, that Bingham presented his first dance work. He and Clarke, with whom he was romantically involved, created a structured improvisation sporting the confounding title, *if two and two still = two all the rest is easy*. During his solo section, he sat cross-legged on the floor and performed a dance with one arm and hand to a gentle song, *Hand-dancing*, by Canadian singer/songwriter Bruce Cockburn.

Also on the bill was an open improvisation called *Emerging Images* directed by Rubin, who performed with Bingham, Clarke, Harwood and Ryan. In a group work by Harwood, the performers first impersonated a washing machine and then the clothes hanging out to dry. It might have been goofy, but it was also a lot of fun, and the audience of about one hundred enjoyed the evening.

Today, Bingham recognizes Linda Rubin's importance to his artistic growth, and to the Vancouver scene in general:

> *Synergy opened people up to the notion of being creative together in an improvisational way. And it was with knowledge, it wasn't just getting together and playing....*

> *I would never have had anything to do with ballet. Neither would most of the other guys there. Linda made it possible for us to dance.*

For athletic men like Bingham, who had attended only one formal dance performance in his life – a modern company at his high school, the details of which he cannot recall – Rubin made dance approachable. More than that, at Synergy athleticism was not out of place. This was dance for real people. A number of the women wore traditional black leotards and tights with stirrup feet, but sweat pants or light cotton trousers were common, particularly for the men.

Dancing at Synergy was, for many, spiritually and emotionally healing. In the improvisations, through emphasis on individual expression and in the demand for openness to others, there was a healthy mix of personal freedom and social interaction. The paradox was that you had to be yourself in order to participate effectively as part of the team. This was the bedrock on which Bingham would build his understanding of what it was to be an artist.

Peter Bingham, Jane Ellison, Linda Rubin and unknown dancer, Synergy, 1976.　　　　Photo: Daniel Collins

Peter Bingham and Jane Ellison, Synergy, 1975.
Photos: Sarah Wellington

First Contact

Sometimes, I think that if Vancouver had not discovered contact improvisation, we would have had to invent it. — Elizabeth Zimmer in *YVR* magazine

In January 1975, the Vancouver arts community had its first experience of a form of movement that would leave a deep, lasting impact on the city's dance scene. Helen Goodwin, with an eye for innovative presentations, brought in two young Americans – Steve Paxton and Nancy Stark Smith – for a daytime demonstration of an athletic style of partnering called contact improvisation. Goodwin set the pair up at the Vancouver Opera's rehearsal hall, where they arrived pretty much ready to go – there was no special lighting, no costumes and not even any seating to arrange. Paxton and Smith were barefoot, wearing t-shirts and drawstring pants, and the audience sat on the floor along the sides of the room.

Their typically casual demonstration profoundly affected two Synergy participants who were in that audience, Peter Ryan and Michael Seamus Linehan. Recalls Linehan: "When I saw Steve and Nancy, they were incredibly centred and free in three-dimensional space, all while in communication with each other – such clean, moment-by-moment, non-verbal communication." Also notable was the fact that there was no difference in movement quality or roles between the man and the woman: each lifted the other, each had moments of being supported and of supporting. Paxton and Smith explored how two people could move together in close contact, taking and giving weight in a constantly shifting, symbiotic relationship. They were on the ground as often as standing or in the air, with nothing planned in advance – through focussing on the physical sensations of their own and their partner's body, they touched and tumbled, and rolled and balanced on shoulders, hips, backs, legs, wherever there was a possibility of being supported.

Afterwards, Linehan and Ryan went to a gym to work out. "We were so rushed from Steve and Nancy's demo," Linehan says. "Linda was enthusiastic as well – she must have been at the demo, too – and she started playing with contact a bit in her classes."

Linda Rubin was indeed present, appreciating what she describes as "a heightened and extended physicality done with explicit detail in connection between dancers." She considered contact improvisation "another colour" to add to her movement palette and to her classes. As for Linehan and Ryan, "those guys were flying off the walls!" she recalls. "It was hard to slow them down so they wouldn't bruise."

Tylar Merrill, Bruce Fraser, Peter Ryan, Helen Clarke, Karen Malcolm, Gillian Lowndes, Peter Bingham and Andrew Harwood of the group Around Nine.　　　　　　　　　Photo: Michael Linehan

Although Peter Bingham missed that first demonstration, Paxton, who had invented contact improvisation in 1972, would become an important mentor. He was drawn to Paxton's questioning and egalitarian spirit, and came to respect his substantial experience with different forms of movement. Born in Arizona, Paxton started in gymnastics before taking dance classes in high school. He joined the Merce Cunningham modern dance company in 1961 and the following year was a founding member of New York's influential, postmodern Judson Dance Theater. In the 1970s, Paxton performed as part of a collective improvisational group called Grand Union. Paxton also practiced the non-aggressive, Japanese martial art of aikido, with its emphasis on the dynamics of movement and perfecting the spirit. As a choreographer, Paxton pushed boundaries when he began making dances with everyday actions like walking, as well as using ordinary people who did not have the typical dancer's body or posture.

Elizabeth Zimmer in *The Vancouver Courier* wrote in 1976 that after that first visit by "an avant-garde dancer named Steve Paxton", interest in contact improvisation was "swelling, and a wave of workshops and performances in what Paxton has called an 'art sport' is taking place around the city." Zimmer (a New Yorker who later became a senior editor for *The Village Voice*) noted that contact improvisation "differs from theatre dance in that it is not an expression or representation of anything. It is what it is, an energy flow between two or more people, a focus on points of communication and sensitivity." She advised her *Courier* readers: "If you find yourself encountering fruitless verbal interactions in your daily round, and you're looking for a better way to communicate, explore contact improvisation, as a spectator or a participant. It's like going back to a vital, fertile source, a refreshing spring of energy and attention."

She also noted the spiritual richness of contact improvisation. "[C]ontact is a kind of moving meditation," Zimmer wrote, one that provides "a sane, social counterpart to the inner-directedness, the privacy of most meditative paths." Spirituality was a popular concern in the 1970s, particularly among the young, who often searched for answers in Eastern meditation practices, and many were attracted to contact improvisation because of the way it reflected their spiritual aspirations.

"Natural" was another key seventies concern, with the public increasingly interested in natural healing and nutrition, questioning the use of additives to food and beauty products. When Linehan and Harwood organized an event called Country Jam on Vancouver Island in 1977, it was "homespun, [with] organic food and jamming every day." Contact improvisation was a "natural", unforced way of moving with another person, one that stressed honest, attentive interaction in the moment.

Inherently, contact improvisation was "about" these and other social beliefs that were transforming contemporary life. Cynthia Novack, in her history of contact improvisation, *Sharing the Dance*, wrote that early participants, audience members and critics

> *viewed the experience of touching and sharing weight with a partner of either sex and any size as a way of constructing a new experience of the self interacting with another person. The lack of conscious compositional focus in the form represented spontaneity in life, a literal "going with the flow" of events, just as the dancers followed the flow of their physical contact. The group with no director symbolized an egalitarian community in which everyone cooperated and no one dominated. Finally, the mode of practicing and performing contact improvisation resembled a social dance, an informal gathering in which anyone could participate who wished to do so; distinctions between amateur and professional dancers were consciously ignored initially.*

Contact improvisation was socially relevant within its own small community in a way that ballet had been when it took shape within the French court in the seventeenth century. The contrast between the two forms could not be greater, however, and contact improvisation was far from the codified movement and huge spectacle of court ballet.

A Contact-Styled Epiphany

Peter Bingham joined the Synergy gang for his first contact improvisation workshop in early 1976. Led by Nancy Stark Smith, it took place in an old Kitsilano studio rented from a small theatre company. It was his second dance epiphany.

Afterwards, he followed up every opportunity he could to join in the burgeoning contact activity. Throughout the 1970s, practitioners from the United States travelled north, allowing the Vancouver contacters to hone their skills and gain technical tools at home, getting past the early, bruising days. American groups like ReUnion, made up of Steve Paxton, Nancy Stark Smith, Nita Little, Curt Siddall and Danny Lepkoff, came to teach and perform. So did Mangrove, an all-male contact improvisation collective who brought to their work a wealth of influences, such as choreographers Anna Halprin and Erick Hawkins, Bread and Puppet Theatre and Grotowski's Polish Laboratory Theatre. Linehan appreciated how the visitors "gave us clear tools to work with as opposed to the haphazard experimenting we were doing. Before they came, we were trying to emulate this thing without having any of the letters or words of the alphabet except what we could guess at from having seen it."

Bingham recalls the early period of learning as "pretty crash and thrash. I remember living with bruises all over me. I didn't care. It hurt if you had bruises but getting them never hurt." Somehow, without any conscious planning or decision-making, dancing was now a full-time affair. University study fell by the wayside. To pay the rent he took time out to drive a truck for the post office on evenings and weekends.

On May 23, 1976, only a few months after that first workshop with Smith, Peter Bingham participated in an afternoon demonstration called *The Dance Dojo*. A dojo is a room or place where judo and other martial arts are practiced, and its use in the title suggests the casual nature of the event. The poster announcing the demonstration took a practical tone:

> *Contact Improvisation is a movement form based on the union of two people through their point of physical contact, both equally assisting each other in movement that follows their mutual "energy paths". Attitude, sensing time, orientation to space, orientation to partner, expanding peripheral vision, muscular development, centering, stretching, taking weight and increasing joint action are some of the elements in Contact.*

Michael Linehan directed *The Dance Dojo* on the grass outside the Burnaby Art Gallery. It was Bingham's first paid performance.

Peter Bingham, Michael Linehan, Peter Ryan and Andrew Harwood in *Four Men Dancing*.

That September, keen to develop his skills, Bingham joined Helen Clarke and other Vancouver contact dancers in Berkeley, California for Focus: 9/76. At this month-long program offered by the Bay Area Contact Coalition, they were exposed to a range of approaches to contact improvisation. The real draw was the chance to study with Mangrove, a company that, according to Andrew Harwood, "took contact into a whole new area, which was much more theatrical, adding storytelling, playing instruments, doing ensemble work as well as contact. It was all improvised but they had a much broader view." The Vancouverites rented a house together, with Bingham and Clarke camping out in a tent in the front yard.

This committed, passionate group became an informal association called Around Nine because, with a few comings and goings, that was the number of core members: Peter Bingham, Helen Clarke, Andrew Harwood, Michael Linehan, Peter Ryan, Bruce Fraser, Gillian Loundes, Tylar Merrill and Karen Malcolm. Around Nine worked at the Western Front, usually for a couple of hours at a time, mostly in silence. Not everyone in the group wanted to perform; for some, it was the physically challenging practice of a meditative state that drew them to contact. For Bingham, it was both:

It was really about becoming a dancer. I loved rolling around with those bodies and getting into it. We'd just dance when we felt like it and stop when we didn't. I think we were into the meditation of it. We were into the soft focus of the eyes, really practicing with the body to move through space and with each other, just getting skilled.

Different configurations of Around Nine gave demonstrations at the downtown Pender Street Gallery, Simon Fraser University, the University of British Columbia, Vancouver Community College and the Western Front, as well as on Vancouver Island. A notable event was *Four Men Dancing*, "An evening of Improvisational Movement and Contact Improvisation" in December 1977, which took place at Linda Rubin's Arcadian Hall studio. Jazz pianist Bruce Cuddeford, a Synergy faithful, provided live music. Dancing with Bingham were Michael Linehan, whose main interest was in contact as a personal practice, and Andrew Harwood and Peter Ryan, who would develop the two strands of improvisation and contact improvisation in their subsequent performing careers.

The rarity of a quartet of men dancing together is suggested by the information being featured in the title. The longstanding shortage of strong male dancers was well known in the dance scene, and contact improvisation was proud of its gender-free appeal.

This colourful description of Bingham and some of his colleagues is found in Elizabeth Zimmer's report of a benefit performance held for the American magazine, *Contact Quarterly*:

After an opening meditation, the dancers take solo turns. Nothing homogenous about this crowd, sometimes called Fulcrum, augmented with friends. Wild-eyed Peter Bingham brings to his dancing a sense of drama, a lean and hungry look. Michael Seamus Linehan and Karen Malcolm are clowns, chasing each other around the space on knees and seat, pushing and shoving, the big woman and the spaniel-faced man abandoning themselves to play. Suddenly I am seeing double – no, it's Susan Mathie and Helen Clarke, well matched in size (relatively slight), hair (blond pigtails) and costume (grey tops, white pants), using a parallel style of movement, folding together, knitting and unraveling a human macramé.

Peter Ryan, solid, somber in rust velour, feeling his thought as immediately as the odor of the nearest body; Andrew Harwood, the gentle lion in his usual motley and many pairs of socks, prime mover of this series of events, recently back from a tour of the continent, opening the mysterious east of Canada to Contact.

Fulcrum

Actually, Fulcrum was made up just of Bingham, Clarke and Harwood. An affinity had slowly grown between this trio, both artistic and personal. Bingham and Clarke were a couple, and for a time all three lived together on Kitsilano's Point Grey Road in a basement suite they rented from Bingham's parents, who lived upstairs. With these two close friends and colleagues, Peter Bingham began to shape contact improvisation into his own vision. From the start, improvisation in theatrical terms was as important as pure contact improvisation. There is no doubt, however, that it was contact that gave Fulcrum its unique identity and energy. Here is how they described themselves in publicity material:

Fulcrum aims for effortless movement through deep mutual trust and a heightened sensitivity to the flow of spontaneous interaction. The performances are informal, revealing the natural moving body as a beautiful instrument free of tension.

Helen Clarke, Andrew Harwood and Peter Bingham of the group Fulcrum, Montreal.

The company's big break was an invitation to perform at the Vancouver Playhouse on a Sunday afternoon in February 1978. Part of the Festival Concert Society's coffee-concert series, this first formal show constituted a real development in their presentation and goals. The hour-long performance, wrote Zimmer in *YVR* magazine

began with an obviously rehearsed series of rolls across the stage by the three performers, interconnected in a corridor of light. They then retreated in the standard contact warm-up, the silent 'stand', which, even though greatly abbreviated, tended to leave the audience, hungry for action, in something of a quandary.

The Vancouver Sun newspaper was more direct: "Contact improvisation is no theatrical spectacle" blared the headline for Max Wyman's review. Until then, contact had been viewed in casual demonstrations. Now, critics and audiences had to rethink their expectations. At this stage, Wyman was perturbed by the theatrical developments:

> [O]nce any hint of performance conventions set in, the purity – the freshness and unexpectedness that is the real charm of the form – simply evaporates, and you are left with a lot of dull and hesitant non-dance. On Sunday, there were long empty stretches. I'm surprised so many of the audience stayed so long.

The *Sun* review was a very public blow but it did not change the course Fulcrum was following toward a professional theatrical practice. By the time of the Dance in Canada Conference, which took place August 13 to 17, 1978, the Fulcrum trio had a few more performances under their belts and things went significantly better. Their fifteen-minute improvisation on the 10:00 p.m. mixed bill that closed the event took place at the five-year-old Vancouver East Cultural Centre, a converted church with just the right formal yet funky atmosphere. Fulcrum gave conference-goers from across the country something very different from the mostly ballet and modern dance they watched all week, and all of these things – Fulcrum's uniqueness, the atmospheric venue, the brevity of their appearance and their greater experience – contributed to the company being received more enthusiastically than had been the case at the Playhouse. At least one Toronto-based modern dancer, Jennifer Mascall, was intrigued enough to stay in town for a few days after the conference in order to do some contact improvisation with members of Fulcrum, who had quickly set up an intensive workshop at the Western Front.

Based on their success at Dance in Canada, Fulcrum was invited to the 1978 Toronto Dance Festival that October. The Paula Ross Dancers and Anna Wyman Dance Theatre were the only other Vancouver companies to appear. Judging from Stephen Godfrey's review in the national *Globe and Mail* newspaper, quoted in part below, Fulcrum made theatrical, though still meditative, sense. The tension between performance and practice, theatre and studio, was being resolved.

> Fulcrum ... is not only one of the best things to happen at the Toronto Dance Festival ... but probably the best possible midnight show the festival could have booked. The movement is not going to shock or jolt, sending one out restless and raring to loll about Yonge Street at 12:30 a.m. on a week night. Instead, this is one of the most serene theatrical experiences imaginable.
>
> As its name implies, the movement centers around balance. It's the kind of balance to make one think that for even the most graceless body, there is hope. Harwood and Bingham meet, and by finding pressure points of the

body — any body — they make a series of flowing motions, which seem to end naturally in precarious positions....

The applause was muted, but not for lack of appreciation. It was the first contrived sound of the evening, the first sound and sight that was sudden. It stopped just as suddenly as it began. A moment longer, and there would have been the risk that the most tranquil mood on Yonge Street would have been swallowed up by the bright lights and unnatural neon.

Later, when Godfrey wrote about Montreal's contact improvisation quartet Catpoto (Gurney Bolster, Dena Davida, Evelyn Ginzburg and Sylvie St. Laurent), Fulcrum was his touchstone: "One misses the variations in speed and daring of Vancouver's Fulcrum Contact Improvisation group, which performed at the Toronto Dance Festival two years ago."

After the Toronto Dance Festival performances, Fulcrum toured to Ottawa, Montreal and Halifax. They billeted with whomever had room for them, performed in studios, taught and felt part of a growing community of creative individuals. In terms of experimental dance, rough-and-tumble contact improvisers were in the forefront, and this Vancouver trio led the pack.

One of the Fulcrum members — Andrew Harwood — had received Canada Council funding for a cross-Canada tour with Michael Linehan earlier that year, further proof of the popularity of these rule-breaking, tradition-busting west coast contact dancers. The pair also travelled to three cities in the United States, including New York where *The Village Voice* guide to events, Voice Choices, listed the two contacters from Vancouver. Their entry was sandwiched below the Joffrey Ballet and above Eliot Feld and Rudolf Nureyev. Jennifer Dunning from *The New York Times* did not review the event but did attend. Afterwards, she wrote Linehan a letter praising the performance, concluding, "Any chance you may relocate to New York?"

Despite this success, many in the dance community remained dismissive of contact improvisation — including many modern dancers, who themselves were considered radical by the ballet establishment. Modern dancers were showing more and more interest in strong technique and ballet classes were increasingly part of their training. It was not obvious what contact improvisers, for whom straight legs and pointed feet were irrelevant, had to contribute. It takes sweat, persistence, tears and long years to master the kind of strength, flexibility and artistry that ballet and modern dance require, and of which dancers are deservedly proud, yet within a couple of years of his first dance class, Bingham had already formed a company and was performing. For many in the dance community, this was an outrageously bold thing to do. However, looked at in context, at the time the contact improvisation movement itself was just five years old, so even the founders were not much more experienced.

From a contact improviser's point of view, they were the happening thing, and they considered even Vancouver's more experimental modern dance companies to be conservative. But when Michael Linehan presented a two-day Festival of Experimental Dance in February 1978 at the Vancouver East Cultural Centre, he sensibly looked beyond his own aesthetic. First, though, the opening night was given over to contact's influential duo, Steve Paxton and Nancy Stark Smith, joined by Linehan, Andrew Harwood, Peter Ryan and Helen Clarke, in an evening of pure contact improvisation. Bingham cannot remember why he was not there, although concedes the others had a few months more experience.

On the second night, Linehan presented works by Judith Marcuse, Savannah Walling, Karen Jamieson (then using her married name, Rimmer) and Peggy Florin. Who were these other "experimental" dancers? Marcuse had a national reputation for her bold, genre-busting mix of ballet and modern dance. Walling and Jamieson, along with Terry Hunter, co-directed Terminal City Dance, founded in 1975 and known for integrating dance, music and theatre. The company's cooperative way of working was very much in tune with contemporary social ideas, and their exciting multidisciplinary focus has had long-lasting impact on the Vancouver scene. Florin was an American who danced with Anna Wyman's company before joining Terminal City.

Other companies active in Vancouver were Gisa Cole and Jamie Zagoudakis' Prism Dance Theatre, founded in 1974, and Mauryne Allan and Freddie Long's Mountain Dance Theatre, founded in 1973. There was also the Paula Ross Dancers and Anna Wyman Dance Theatre. The latter was admired for its high professional standards but was also resented because for years it was the only Vancouver group receiving operating funds from the Canada Council for the Arts. On the ballet side, Vancouver had its long-desired professional company in Pacific Ballet Theatre, founded by Maria Lewis in 1976.

Fulcrum folded after two years. Helen Clarke was more interested in performance art and, according to Bingham:

> *Helen thought Fulcrum had become too gymnastic and "show-offy". I have to say I was disappointed that she wasn't more interested because it was so successful. I think Fulcrum could have commanded a lot of attention. But now I'm kind of thankful to Helen for forcing me to be more of an artist and not going for the easy high.*

Fulcrum had never been officially incorporated as a company, so the trio simply stopped performing together. Bingham, however, still performed with

Clarke in her performance art-styled choreography. He recalls:

> Helen and I did a lot of work together. We were partners, so I was always facilitating her work and she would help me with mine. She'd tell me her dreams and we would try and manifest them.

Like Bingham, Harwood was disappointed by the break up: "I'm convinced Fulcrum could have gone quite far on the dance map had we stuck together for a while. In a short period of time we left a real imprint, and if we'd stayed together for eight or ten years, who knows what would have happened." He left to forge his own path, travelling to San Francisco for further training with Mangrove.

Peter Bingham and Helen Clarke in Clarke's *Oeufs Fragile*.
Photo: Chris Randle

After a year studying and teaching, Harwood settled back in Montreal.

Bingham credits the success of Fulcrum to the wide training Rubin gave them in improvisation: "We liked to do contact, but we also knew about improvising [in general]." He considers Synergy to have been the catalyst for his discovery of himself: "... of who I was and, through that, potentially who I might be. And allowing myself to physically investigate those possibilities." Peter Ryan echoes Bingham's comments: "Linda opened you to the possibilities of dance. There's no question – it was a great place to start." Nonetheless, disagreements slowly emerged as students developed their own ideas and directions. "There was never a decision to stop," Bingham recalls. "The situation just slowly wore itself out." The role of Synergy had been to offer an effective introduction, and it is remembered with respect.

Bingham finally decided to have a second knee operation. The first, at age seventeen, had been to stop the knee joint from continually slipping out of its socket; now, the anterior cruciate ligament had snapped and muscle needed to be moved to help stabilize the knee. Once the cast was taken off, he was told he probably would not be able to return to dance, so it seemed a good time for a change of focus and in November 1979 he set off on a year-long trip with Helen Clarke to Japan and Southeast Asia. They also spent time with Clarke's family in Australia, body surfing in the ocean for four or five hours at a time and going on long hikes, which was good therapy for his knee.

Back in Vancouver, Bingham threw himself into renovating a house he bought with his younger brother John, funded through a small family inheritance. The house was on a quiet residential street not far from the downtown core, and the project consumed much time and energy. Any fears over the success of his knee operation were dispelled when he took time off to work with Jennifer Mascall, who was dancing with Paula Ross' company, and Jay Hirabayashi, who had recently left the same group. Mascall created a duet for the two men as part of what became a trio called *Broken Up*. First, she orchestrated a dance that resembled a fight, keeping the men in close physical contact. Then she separated them and set the choreography, in which they performed the same moves as simultaneous solos, featuring an athletic force that came naturally to them both. An expressive "face dance" performed by Clarke alongside the men completed the trio.

Although he enjoyed being part of such experimental work, Bingham was still uncertain about where his dance career was headed. A choreography called *Coming Out of Chaos* would put him firmly back on the dance track.

Making EDAM

EDAM was a phenomenon.
— Barbara Clausen

EDAM was the supertroupe.
— Daniel Collins

Peter Bingham, by the age of thirty, was an experienced performer who had received acclaim for his avant-garde work in contact improvisation. As part of Fulcrum, he had weathered one devastating review in a local newspaper and gone on to the glory of a rave in the national *Globe and Mail*. However, as the hard labour of upgrading the two-storey, wood-frame house he had bought with his brother, John, progressed, he felt that taking time out to dance needed to be justified with a decent wage. Renovations were costing more than they had expected and, engrossed in ripping out walls and installing plumbing, life took on a practical rather than a creative drive. He did not feel any immediate need to dance, although now that his knee had recovered from surgery, there was no reason not to. So, when choreographer Karen Jamieson offered Bingham a job, the only question he asked was the straightforward one of salary.

First, *Chaos*

Bingham had met Karen Jamieson when she came to the Western Front to practice contact improvisation with him and Peter Ryan. Jamieson, like Bingham, had discovered dance while a student at Simon Fraser University. At age twenty-two, in 1968, the Vancouver-born education student had taken her first dance class: a non-credit workshop taught by Iris Garland. After studying and performing in New York, where she had been a member of the Alwin Nikolais company, Jamieson returned to Vancouver. Here, with Savannah Walling, she co-founded the multidisciplinary Terminal City Dance Research collective.

Familiar with Jamieson's reputation as a collective creator, Bingham presumed she was hiring him for the kind of collaborative work he always did. What he did not know was that Jamieson was in the throes of questioning the whole idea of collective creation and was ready to find her own voice. "Every aspect of my life was in a collective," she explains. "I owned property up the coast collectively, I sent my son to a collective daycare and I was in the Terminal City collective. There was no 'me' anywhere." What she needed was a group of dancers who supported her vision, but no one – including Jamieson herself – knew this yet.

Besides Bingham, Jamieson hired Walling, contact improviser Peter Ryan and a recent SFU dance program graduate, Lola MacLaughlin. Musician Ahmed Hassan, who had worked with Terminal City Dance Research, was

Karen Jamieson, Savannah Walling and Terry Hunter, 1980.   Photo: David Cooper

also in the group. Barbara Bourget was with the project for a time, but left to join the Paula Ross group; Jennifer Mascall, whom Jamieson had met at York University during the first of Grant Strate's Choreographic Seminars, was her replacement. Although the salary proved disappointing, Bingham was soon bicycling every morning to the Jamieson studio at 531 Carroll Street in the heart of Gastown and putting in drywall at night. On a purely physical level, it was hard going.

It was hard going for Jamieson, too. Throughout the creation period of what became *Coming Out of Chaos*, she was torn between forces of collective need (her dancers) and individual agency (her own). Jamieson recalls:

> *I would bring in these ideas and the dancers would say, "Well, no, we don't want to do that." I'd be totally stymied. Of course it never occurred to me to just fire the lot and find some other dancers.*

Instead, she worked with the performers' desire to follow their own direction, seeing where this could fit in with her imperative to find herself. The piece began to come together when Jamieson brought a ladder into the studio, which she would climb and then sit on in order to observe them improvising. "They did what they wanted, which was the chaos, and I would come down from the ladder and dance with each one. That was basically it." To honour their input, she credited the dancers with "choreographic assistance".

Coming Out of Chaos premiered in April 1982 at the Waterfront Theatre on Granville Island. *Vandance* magazine described it as a "blending of dance, drama and music, combining highly structured choreography, contact improvisation, dramatic lines and characterization and every imaginable non-verbal vocalization." There is humour, as well as "madness", as when "Peter Bingham screams at his finger."

Program for *Coming Out of Chaos* by Karen Jamieson Rimmer.

The work toured to Victoria, Toronto and Quebec City, receiving international attention in *Dance Magazine*. After the Toronto performance, writer Selma Landen Odom described it as a "tour de force of contrasting moods and textures", with the contact improvisation by Jamieson, Bingham, Ryan and Mascall containing "awe-inspiring surprises of balance and weight." As always with a work of art, there were different opinions. Bingham remembers one Toronto dance artist complaining, "You guys aren't dancers, your legs aren't even straight!"

As the choreographer and a few of those involved admit, some performances of *Coming Out of Chaos* were less than satisfactory. The dancers were not always at their most committed: they had their own aesthetic agendas and beliefs, which limited their ability to commit to another artist. The professional dancer's generosity and ability to suspend any disbelief they might feel toward a project did not come easily to them.

During the creation and performance of *Chaos*, the independent dancers became close. Together, they could vent frustration at not being in charge, and at having to undergo a creative process that was not like their own. Various members of the group were already friends after performing together as independents. In April 1981, Bingham had coordinated Four Concerts in Contact Improvisation with Mascall, Ryan and Diane Moore, presented at the Terminal City Dance studio. In May 1982, some of them were part of the Western Front Independent Choreographers Series. Presented at the Firehall Theatre by Jane Ellison and Barbara Clausen, this was the inaugural dance event at the newly opened Firehall Arts Centre. Bingham shared a bill with MacLaughlin and Ryan, and the next night Mascall performed solo. The only non-local performer was Quebec's Marie Chouinard.

In Max Wyman's review of the Independent Choreographers Series, published in *The Province* newspaper for which he now wrote, he devoted much space to the contact improvisation work of Bingham and Ryan. Their first piece was humorous, with vocal and percussion accompaniment by Ahmed Hassan, while the second was "a silent, intense working-together in practice clothes, framed by an artful slow arc of light from dark to bright to dark again." Wyman called the pair "exceptions" in terms of using contact improvisation, having "developed an instinct for the moving moment that sustains their work in something close to theatrical terms." He found the performance by Bingham and Ryan "underlined their deep understanding of the form's possibilities." This was heady praise for the two men, who were keen to develop their own work further, and who felt like they were marking time working for someone else.

Shortly after *Coming Out of Chaos* closed, Jamieson made the break from the collective situation of Terminal City Dance Research to birth the Karen Jamieson Dance Company, leaving Walling and Hunter to regroup as Vancouver Moving Theatre. Bingham and Ryan, with other survivors from *Chaos*, banded together and thus the seven-headed *enfant terrible* known as EDAM came into being.

EDAM Seven

The story of the founding of Experimental Dance and Music, or EDAM as it was soon called, has more than one telling. According to Peter Bingham, one day he and Jennifer Mascall were on their way to visit Lola MacLaughlin and Ahmed Hassan in their studio. As they walked along, trying to figure out how to survive as dancers, Bingham remembers arriving at the conclusion that they should all band together to form a company, thus becoming eligible for support at a time when independent dancers did not fit into government funding categories.

Mascall remembers arranging a number of performances at the Terminal City and Western Front studios. After one concert involving pretty much everyone who became the EDAM gang, she recalls suggesting they get together on a more permanent basis, and then discussing with Peter Ryan how to create an entity that could support independent dance artists within a company structure.

MacLaughlin says that after working together in *Coming Out of Chaos*, the idea itself was "in the air". This is reinforced in a letter Barbara Bourget wrote on behalf of EDAM to the Canada Council, in which she states: "Most of us had worked together previously, but we were encouraged by the suggestions from several of our members that a collective/cooperative would be a more effective and efficient solution to our individual concerns."

In any case, the telephone calls seem to have come from Mascall, which is what Jay Hirabayashi remembers. He had not been part of *Coming Out of Chaos*, but the only member of the proposed collective he did not know was Hassan, the sole musician, who worked as an accompanist. Hirabayashi had taken contact improvisation classes with Bingham and Ryan, and had seen one of MacLaughlin's early pieces at the Paula Ross studio when he was with the Ross company. He had worked with Bingham and Mascall on *Broken Up* and was married to Bourget, so it was natural to invite him to join them.

The initial meeting took place during the summer of 1982, either at MacLaughlin and Hassan's studio, at Bourget and Hirabayashi's Kitsilano home, or in the basement suite Bingham and his brother had built in their house on 15th Avenue, which was where Bingham lived. These were the three places where the group usually met. All seven founding members were present: Peter Bingham, Barbara Bourget, Ahmed Hassan, Jay Hirabayashi, Lola MacLaughlin, Jennifer Mascall and Peter Ryan. It was Hassan who coined the name Experimental Dance and Music, or EDAM, eager to have the music side of things acknowledged, although not everyone liked the acronym's association to cheese.

On September 10, 1982, EDAM Performing Arts Society was incorporated as a non-profit charitable organization. A description of motives and operations is found in Bourget's letter to the Canada Council:

> We intend our organization to allow for our development as individuals, yet we see it as being in no way detrimental to the company's evolution. The image of the independent dancer in Canada is often that of a person who is disorganized and not genuinely professional; we have united in order to avoid those connotations and to work from a position of cohesion and of responsibility.... EDAM will evolve as each member achieves individual goals and incorporates them into the structure of the whole.

The group had no manager or administrator, so Hirabayashi took over much of the paperwork. He recalls numerous meetings, which tended to be lengthy, with consensus seldom easy to reach. Choosing a bank became a major dilemma when one member refused to conduct business with any institutions associated with questionable third world practices. Hirabayashi recalls:

There was one meeting where we talked for three hours about whether to buy a cash box that cost $17. Some people thought it was a complete waste of money; you could just use an envelope. Some of us said, "Well, no, the point of a cash box is it's more secure and identifiable." Finally everyone was exhausted and we all agreed to get the cash box.

On the other hand, Mascall remembers a meeting – "Jay wasn't there" – where "we sat for hours and hours to arrive at a title, *Naked and Unafraid*. Well, on my own it takes me a good couple of weeks to find a title so this session was arduous but also inspiring." She admits, however, that at some point, "dealing with the other people took too much time away from the creative work. I felt what we needed was four companies and one manager."

Both Bingham and Ryan used the term "marriage of convenience" to describe EDAM. Certainly, from the beginning members pursued their individual careers with diligence, even when these took them out of Vancouver for extended periods. Hassan left almost immediately after the company's formation to study in New York, and then went to Toronto with MacLaughlin to perform with Desrosiers Dance Theatre. Hirabayashi danced for Karen Jamieson in the first year. Mascall kept up her solo career throughout. Ryan continued writing for *Vandance* and *Dance in Canada* magazines, and taught contact improvisation through the Vancouver School Board and at various theatre schools. Bingham taught contact improvisation, both at the Western Front and at Dean Fogal and Catherine Lee's Room to Move studio.

Affinities between individuals, as well as their variety of dance training, led to tension within the group. Alliances were formed through personal partnerships (Bourget and Hirabayashi, MacLaughlin and Hassan), as well as through artistic ones (Bingham and Ryan as seasoned contact improvisers; Bingham, Ryan and Mascall as the keen improvisers in a broader theatrical sense). Although Bourget had the most extensive professional experience, having performed with the Royal Winnipeg Ballet, Les Grands Ballets Canadiens, Mountain Dance Theatre and Paula Ross' company, Mascall and MacLaughlin had the credentials of undergraduate degrees in dance from York and Simon Fraser Universities respectively. Strong verbal and writing skills, as well as advanced academic credentials came from Hirabayashi, who had an MA in Buddhist Studies from the University of British Columbia, and Ryan, with an MA in English from the University of Western Ontario.

Members of EDAM offered classes for the public at the Western Front studio and, partly to facilitate their work in each other's choreography, the group took turns leading a company class on an irregular basis, usually during periods of rehearsal. This sharing of knowledge would be invaluable to everyone. Bourget, Hirabayashi, MacLaughlin and Mascall gave classes in modern dance. Bourget also taught ballet. Bingham and Ryan offered their experience in contact improvisation and improvisation. Bingham says:

> I remember standing at the barre doing a hundred battements with Barbara and I remember Jennifer trying to teach me how to keep my pelvis still doing pliés. Really basic technical stuff. Jay taught, too, and I remember doing "crab walks" with him.

Bingham had begun expanding his technical skill in the late 1970s by taking ballet with Peggy Florin, whom he had met when she came to his contact classes. When Florin began teaching ballet at Capilano College, he travelled to North Vancouver to study with her for a period. Then, while he worked on *Coming Out of Chaos*, Bingham joined Karen Jamieson in her private ballet classes with Dianne Miller. "One of the first things Dianne said to me," recalls Bingham, "was 'Oh my god, you have an intelligent body.' It was because she could touch me and talk to me and my body would respond directly." He was impressed with Miller's ability to grasp what was going on for him physically, and to help him open and grow as a dancer. Gradually, Bingham's dismissal and distrust of ballet grew into a respect for the depth of anatomical understanding on which it is based.

It was MacLaughlin and Hassan who organized the inaugural EDAM performance. This was in October 1982 at a small club on West Hastings Street, the Dub Club. The couple improvised together, and there were contributions from Bourget, Hirabayashi and Bingham. There is no record of what was performed and none of the individuals interviewed have clear memories of the event. In fact, Bingham did not recall being in the show at all, until a poster turned up in a pile of papers he found in a closet at his home. Over the next two years, a variety of appearances kept EDAM busy, including fundraisers for the company and a performance at the Vancouver Children's Festival.

Terry Hunter, Peter Bingham and Helen Clarke in *All Flames are Waiting to Kill All Moths.*   Photo: Chris Randle

In 1983, Helen Clarke joined EDAM for Performance Exchange. Bingham had hoped Clarke would be part of EDAM but she had other plans, and would soon move to the United States to attend university. While Clarke continued to support Bingham by performing in his choreography, just as he continued to appear in hers, their open relationship was slowly unravelling. Once in the United States, Clarke became involved with the man she would marry and with whom she would return to Australia.

Performance Exchange was a multidisciplinary series at the busy Terminal City Dance Research studio. In January, Bingham, Clarke and Mascall performed in *All Flames are Waiting to Kill All Moths*, a structured improvisation devised by the three performers.

The second show, in April, included one piece by Ryan and three by Bingham: *Reflect, Wangarata Crawl* and *Ray De Us* (Bingham calls the title his "first stupid joke" and later changed the spelling to *Radius*). *Reflect,* a sinuous solo combining choreography and structured improvisation, was performed by Jay Hirabayashi,

Jay Hirabayashi in *Reflect*.   Photo: Chris Randle

dressed in black, with red gloves and a red hat. *Wangarata Crawl*, titled after a place
in Australia Bingham passed through during his travels, was a duet he performed
with mime artist Philip Maxwell, with movement based on Australian animals.

Ray De Us, which featured him and Clarke, is the only piece Bingham
remembers in any detail. Much like their relationship, *Ray De Us* was about
mutual support. It began with Bingham standing in the centre of a circle
defined by eight lines marked out in tape on the studio floor, like the rays of
the sun in a child's drawing. Clarke ran along one line and hurled herself at
Bingham, who delivered her to the next line, where the action was repeated
until the circle was complete. Then it was Bingham's turn to be caught and
supported.

Throughout *Ray De Us*, a quartet of black-clad performers carried mirrors
to various spots on the stage. This served numerous functions. First, it gave
the audience a different view than just the straight-ahead one, reminiscent
of the casual contact improvisation demonstrations that took place in studios
with people sitting on all sides. As well, the audience could see themselves in
the mirrors, which made them a part of the performance. This was meant to
suggest the spectator's role in the experience of a work of art by encouraging
the idea of self-reflection.

The quartet were members of Bingham's "work group". Made up of proficient students who performed together as an improvisational ensemble, work group members included jazz pianist Bruce "VJ" Cuddeford, from Synergy; Mark Lavelle, who was desperate to dance after he saw a performance by Bingham at the Western Front; Monique Léger, a young dancer from Moncton, New Brunswick; Lee Masters, later a member of Rebound Dance Collective; mime artist Philip Maxwell; and Irene Franco, an art school student. At informal studio presentations, the group gave a number of improvisations, including one structured around flocking called *The Great Ock*.

Right from the beginning, Bingham came up against his fellow "EDAMites" when a piece he wanted to present with his work group was cut from one of EDAM's mixed bills. Some members of the work group had rehearsed an ensemble version of the duet from *Ray De Us*, perfecting a series of jumps and catches using contact improvisation. Despite the hours of rehearsal put in, the EDAM collective judged the work inappropriate for their professional program. The dancers were not polished enough and the company felt their image would be tarnished. Bingham argued that the piece was a postmodern one with its own vocabulary and style. When this fell on deaf ears, he was furious, and never forgot this slight to his artistic voice.

After this incident, Bingham was no longer involved with the work group, recalls Lee Masters, who regretted losing "such a great leader. He didn't put himself above us, he was down-to-earth and matter-of-fact. I always felt comfortable with Peter because he was so accepting of people." Mark Lavelle, who entered the dance program at Simon Fraser University shortly afterwards recalls the whole thing as disheartening. "We continued as a group," he says, "but our aspirations changed. We knew we couldn't perform with EDAM."

Despite such clashes, two men at EDAM, Hirabayashi and Ryan, remained close colleagues of Bingham's. In February 1983, when EDAM presented a half-dozen works on a mixed bill at the Western Front, their contribution left a strong impression on critic Max Wyman. The bill included *Orbits*, a contact improvisation-based choreography co-created by all three, as well as Hirabayashi's study of conflict and cooperation, *Blind Fraternity*. This was a duet for himself and Bingham with numerous lifts derived from contact improvisation.

By comparison to the women, the three men were relatively inexperienced, a fact they made no attempt to hide. In fact, it was the raw athleticism and kinetic excitement of their movement that so impressed audiences. In his *Province* review, Wyman attributed much of the evening's "sense of explosive energy harnessed to a rich imaginative expressiveness" to "the sport-and-dance crossover." He noted the athletic backgrounds of Bingham, Hirabayashi and Ryan, calling them "important elements of a vigorous new wave of creative freshness and imaginative force that is sweeping the small community of Vancouver independent choreographers."

Such enthusiasm for their first shared efforts was exhilarating. The show acted to whet the appetite of the city's dance audience for a larger project in which the crossover between dance and sport would be explored in more depth. Bingham, Hirabayashi and Ryan had already applied for a Canada Council Explorations Grant to fund what would be EDAM's first collective creation, a sport-derived choreography. An Explorations Grant did not require formal peer assessments of artistic quality; geared for cultural development, it was open to any Canadian with a groundbreaking idea. They were sure they had one.

Running Raw

In their Canada Council funding application, Bingham, Hirabayashi and Ryan wrote:

> We intend to utilize our collective athletic experience to create a dance work that will reflect the aesthetics of the competitive athlete within the medium of dance performance. It is not our intention to create a work that neces- sarily resembles, caricatures or otherwise imitates sports, but rather one that incorporates aesthetic considerations derived from sports. Our purpose is to enlarge the vocabulary of the dance medium through this introduction of sports-derived movement.

The men's athletic experience was the common denominator around which the group rallied: Bingham had played competitive school sports, Hirabayashi had been a downhill ski racer and Ryan had competed in international row- ing.

The trio's Canada Council application, under the working title *Athletic Aes- thetics in Dance*, proposed an eight-week training period beginning in January 1983. The first two weeks would be devoted to researching sports movement, out of which a training and rehearsal schedule would be designed. The ath- letic training would include endurance, strength and motor skills. The second stage was abstracting the movement into dance. A finished performance, with two additional dancers and music by Ahmed Hassan, was promised for March 1983.

As it turned out, Hassan was not involved in what became *Run Raw: Theme and Deviation*. He was in New York, auditioning and learning to play a single stringed, bowed Brazilian instrument called the berimbau. Salvador Ferreras, a newcomer to Vancouver working as an accompanist for Karen Jamieson, re- placed him. Four, not two, additional dancers were hired: EDAMites Bourget, MacLaughlin and Mascall, plus the independent Léger.

In addition to the company dance class, Bingham, Hirabayashi and Ryan set up a regimen of weight training, timed circuit training, cycling and running to increase the group's strength and endurance. Basketball, including passing and shooting drills, frisbee throws and catches, and high jumping were also scheduled.

The extreme training regimen "was a kind of bonding thing," says Hirabayashi, adding:

> Circuit training is hard. There are times when your body just doesn't want to go, yet people around you are shouting, "Go, go, go!" We had to convey to the women what it's like to have a coach pushing you all the time, which was a kind of training they weren't used to.

The piece was created collaboratively, using improvisation to generate material in the early stages of rehearsals. Bourget, MacLaughlin and Mascall, more experienced as choreographers than the men, shaped the material into individual sections that were later ordered into a cohesive structure. The percussion score by Ferreras was performed live.

After a late-night preview at the Vancouver East Cultural Centre on May 20, five minutes were cut, bringing the work down to thirty minutes. *Run Raw: Theme and Deviation* premiered on May 30, 1983 for a four-night run at the Western Front studio where the company was now resident. Each evening opened with a different selection of dances by EDAM members; then, in preparation for *Run Raw*, during intermission the seating arrangement was changed to resemble a gymnasium, with spectators along two sides of the studio.

Susan Mertens in *The Vancouver Sun* wrote:

> Run Raw *begins with a variation on speed sprints around obstacles — a kind of human barrel race with an interweaving pattern of six bodies moving flat-out. The seventh dancer, stopwatch in hand, hurls out instructions, corrections. The speed increases. Time is the competition. Personal best is the name of the game. It's dance class with the gloves off.*

The *Province* newspaper found room for not just one, but two reviews by Max Wyman; clearly, EDAM was hot. On May 31, after the opening night show, Wyman wrote: "There's an Olympian nobility to their strenuous achievement. It holds you fascinated and it leaves you exhilarated ... and wondering exactly who has won."

A week later, on June 8, Wyman's remarks are more considered, perhaps due to the injuries sustained during performance by Hirabayashi (torn ankle ligaments) and Bourget (a broken wrist), which are noted in the article. At the two evening shows Wyman saw, the group "drove themselves literally to the point of dripping exhaustion — and it's no surprise that they had to pace the performances over a period of six days, the way opera companies do, to allow the organism a day of rest and recuperation between the immense demands." However, "repeated exposure to extreme exertion deadens our surprise" and he offers advice: "What the EDAM people need to find now are ways to shape and harness that kinetic explosiveness to the service of kinetic form – to impose dance craft."

EDAM's final report to the Canada Council sums up the project:

> ... the work accomplished a number of goals: dancers were able to gain immeasurably from exposure to athletic training methods and thinking, then to evoke a combination of dance and athletic experience with sufficient skill and intensity to create a new context for viewing by audiences that previously had not connected the two disciplines in anything other than superficial terms. We were also able to perform a dance work possessing the tension and moment-to-moment excitement (as well as some of the calm and concentration) of athletic situations.

The report did not mention the two accidents. When Bourget broke her wrist on opening night, she managed to finish the show but Debra Brown replaced her for subsequent performances. On the final evening, Hirabayashi's ankle was crushed. It is possible these accidents were caused by last-minute changes to the choreography, leaving the dancers under-rehearsed. Yet it seems hardly surprising that accidents would happen in a piece about endurance and pushing the body to the limit, an aesthetic whose time had come. Endurance training was something Paula Ross stressed in her modern dance classes, with non-dance exercises like push-ups, running on the spot and "crab walks" across the floor. As a choreographer, too, Ross used elements of repetition and exhaustion, notably in her 1979 work, *Coming Together*, in which Hirabayashi performed. In 1985, Montreal's Édouard Lock toured *Human Sex*, a choreographed blast of athletic energy, something his company, La La La Human Steps, became famous for. Later still, in the 1990s, Vancouver's Holy Body Tattoo became internationally known through choreography based on frenzied, repetitive energy and effort.

As for EDAM, *Run Raw* had pushed raw energy to its limit. The high impact, go-for-broke physicality, with its mix of task-like focus and wild abandon, offered exactly the kind of shake-up the well-behaved dance world needed. The company was playing its role as new kid on the block to the hilt and the generous amount of Vancouver press kept them in the public eye.

8:00 pm
JUNE 28 & 29
JULY 3-6

Reservations and Information:
876-9559
Admission: $10/$9

Western Front Lodge
303 East 8th Ave

Project Funded by Canada Council and the Province of British Columbia.

poster design: Alix Hirabayashi

Coming and Going
In the Garden of EDAM

EDAM is a cooperative – I don't understand why you're being so uncooperative.
— Jennifer Mascall to Jay Hirabayashi during a company meeting

EDAM's new home at the Western Front was the same high-ceilinged studio with large sash windows and a beautiful maple floor where Peter Bingham had taken his first dance class with Linda Rubin. It was located on the ground floor of a three-storey, wood-clad building constructed in 1922 by a fraternal organization called the Knights of Pythias. When the hall was purchased in 1973 by a group of artists, they transformed the dark, somewhat gloomy rabbit warren of rooms into a shared live/work space and named it the Western Front Lodge. According to *Whispered Art History: Twenty years at the Western Front*, this was in reference to the Vancouver-styled "'pioneer' false front façade, an architectural device that made a gable-roofed building appear more imposing." The name also "conjures up images of World War I and the creation of alliances that did battle with the 'enemy'. Although there were no major art battles being fought in Vancouver during the early 1970s, alliances were indeed being formed...." On a residential street bordering a light industrial area, the Western Front was a busy artist-run centre, known for its avant-garde performance art, video, music, visual art and literary activities.

Filmmaker Peg Campbell describes an evening at the Western Front circa 1980, which she videotaped as a member of the Women's Media Alliance:

> *Willoughby Sharp, a performance artist from New York, sits in a cage in the attic of the Western Front, banging a tin plate on the bars. Crowds gather in the Lux theatre, watching Hitchcock's* The Man Who Knew Too Much, *running forwards and backwards on two projectors. Paul Plimley plays cacophonous notes on a grand piano, Taki Bluesinger takes photographs from a restricted square in the middle of the room. Live video from everywhere in the artist-run-centre [is] fed into a bank of monitors. It is all very exciting.*

It was here that Bingham would receive his art-world education. Jane Ellison, who lived at the Front for a time and was involved in many of the activities, says:

> *Peter always checked out what was going on upstairs [at the Lux Theatre]. You very rarely see dancers coming to new music, but Peter was interested. He came to performance art events, too.*

"I had never run into the art world before," Bingham explains. "It was amazing to me." He first heard local poet Gerry Gilbert at the Western Front, and caught the Vancouver debut of American musician and performance artist Laurie Anderson there. Bingham enjoyed the irreverent, tongue-in-cheek quality of performance art and appeared in a number of pieces, including one by a visiting Ottawa artist who asked him to read some text aloud and smoke a cigarette while a silent film was projected. As recently as 2001, Bingham played a character called

Sleuth Lips for a performance art piece presented at the Vancouver Art Gallery by Glenn Lewis, one of the original eight shareholders who founded the Western Front. Bingham says: "My character was an FBI agent trying to figure out performance art – well, you know what? That's what I was doing at all those early performances."

For the artists living at the Western Front, it was easy to attend the various events at the second floor Lux Theatre or in the downstairs dance studio, but the latter was of no particular interest to them. "At that time," says Ellison, who was the exception and had a solid background in dance, "there was very much an upstairs/downstairs mentality [at the Front] …" When well-known names like Deborah Hay, Yvonne Rainer and Steve Paxton came to the Front in the 1970s, Ellison's colleagues "were down there checking it out." But most of the local work "wasn't that interesting from an art point of view. The dance community in Vancouver just had no relationship with the art world."

Ellison recalls how the studio constantly came under threat:

Every once in a while someone at the Front would say, "Oh, that dance studio – you know, we really need another gallery space. We could just

knock out the wall and have the whole main floor as a gallery." So it was really important to me to keep the income coming in so that the space could justify its existence as a dance studio.

In 1983, she was happy to relinquish the chore of handling studio rentals when EDAM moved in and programming became their responsibility.

Early Days

After *Run Raw: Theme and Deviation*, EDAM hired its first manager, Sheenah Andrews. Although experienced in arts management, including a stint as general manager with Pacific Ballet Theatre, she had her hands full with seven artistic directors. "They were all strong personalities," she recalls, "and all uniquely gifted." Andrews stayed for eight months. EDAM would go through three managers in six years.

"We were pretty anxious to keep working," says Bingham of this period, "and to build the company." Only two months after the marathon of *Run Raw* had ended, EDAM mounted a mixed bill in August 1983, *True Lies*, at the Western Front studio, featuring an excerpt from Jennifer Mascall's new work of the same title, and another showing of Bingham's *Ray De Us*. By mid-August, most of EDAM, except for Bingham, were in Toronto for various reasons and gave three performances there.

When the full company toured to London, Ontario and St. John's, Newfoundland in 1984, the press was wildly complimentary. In *The Newfoundland Herald*, the reviewer called the visit "fabulously successful" and enjoyed everyone's contribution. The enthusiastic review noted Bingham and Ryan's "tour de force", *Sui Generis* (Latin for "of its own kind; unique"), "a combination of contact and improvisation that clicked in and out with superbly timed precision."

The reviewer from the University of Western Ontario's newspaper, *The London Gazette*, enjoyed the choreographed pieces but found the improvisations "the most absorbing works of the programme." The closing improvised duet by Bingham and Ryan "exploded with the sheer physicality of the two athletic bodies in motion." There was also a group improvisation, and another performed by Bingham and Mascall, in which the two "worked together so beautifully and instinctively that it was difficult to believe that the movement was not choreographed beforehand."

There was one dissenting voice – the *Daily News*' Linda Rimsay, who had moved to Newfoundland from the United States in 1978 and was co-director of Newfoundland Dance Theatre at the time of EDAM's visit. Here is the penultimate paragraph of her review:

This is a group of very finely trained dancers. There is little question about their technical ability. They have power and control but they are stuck in the trendy ruts of the 50s and 60s which probably wouldn't annoy me so much if the works were performed as period pieces rather than experimental pieces of the 80s.

Rimsay's compliment to their training might almost be enough to cancel out her negative comments, at least for the majority of the group, who had come to dance late in life. The men in particular had a minimum of technical dance training and were sensitive about this. Bingham feels some of his colleagues considered it difficult to choreograph on him because he was not technically proficient aside from his expertise in contact improvisation. This, however, was not really considered proper technique, which had to come from ballet or modern dance. "That was one of the issues I had with EDAM," Bingham says. "I found it a bit weird that we were supposed to be postmodernist but wouldn't let go of [modern] technique."

As late as 1995, Ryan wrote in *Dance Connection* magazine: "… the policy of the Canada Council has been that contact improvisation does not suffice as a dancer's basic training. Apparently (and partly as a result of inquiries made to the Council during the writing of this article), this situation has changed."

Despite their successful partnership and the buzz surrounding the company's improvisations, Ryan believes that both he and Bingham were merely "tolerated" at EDAM:

There was a feeling of resentment because the others would toil at choreography. Peter and I would improvise – they would say we "just" improvised. There was a real split between the choreographed and improvised sides.

What probably made it worse was how easy the two found it to perform together. Ryan recalls of those early days:

We didn't need to talk. We just knew [what to do] because we were on the same page. Each year we'd give our dance a new title and walk out into the wings. I'd look at him and say, "You ready?" "Yup." "Okay, who's first?" And off we'd go.

Bingham agrees there were issues with regard to his and Ryan's lack of rehearsal prior to performances. From his point of view, what mattered more were the almost daily contact improvisation sessions, which kept their instincts for creating in the moment sharp. For the two improvisers, preparation for shows was not about polishing and perfecting a particular repertoire: rehearsals were simply part of their on-going practice. As Bingham says, "It's hard for people who make choreography to recognize that improvisers do their work long before a show. You just don't iden-tify that the rehearsals are for a particular show. You're always rehearsing when you practice."

While Bingham may not have won contests over whose legs lifted the highest or who had the most turnout, he had what manager Andrews called "charisma", both on stage and off. As Jane Ellison put it:

Steve Paxton rehearsing with Michael Linehan, EDAM studio/theatre.

Peter never had great
modern dance technique,
and I think there might have been a hierarchy within the group on that.
On the other hand, Peter had skills none of them had — he had the charm
and the ability to work with people. Some of them had these egos, and in
a way that's what you need to get a higher profile, but Peter has this other
way of getting things and getting to places.

For everyone, it was an enormous undertaking to try and master the stylistic variety EDAM presented. EDAM's Lola MacLaughlin admits that contact improvisation and improvisation were never easy for her, except when she was dancing with Bingham:

I was new to contact improvisation and kind of had it rammed down my
throat. Honestly, I didn't like it very much — it always came down to per-
sonal space .... But I always enjoyed dancing with Peter. He was gentle and
caring about his partnering. I had other experiences with some EDAMites.
We did improvs all the time and there would be these rules, but when you
got out there, no one ever played by the rules. It was a free-for-all, it was
always sabotage; I hated it. Improvisation at EDAM was never a safe place
to be. But a duet with Peter was different.

Peter Ryan and Peter Bingham in *XYZ*.   Photo: Chris Randle

While guest dancers were brought in for specific choreographies, the EDAMites were all expected to perform in each other's works. Bingham, who had to stretch his understanding of what it meant to be a dancer, admits:

> It wasn't all my cup of tea, by any means, but I was supportive of the idea of the company. Of course the work was challenging because a lot of it wasn't in my style. During a feedback session after one performance, I asked why they had me dancing like that, because I didn't look great doing that kind of work. I knew what I was good at; I wasn't carrying any illusions around about myself.

It was his partnership with Ryan that most fulfilled Bingham's potential as a performer. As Deborah Meyers wrote about Bingham and Ryan: "It is a pleasure to watch these two move together." This sentiment was a common one.

It is also important to realize how key their improvisational work was to EDAM's reputation for being experimental. That was what gave them the edge on other modern dance companies. Over and over, the open, fresh and unpretentious improvisations by Bingham and Ryan endeared the duo to the public and press. When EDAM embarked on another tour to eastern Canada in March 1985, their improvised *XYZ* was one of the company's most successful works, and contact improvisation was commented on in every review.

The *Ottawa Citizen*'s Charles Pope noted the company's "high degree of general professionalism and polish," as well as their "genuine originality". He called contact improvisation the "basic skill" within the company, and declared " ... the most startling example" of that skill was *XYZ*.

Deirdre Kelly in *The Globe and Mail* wrote: "EDAM is perhaps the country's most skilful practitioner of contact improvisation." She enjoyed Bourget's trio work, *Hitting the Wall*, noting: "the hallmark of the dance was a dazzling display of contact improvisation. Bingham and Hirabayashi, though less confident in their movements than Bourget, nonetheless demonstrated the graceful athleticism of contact." *XYZ*'s "lush physicality and delightful spontaneity of dancing" was also praised.

The Toronto Star's William Littler described the "look" of EDAM as being "the look of contact improvisation, a technique taught by some of its members and practiced explicitly in one of the pieces by the Peters Bingham and Ryan." In their *XYZ*, he continued, "contact improvisation provides a way of freeing the choreographic mind of its ordinary patterns of thought."

Yet some company members, though willing to take on board a part of what contact improvisation had to offer, also felt it necessary to keep the form at arm's length. It was not, after all, the primary means of aesthetic expression for all of them. Perhaps contact improvisation was too grassroots, too untamed, and thus too liable to compromise the company's professional image. EDAM was competing for funding and for audiences with modern dance groups like Anna Wyman's, whose dancers were proficient in the recognizable technical vocabulary that made it clear they were professional, well-trained artists, and that gave them high status within the dance world. This was not, however, the aesthetic Bingham was after – and he felt keenly this disconnect with both his fellow EDAMites and the larger dance community.

Behind the scenes, too, Lola MacLaughlin notes how competitive the members of EDAM were: "It was never a harmonious group, it was always hard on the health. There was a lot of conflict, because everyone wanted different things and were determined that no one was going to get ahead of them."

As well, the sheer number of meetings was wearing, and decisions reached by the group often did not satisfy individuals. From the beginning, Jay Hirabayashi found it difficult to accept the compromise that was necessary to reach group agreement. For him, the meetings were onerous and often infuriating. Aside from Barbara Bourget, his life and work partner, Hirabayashi felt increasingly alienated from his colleagues. He wanted more administra-

THREE NIGHTS IN THE GARDEN OF

EDAM

THE WESTERN FRONT   303 EAST 8TH AVE.

MAY 25 - 27

8:30 PM

$6/$5

RESERVATIONS & INFORMATION 876-9559

EDAM · EXPERIMENTAL DANCE AND MUSIC

photo: jay hirabayashi

tive structure and formal curation, feeling the lack of evaluation of the company's mixed bills was damaging to EDAM's reputation. Unable to effect these changes, he decided to leave.

In his May 9, 1984 letter of resignation, Hirabayashi describes himself as having "a relatively low tolerance level for compromise." With characteristic forthrightness, he criticized his colleagues for lack of discipline in technical training, disrespect for others and a "me first" attitude, closing with a "capsule view" of EDAM:

> *Ryan: in retirement*
> *MacLaughlin: in distress*
> *Bingham: everything's cool but it's important to be late*
> *Mascall: no longer interested in moving, baby x is coming*
> *Hassan: running after the train*
> *Bourget: life is a shithole*
> *Hirabayashi: gone*

Less than a week later, in another letter addressed to EDAM, Hirabayashi describes how he was persuaded to attend yet another meeting, "the kind that I'm really sick of participating in." The dialogue "was more vitriolic, pernicious and mean than usual." At the core of the disagreement was the group's dismissal of his suggestion to appoint a company director on an annual basis to arbitrate the interests of individual members and to produce the season's artistic program. Hirabayashi was also adamant that an artistic director needed to be appointed for each show.

A Night in the Garden of EDAM

During this turmoil, the group was in the throes of creating a site-specific spectacular, A Night in the Garden of EDAM, which would premiere in May 1984. Hirabayashi backed down from his resignation but refused to participate. He felt the work was unfinished, with inadequate artistic direction. In yet another letter, written a few days later and this time addressed to Mascall and Hassan, he criticized the quality of the improvisations: "I do not think that EDAM as a group has the training and experience to successfully pull off three nights of mainly improvisational group pieces." Of particular concern was Hassan's *Psychobabble*, a sound piece using percussion and vocalization. Hirabayashi felt it "had no discernible structure and was being rehearsed with people who lacked pitch control, dynamic sensibility and rhythmic consistency."

Hirabayashi's fears proved unfounded. A Night in the Garden of EDAM was the first of a number of successful "environmental shows", a phrase that referred to the way in which the Western Front studio environment was completely transformed. There was dim, atmospheric lighting, dozens of plants, and hanging nets and mirrors. The audience was asked to take off their shoes before entering. The evening's different sections flowed seamlessly into each other, with group improvisations broken up by Bourget's solo for guest artist Aaron Shields. This was performed three times to three different scores in three different costumes, including whole-body bandages.

Agnes Stevens in *The Vancouver Courier* felt "there was a marvellous feeling of unity about the whole performance" and "the dancers were closely attuned to one another, moving and reacting as a natural whole unit rather than as individual dancers performing together." Max Wyman in *The Province* was uncertain how much was improvised in the group works but "found some of it surprisingly touching and mysteriously exotic" although other bits were "tiresomely arch and trite." Alanna Matthew noted a few highlights, including "Peter Bingham … trapped behind a swaying human barrier, finding a way through and becoming part of it himself."

A few months later, EDAM received a standing ovation from a close-to-capacity crowd at the Queen Elizabeth Playhouse, a downtown civic theatre seating almost 700. Clearly, to be able to fill this mid-size theatre with so many happy patrons, they were doing something right. The September 1984 bill was typically ambitious and showed the company off at their most hyper-creative, unpredictable best. In EDAM's boundary-busting style, things started in the lobby with a remount of Hassan's chant and movement piece, *Jabberwocky*. Then, in the auditorium, Hassan played the berimbau in front of the curtain in *Rapatak*, which Agnes Stevens in the *Courier* described as "a rapid-fire rhythmical talk on everything from relationships to the arrival of the Martians."

Bingham danced in a number of works. One was Mascall's 1982 *Still Bound to Earth (I Refused)*, a solo set to Debussy that was remounted as a duet for him and MacLaughlin. To accompany the earlier solo material set on MacLaughlin, Mascall created static poses for Bingham, who was placed upstage, that were intended to act as a balancing force. When Bingham complained about his lack of movement, Mascall added some business with the hands. Bingham recalls:

> *I had to do a lot of freezing in very difficult positions. Like balancing upside down on my forearms for five minutes, and standing on my tiptoes in an X with my back to the audience for a long period of time. A looong period of time!*

Although he believes the reason Mascall gave him such minimal movement was because he was not one of the "pyrotechnical dancers" she preferred, the effect worked. Agnes Stevens found *Still Bound to Earth* "strongly danced" by both performers and Deborah Meyers in *Vandance* wrote:

> *[Peter Bingham] is an impassive and rigid figure in perfect, preppy white, propping up the woman but not supporting her. She, in shapeless black, moves in circles of arms, torso, jumping turns, floor rolls, but always with a quirk, something which warps the roundness. She is the obvious victim, but she continues her circlings, while he, hanging motionless and alone in a shoulder stand, is frozen like a still white moon…. It seemed to me like a dark but tenacious assertion of self.*

Bingham was more active in the remount of an early choreographic work by contact improvisation's founder, Steve Paxton. In Paxton's *Jag Ville Görna Telefonera*, a 1965 duet that pre-dates the birth of contact, Meyers describes how Bingham and Ryan "run in unison, they change direction, they do Kung Fu kicks and finish in muscle man poses or a judo hold." The popular duo also improvised their way through a light-hearted version of *XYZ*, this time to live accompaniment by Hassan, who wore a mask. Finally, in Hirabayashi's

Peter Bingham in Steve Paxton's *Jag Ville Görna Telefonera* at Véhicule Art, Montreal.

Runaway Horses, inspired by the Yukio Mishima novel of the same name, Bingham was part of the ensemble.

Rounding out the program was a solo by MacLaughlin, Bourget's duet for herself and Hirabayashi, and a trio by Mascall for Bourget, Debra Brown and Kathryn Ricketts. As Meyers wrote: "Both the number and diversity of new works seen this fall – six of the eight pieces on the programme were made this year – suggest that this dynamic performing collective is living up to its goals."

Less than half a year later, in February 1985, EDAM was back at the Play-house as part of the Sunday Coffee Concert series. Ryan and Bingham opened with one of their acclaimed improvisations, after which Bourget, Hirabayashi, MacLaughlin and Mascall presented choreography under the title *For the Children*. A group improvisation directed by Bingham closed the concert. To have appeared twice at the Playhouse was a great accomplishment for a small experimental dance company. EDAM was on a roll.

Hilda's Valiant

The same February, the energetic EDAMites mounted yet another group environmental show, called Hilda's Valiant, designed to burst the bounds of their studio environment. Bingham and Hirabayashi created the major set piece, using torches to cut up dancer Hilda Nanning's Dodge Valiant automobile, and

Peter Bingham and Peter Ryan in *Laughter is a Serious Affair*, Vancouver Fringe Festival, 1987.   Photo: Robert Meister

hanging the parts, along with some old street lights, from the studio's ceiling. Musicians were on risers next to the walls and wire mesh hung between the performers and the audience.

One of the works mounted on the mixed bill was *Necropolis*, with Hirabayashi taking credit for both choreography and "imprography". The word did not fly (although in 2003, the American tap artist, Savion Glover, premiered a show called *Improvography*) but the concept was crucial in much of EDAM's work. Hirabayashi described the thirteen-minute piece for five dancers:

> *The initial three-minute section allowed improvisational movement restricted to a limited vocabulary. The remainder of the piece was choreographed with the exception of a two-minute duet again improvised to specific vocabulary. The aim here was to allow a certain amount of spontaneous freedom without deviating from the overall aesthetic quality of the work....*

Today, improvisation using a set vocabulary would be called either "structured improvisation" or "open choreography", and is integral to the work of many contemporary dance artists. Whatever name is used, the concept is actually an old one, and legendary soloists such as Isadora Duncan performed in this manner: her dances, though carefully prepared, were often improvised.

For this bill, "the two Peters", as Peters Bingham and Ryan were sometimes called, gave another outing to the more straightforward improvisation called *XYZ*. This contact-based work had no concept or structure beyond the hint of character given by the costumes and, in this version, by the atmosphere created through the Hilda's Valiant set.

In a videotape of their performance, Bingham and Ryan give easygoing but committed performances that fully engage the audience, who chuckle appreciatively throughout. The eight-minute improvisation, performed in silence, is casual but focussed, moving quickly from one episode to the next. Ryan wears a light blue t-shirt and grey trousers, while Bingham's outfit is more theatrical, with pants cut just above his ankle and held up by suspenders. Both men wear natty white jazz shoes.

A long-limbed Bingham skips and hops easily and often, with a hint of gawkiness lending texture to the smooth elegance of his movement. His consciousness moves fluidly around his body: one minute it is in an outstretched hand; the next, in a foot extended in his partner's direction. He is aware of the space in front and behind, above and below, and tends to fill more than one direction at the same time: if a leg stretches back, an arm reaches forward. There is an innocent readiness in his approach, an eagerness, which plays well next to Ryan's more solid, solemn presence.

According to Max Wyman in *The Province*, the work showed "… just how skilled these individuals have become at creating compelling visual theatre out of the movement of the moment." Earlier, when the duo presented *XYZ* at the Playhouse, it met with equal success (it was then a trio with musician Hassan). At that time, Agnes Stevens in the *Courier* praised the pair's "great sense of comic timing", and a *Sun* reviewer felt that *XYZ* was "made vital by their all-risks-accepted, no-holds-barred attack."

EDAM/MADE

EDAM/MADE, the third evening designed to radically transform the performance environment, took place throughout the Western Front over six nights in June 1985. Members of the audience were major improvisers, freely wandering about at will during the four-hour event. More than a dozen individual performances and interactive installations happened at various sites within the building, making it impossible to see everything in one night. There were twelve guest dancers, five guest musicians and more than a dozen production assistants.

In *Day Leaves*, poet Gerry Gilbert, wearing a huge codpiece, read his stream-of-consciousness poetry as he perched on a shelf in the ground floor hallway, while Yvonne Parent painted in a room on the second floor. Two software developers, Douglas Collinge and Steven Parkinson, were in the stairway, where their movement-sensitive computer system activated an electric eggbeater and strings of Christmas lights. Another guest was New York choreographer and visual artist Mel Wong, who had been in residence at EDAM the previous three weeks. His *Buddha at the Mount*, for thirteen dancers, included exterior scaffolding placed outside the windows, enabling the performers posed on it to be visible as part of the dance going on in the studio.

Bingham and Ryan, in *Laughter is a Serious Affair*, worked with the concept of free will and determinism explored through the intellectual, the physical and the emotional. With this theme to guide them, the improvisation had a certain amount of structure and direction that was new to them. The work developed over time and when they performed it two years later at the Vancouver Fringe Festival, had become quite refined. At that stage, during part one, "The Body", Bingham and Ryan danced in a sandbox filled with broken glass, protected by costuming: long johns and undershirts under three-piece corduroy suits, wrestling boots and safety glasses. "Glass is sand," explains Ryan, "so we were adults playing in the sand." Part two, "The Head", took place in an arena formed by broken bottles; and part three, "The Heart", within a diamond-shaped space around which the audience was seated.

There was a lot of talking in the piece. Ryan describes Bingham as able to think on his feet "amazingly quickly" although, he adds, his philosophical arguments "were not always accurate. But quick, for sure. It was highly entertaining for the audience who had a great time jumping in and saying things. And we would ask them questions."

A review in *Vanguard* magazine of the Fringe Festival performance described how the artists "demonstrate the complexities of laughter – particularly the uneasy relation of laughter to risk. They thus broke down the barriers laughter creates so their audience was engaged intellectually, spiritually, and emotionally with the performers."

For EDAM/MADE, Bingham also performed as part of a quartet in an improvisation directed by Ryan, in a co-created improvisation with Bourget, Mascall, Ryan and Gilbert, and in an ensemble choreographed by Mascall. Bingham choreographed a solo, *Chatterbox*, described by Susan Mertens in the *Sun* as carrying an overt social message, "an indictment of television with Barbara Bourget as a kind of moving couch potato pursued by projected television test patterns to electric guitar and synthesizer accompaniment."

And Unmade

Soon after EDAM/MADE, the company was at the Seattle Children's Festival in the United States performing *Dance, Stuff and Nonsense*, choreographed by

Barbara Bourget, Jay Hirabayashi and Lola MacLaughlin. Bingham was not happy to be there – he did not see himself as a children's performer, and he was frustrated by the fact that any increase in revenue resulting from these shows was absorbed by the costs of production.

As well, he still harboured resentment toward his colleagues for their earlier dismissal of his work group, which he saw as indicative of their attitude towards his aesthetics in general. So, back in town during yet another long, argumentative meeting held at his home, Peter Bingham resigned. It seemed the only way to remove himself from the ongoing, unresolved issues that plagued EDAM. Ahmed Hassan, too, left at this time, and although he returned briefly, it was in name only.

In a document titled "EDAM as a Cooperative: A Statement of Position", Jennifer Mascall, Lola MacLaughlin and Peter Ryan suggest the potential of EDAM had been sacrificed "to the interests of efficiency and control". Hirabayashi was furious, feeling this was a veiled reference to losing Bingham and Hassan, and that he was being blamed. The three-page document discusses the need for all the artistic directors to be trained in artistic, administrative and financial roles in order for EDAM to become an equitable organization.

After a July 21, 1985 meeting, Hirabayashi wrote a two-and-a-half page response, complaining: "EDAM has never been a cooperative. A cooperative is an organization where people willingly cooperate." His only praise is for Bingham, who did cooperate "but took so much on it burnt him out." Hirabayashi felt the statement by Mascall, MacLaughlin and Ryan "serves as a rebuke to my proposal and to me personally. You go so far in your distaste for my expressed interests that I am denied even a suggestion as a possible coordinator."

This was a reference to Hirabayashi's earlier document, titled "Proposal to EDAM's Board of Directors", which contained the suggestion that he be appointed as company director for the upcoming season. His tasks would include liaising between the co-artistic directors and the manager, scheduling performances, teaching and grant writing. "My proposal," he had written, "is to reify the role that I unofficially assumed in 1984/85." He also requested a salary of $400 a week for twenty weeks (the minimum necessary to qualify for Unemployment Insurance).

Hirabayashi perceived the comments in his colleagues' "Statement of Position" to mean that his proposal, and his past work, was not taken seriously. His July 21 letter claims his contribution in terms of performance, choreography and administration was "responsible in a disproportionate sense for EDAM's budget rising from $8000 in 1983 to over $150,000 this year." The letter concludes with Hirabayashi's resignation.

Returns

Hirabayashi did return to the fold once more when his wish to appoint a company coordinator to liaise between the artistic directors and the manager was finally implemented. In fact, they appointed two: Lola MacLaughlin and Peter Ryan. Despite this slight to his own leadership, Hirabayashi continued to do most of the onerous grant writing with Ryan, something they had tackled together from the beginning.

Bingham, too, returned to EDAM although at first it was only to fulfill performance obligations. In the few months he was away, he had auditioned in Montreal for Ginette Laurin, having admired Kenneth Gould in Laurin's work and wanting a chance to dance with him. While he was unsuccessful, Bingham felt his strengths had been noted and appreciated, and he returned wiser for the experience.

In September 1985, Bingham joined the company for another high-profile evening at the Queen Elizabeth Playhouse. His sole contribution was a duet, *Stuck on You*, choreographed and performed with Lola MacLaughlin and set to music by Toronto composer Kirk Elliott. An acrobatic sparring match that ends in a free-flying waltz, it was exactly the type of work where Bingham's partnering skills shone. MacLaughlin recalls that when they presented the group with their first idea for a title, *Perhaps if I Crawled*, it was declared unacceptable. "EDAM was like that," she says. "You could get shot down."

Yet another opportunity to perform at the Queen Elizabeth Playhouse arose during the Third Annual Dance Week in February 1986. It was the beginning of a high profile year for the city, which was celebrating its 100th birthday and preparing to host the Expo '86 world fair. Dance Week was co-produced by The Dance Centre, a newly formed service organization, by Dance in Canada and by the Firehall Arts Centre. The event's prestige was boosted when the mayor declared the week of performances as Vancouver Dance Week.

Only one show took place at the downtown Playhouse theatre and EDAM was on the bill, along with the modern dance companies of Karen Jamieson, Judith Marcuse, Paula Ross and Anna Wyman. EDAM presented the premiere of Steve Paxton's *Ankle On*, created during a company residency that once more brought the contact improvisation legend to Vancouver. *Ankle On*, in which Bingham was one of eight dancers, was set to an electronic score by Western Front co-founder Martin Bartlett. Stephen Godfrey in *The Globe and Mail* described it as a "hypnotic, pristine form of improvisation in which dancers traced an endless series of overlapping squares on stage." The other EDAM presentations were Hirabayashi's *Rage*, performed by him and musician Robert Rosen, and Mascall's solo, *Melt*.

Bingham appeared in other Dance Week shows, too, as an independent artist. He was in a contact-influenced quartet by choreographer Lisa Cochrane, presented on the West Coast Trends bill at the Firehall Arts Centre, and in two improvisations. The first, a remount at the Firehall of his and Ryan's *Laughter is a Serious Affair*, was on a program called Men at 11:00. The second, a studio performance at Main Dance Place, was an untitled improvisation with Mary Craig, who had taken over the Synergy studio in 1982 when Linda Rubin moved to the prairies.

In his reflections on Vancouver Dance Week in *Dance in Canada* magazine, Jamil Brownson wrote: "The value of EDAM's influence, specializing in a contact improvisation tradition, has meant much to this dance scene." Once again, Peter Bingham and Peter Ryan's skill was being noted, this time in the context of the wider city.

Resignations

In 1986, Hirabayashi was finally appointed to the role of company coordinator. He managed to raise money for a marley floor, stereo equipment and MIDI music gear. This was used in EDAM's high-tech Expo '86 piece, *Bach to the Future*, featuring the Movement Sensitive Sound System.

Only three EDAMites were part of *Bach to the Future*: Hirabayashi, Bourget and Ryan. Four dancers were hired. Bourget was pregnant and did not want to perform so she became choreographic director. The others developed movement and Hirabayashi worked with the computer. The piece, which had the dancers manipulating the music via live video feeds to a computer, was complicated. The tempo of the Bach music constantly slowed down and was in need of restoration by visible signals from the dancers, who had to run to a certain area of the stage and move rapidly to restore the music to its normal speed. Then they would try to return to their place in the choreography. "We didn't know whether to tell the audience what was happening or not," recalls Hirabayashi. "We decided not to, which was a mistake because it looked like we had these people who couldn't do choreography to this really awful music."

When Hirabayashi made the credits, which were projected onto a screen at the end, he felt it was fair to designate Bourget as choreographer. This, he says, led to bitter arguments with the five dancers. "They came to us and said if we didn't change Barbara's credit they weren't going to perform. But after the piece was performed and was a big bomb, we never heard a word from them."

Exhausted from the unsatisfactory Expo piece, Hirabayashi resigned for good in May 1986. Bourget accompanied him. Bingham recalls that just before his resignation, Hirabayashi had convinced him to rejoin the company.

Despite his avowed belief in EDAM, Hirabayashi felt the others were too involved in projects outside of the company, some of which took them away from the city for extended periods or during crucial projects. Mascall, however, insists EDAM was supposed to be "a fluid structure" meant to facilitate its members' careers. "There wasn't enough money to work all year round, so everybody did whatever else they could," she explains.

In any case, in a letter to Monique Michaud at the Canada Council for the Arts dated May 12, 1986, Bourget and Hirabayashi announced their plans to form their own company, Kokoro Dance Theatre, which would "stress having polished works with trained dancers and high production values...." EDAM, they wrote, "now seems at a point where the individual interests of its members have outstretched the common aims of the group and if it is to survive, its focus must be sharpened ... Our leaving should help EDAM to redefine its purpose – consensus amongst four [Peter Bingham, Lola MacLaughlin, Jennifer Mascall and Peter Ryan] is certainly easier than consensus from six...."

Peter Bingham, Barbara Bourget, Ahmed Hassan, Jay Hirabayashi, Lola MacLaughlin, Peter Ryan and Jennifer Mascall, 1983.   Photo: Chris Randle

And Then There Were Four

You let yourself go, and then get out of it your own way.
— Peter Pan in Patricia Ludwick's *Neverland*

L et's just get on with being artists." That, says Jennifer Mascall, was the feeling at the new EDAM. Yet while the quartet of Mascall, Peter Bingham, Lola MacLaughlin and Peter Ryan may have had fewer outright disagreements, they continued to forge separate artistic paths.

Their individual artistic statements are heard in a promotional video made in 1987. MacLaughlin states her interest in Expressionism: "Basically you can dig deep down inside yourself and you don't know what's going to come up." Mascall talks about beauty. Ryan's preference is "for movement you would call pedestrian." Bingham explains that through "understanding the exact centre of a spiral in the body" an artist can make potent images. Bingham and Ryan also discuss improvisation. Ryan likes the fact "that it is the art of the ephemeral." Bingham's comment is personal: "I love to improvise – it's really an exciting place to be in front of people and not know what you're going to do."

Bingham also states his desire "to make dances that read full and read fast so people can't stop. They can just take in." He had begun exploring this collaboratively with *Run Raw* and now was ready to dive into his own elaborate ensemble work. In *Teller of Visions*, Bingham would develop the previous year's solo, *Chatterbox*, into a complex multimedia group work. Perhaps this ambitious undertaking came from the feeling of being more in control at the new EDAM, where there were fewer agendas to satisfy and he could concentrate on his own needs. Perhaps it came from the fact that he was in his late thirties and knew that despite the popularity of his work with Ryan, it was time to leave behind their youthful partnership. Peter Bingham was ready to find out who he was – not in a duo, not in a trio as in Fulcrum, not as a dancer performing in his colleagues' work – but as an individual artist.

Teller of Visions

Bingham began to develop his choreographic vision, though he did this without ever forgetting his gift for improvisation. *Teller of Visions* would be a formal work containing situations where both strategies co-existed. Nothing was completely improvised because, as Bingham explains, "We rehearsed everything over and over to recognize the things that worked and didn't work." Nor was anything completely choreographed. Performance artists had taught him a looser approach to creating movement; in most performance art pieces, it is not the exact angle and position of the body that is of interest,

Dawn Trudeau in a remount of *Teller of Visions*.   Photo: Chris Randle

but the way an individual expresses an inner compulsion or idea. In *Teller of Visions*, Bingham directed the dancers in choreography informed by various ideas he developed to express his theatrical goal.

The work premiered at the EDAM studio/theatre in November 1986 on a double bill with Peter Ryan's *Honourable Mention*. The two men created a flyer in which Ryan announced his full-length improvisation featuring an actor, Norman Armour, along with four dancers and eight musicians. Bingham's *Teller of Visions* was described as "a multi-media performance collage with the participation of over thirty performers, [as well as] musicians and video, computer graphics and visual artists." The work was touted as "high-impact entertainment just like on T.V.!"

The reference to television was deliberate: Bingham is frank about his compulsion to watch the often trivial offerings found on TV, an addiction that inspired *Chatterbox* and now *Teller of Visions*. "I've lived with a number of women who have kept me away from TV," Bingham says, "but I'm still addicted to it. *Teller of Visions* is not just about me, though, it's about television culture in general, and the non-stop feeding of information, much of which is useless."

The theme was playfully evident in the costumes, which resembled art installations, and were created by Emily Carr Institute of Art and Design instructor Sylvia Scott and her students. One costume, for Jennifer Mascall, featured a large satellite dish perched on her head. The students also constructed "TV heads", which were boxes lit by tiny fluorescent lights worn by some of the performers.

This was a huge collaborative piece and Bingham was appreciative of the input from his performers in rehearsals, giving nine of them credit for movement invention by listing them as choreographers. Bingham credited himself as one of the choreographers and as the director. It might have been cannier to assert full choreographic control and just give thanks to the dancers for their input, as was occasionally done, in order to avoid any doubts about who made the piece. In other spheres – film, for instance – the director's credit would have left no doubt whose vision it was. However, as Bingham explains: "In those days, I was more of an improviser than a choreographer. I wasn't really thinking in those terms."

Making up the disparate team of performer/choreographers was EDAM's Mascall; Chick Snipper, who settled in Vancouver in 1983 after performing with Edmonton's Brian Webb Dance Company; Monique Léger and Lee Masters from the work group, which was still active though without Bingham's participation; Peter Boulanger, a gymnast who discovered contact improvisation at EDAM; Mary Craig, now running Synergy; Robert Meister, who had been with the Synergy Performing Association; Florentia Conway, a Simon Fraser University dance graduate; and new contact improvisation enthusiast and member of EDAM, Jaci Metivier. Filling out the ranks were students from the Emily Carr Institute, who performed the more straightforward physical scores.

Lee Masters recalls the piece as being fast, fun and, due to the bowling shoes worn by the dancers, slippery. During wild zigzag raids across the EDAM studio floor, or when crash landing flat against the back wall onto which they threw themselves, there was the real threat of slipping and falling. Eventually, rubber heels were glued to the shoes to allow the dancers some control.

Simultaneous large group movement was created through a physical score that specified loosely how that movement was expressed. At one point, everyone sat cross-legged on the ground, facing the profile of the person in front of them and copying what he or she did. The effect was perfect unison although the movement was improvised, with the original ideas coming from a designated leader.

Jeff Corness, in his first work with Bingham, composed a soundtrack that used a recorded score augmented with live improvised music. Corness stood on a platform behind an electronic keyboard, joined on stage by harp player and electric guitarist Dean Hart. Also on guitar was none other than Peter Bingham, an enthusiastic musician since his teen years.

Peter Bingham, 1987.

Photo: Chris Randle

Province reviewer Renée Doruyter loved Ryan's *Honourable Mention*, but, she wrote: "Even more mind-boggling and quite wonderful is the complex *Teller of Visions*." Agnes Stevens in the *Courier* said it would require "a novel-sized book" to analyse both works on this "fascinating program".

Teller of Visions was too big to travel, so Bingham took a much leaner version to the Canada Dance Festival in July 1987. For the set, Bingham borrowed a portable wall from Karen Jamieson, which had been built for her 1983 work, *Sisyphus.*

There was a buzz around *Teller of Visions* and it was remounted again the same summer at Artropolis, an annual curated art exhibition held that year in a downtown office building on Beatty Street. *Teller of Visions*, with its performance art overtones, enlivened the event, and its acceptance by the art world was a welcome vote of confidence in Bingham's aesthetic.

In January 1988, Bingham presented the fourth version of *Teller of Visions* when he, Lola MacLaughlin and Peter Ryan mounted a mixed bill at the Arcadian Hall while Jennifer Mascall spent a year in France with her new baby and toddler. In this remount, Bingham had another hyperactive ensemble and the *Sisyphus* wall was called into action once again for them to climb over. The single "couch potato" of the premiere was now a trio sitting on a raised space at the back of the stage, watching television and drinking beer. Another new element was a large video monitor that projected live images of either the dancers or the couch potatoes. Also new was a woman wearing sunglasses inside a mock-up of a TV set, where she read poetry written by Bingham, with lines such as "Television is meditation" and "It's imagination's toilet."

The breadth of the press coverage for the shared bill is testament to EDAM's prominence, although the opinions expressed were mixed. Michael Scott, who had recently taken over the *Sun* dance beat, weighed in negatively. In his first review of EDAM, he wrote that they "served up enough self-indulgent non-choreography to leave anyone's mind numb."

Others were more positive. Agnes Stevens of the *Courier* had an entertaining time, enjoying the "shorter, faster-moving, less gimmicky" remount of *Teller of Visions*. Raewyn Whyte in *The Georgia Straight* provided

Suddenly, you can fly!
TAMAHNOUS THEATRE/EDAM PRESENTS
NEVER-LAND
the adventures of peter pan & wendy
by Patricia Ludwick Directed by Susan Astley
FIREHALL THEATRE-280 EAST CORDOVA ST
RESERVATIONS 689-0926-previews December 10th and 11th
DECEMBER 12 to JANUARY 4
Tuesday to Sunday at 7:30 pm
Design by Barbara Clayden & Phillip Tidd • Music by Sergio Barroso • Lighting by Gerald King
Film Sequences by Peg Campbell & Steven De Nure • Choreography by EDAM
PETER BINGHAM as Peter Pan PETER ANDERSON as Captain Hook
with Karen Draisey, Kim Horsman, Susan McKenzie, Jennifer Mascall, Jaci Metivier and John Ormerod

an apt description of this work when she wrote: "… the visual chaos is much like flicking through the channels in search of something worth watching, its impact underlined by a mix of text, vocalization, and synthesized music."

Neverland

In 1986, during the creation of the original *Teller of Visions*, Bingham was also involved with Jennifer Mascall in a co-production with Tamahnous Theatre. *Neverland: The Adventures of Peter Pan and Wendy* was a children's show written by Patricia Ludwick that would earn EDAM a Jessie Richardson Theatre Award for "outstanding achievement in choreography". Barbara Bourget had set up the collaboration when she was still a part of EDAM and Bingham felt trapped into doing another children's show. "Barb would have been perfect as Peter Pan," he says ruefully.

Despite his reservations about doing youth shows, the company's efforts in this area had been successful. *Dance, Stuff and Nonsense*, which premiered at the 1985 Vancouver Children's Festival, was described on CHQM Radio as "a potpourri of modern, classical and improvisational techniques, melded together by an abundance of collective energy." Moreover: "There are many elements that help make EDAM a fine dance company for young audiences: the dancers are unafraid to make use of clapping, vocal sounds and facial expressions, and the choreography is full of rapid changes and frenzied movement."

Neverland, which premiered at the Firehall Arts Centre in December 1986, was difficult on many counts. Bingham was embarrassed to be portraying Peter Pan at age thirty-five with a receding hairline, and he also felt he needed more direction as an actor. As well, "there was a bit of a struggle between Jennifer and I. We were supposed to be choreographing it together but…." Mascall would only say: "Peter Bingham is charming, a wonderful friend, a very supportive partner, but he's not an easy personality to work with."

As for *Neverland*, it offered three weeks of employment, with the dancers (Bingham, Mascall, Susan McKenzie and Jaci Metivier) working alongside the actors (Peter Anderson among them, as Captain Hook). It also offered the chance to gain first-hand insight into the more formal structure of theatre production, particularly the hierarchical teamwork of a director, assistant director and technical director.

Central to the story, of course, is the fact that Peter Pan flies. In a video recording, Bingham embodies the spirit of flight in the light, carefree way he moves about the stage; in the way he facilitates Tinker Bell (McKenzie) as she climbs on, over and around him; and, most of all, in the way he teaches the three Darling children to fly. Through Bingham's easy physicality and ability to partner using contact improvisation skills, the idea of flight is beautifully enacted without a single special technical effect. "You let yourself go," Peter

Pan explains as he back flips over Tinker Bell, "and then get out of it your own way." And he sits triumphantly cross-legged on the floor. As the children try to copy Peter Pan, he helps each one individually – and in the ease with which he moves them through space, they seem to truly fly.

In the role of Peter Pan, Bingham's explanation of flying – of letting yourself go and then recovering in your own way – also works as a description of how to perform contact improvisation. In the freedom and ease of Bingham's dancing, in the way he floated or propelled individual limbs or his entire body through space, he seemed to have discovered a form of flying. It was based in reality and gravity, which made the soaring all the more remarkable.

Burnout

A milestone evening – the first dedicated solely to Bingham's own work – occurred in January 1989. This was mounted not as a studio event but at a formal theatrical venue, the Vancouver East Cultural Centre. For this two-part evening, Bingham continued to develop his interest in both improvisation and choreography through a contact-inspired group improvisation and a second major multimedia collage.

For the improvised *Burnout*, Bingham brought together dancers from his past and his present. These were good friends he enjoyed dancing with and, while none were highly trained in modern dance or ballet, all three were proficient contact dancers. They were also strong performers who approached movement with inner conviction. Jaci Metivier had come to dance from a theatre background and had her first taste of contact improvisation in a workshop with Bingham in 1983; Mark Lavelle, a member of Bingham's work group, had recently completed an undergraduate degree at Simon Fraser University, studying dance and theatre; and Michael Seamus Linehan was an old friend from Synergy.

This was not your average group of dancers and Bingham was not interested in creating your average modern dance choreography. He proved this in the way he staged the work. For *Burnout*, he took the entire audience upstairs to the balcony, where they looked down on the stage. As well, although he was in a well-equipped theatre, the work was lit primarily by candles placed on the floor to form a square inside of which the dancers performed. Standing at each of the four corners was one of the improvising musicians from the Lunar Adventures quartet, which included Coat Cooke and Ron Samworth in their first appearance with Bingham.

The intention in *Burnout* was for Peter Bingham to dance to exhaustion, with the other three performers taking turns partnering him, while the candles burned out. In the program, Bingham credited himself not for choreography but for "concept", referring to the idea of what he called the "endurance score" and to his direction of the overall staging. Contact improvisation was the main vocabulary but during rehearsals certain moves were practiced and fine-tuned.

In performance, details like how long the candles would take to burn down proved hard to control. As well, Bingham says, "it felt like dancing at the bottom of a swimming pool. It was weird trying to relate to an audience that was all above us."

Critical Mass

In contrast to the simplicity of *Burnout*, *Critical Mass* was designed to overload the senses. With its rich collection of images, the work lived up to its title, which references the mass necessary to set off a nuclear chain reaction. It was danced by that season's company members – Noam Gagnon, Dana Gingras, Jaci Metivier and Dawn Trudeau, joined by guest artists Mark Lavelle and Mary Craig. This group of dancers offered a range of talents, from the charismatic Gagnon and Gingras, who later co-founded the hugely popular Holy Body Tattoo, to young Trudeau, to Bingham's protégé Metivier. Lavelle and Craig were familiar faces, knowledgeable about Bingham's way of working, and it meant a lot to Bingham to have them participate.

This ambitious multifaceted undertaking involved movement, music, poetry, film, numerous props, a full set and dramatic lighting by John Macfarlane. Bingham gave his imagination free reign and was guided by visual images loosely inspired by the ongoing political unrest in the Middle East. He intended to layer images of the conflict and the desert one on top of another, which would create a surrealistic montage. The dance, although central, was only one element of the whole and, during the creative process, it was difficult for the performers to envisage the final result. Bingham admits, "Some of the dancers had a hard time with this piece. When it rocked the house, they were surprised."

Critical Mass is structured around solos for each of the company members with one major quartet. There is some dynamic, precisely set movement, including fast spins and jumps, and spiralling falls with flowing arms and torso. There is also improvisation. One solo for Gingras is only loosely choreographed: her undulating arms and tiny steps are set in a certain space and direction, but not count by count. By the end of the rehearsal period, however, there was little variation in her performance. Craig and Lavelle had set moves, while Jeff Corness was directed in more theatrical terms: he was asked to mock conduct the commissioned score that he had composed.

The theme of conflict is set up from the start when Metivier, eyes shut, struggles to free herself from Gingras and Trudeau. An Eastern setting is suggested by the costumes worn by the principal dancers (Gagnon, Gingras,

Dana Gingras in *Critical Mass*, 1989.   Photo: Chris Randle

Metivier and Trudeau) who are dressed in colourful silk pants and halter-tops. The score features tabla and chimes. A decanter of water is a key prop. But place is only suggested, and Gerry Gilbert's stream-of-consciousness poetry is filled with images and ideas based on ordinary Canadian life.

During the performance Gilbert is present on film, visible only from the neck down, clad in skimpy black underwear. Fluid and graceful, he recites poetry about kitty litter and socks. He also plays nonsense games such as: "This is not what I want to think. This is what I think", which later becomes "No, this is what I want to think. What I think is unthinkable."

The stage is dark throughout, with lights illuminating different tableaux. Besides the main ensemble and the poet, a woman and a man dressed in white (Craig and Lavelle) take cradling poses in a niche four feet above the floor behind blue streamers. Another tableau features a tall, longhaired man in a shiny red and gold brocade coat (Corness) who "conducts" the recorded music from his red-lit niche, confined by a tangle of fluttering red streamers. Adding yet another layer of visuals are the three mirrors on the stage floor, which reflect the performers.

Surprisingly, neither *The Vancouver Sun* nor *The Province* newspapers reviewed this full-length evening. Susan Inman in The Dance Centre's *Dance*

Update newsletter and Alanna Matthew in *Vandance* magazine gave some coverage, but their descriptions are guarded. Perhaps they remained distant because neither felt the work spoke to them, although both writers are generally positive. Matthew is somewhat bemused by the "multi-media choreographic trend" that Bingham has "embraced", while Inman thinks both *Burnout* and *Critical Mass* should definitely draw young people looking for "far-out, groovy new headspaces." In the University of British Columbia's student newspaper, *The Ubyssey*, Olivia Zanger's comments suggest Inman might have been right. For Zanger, *Critical Mass* "blazed triumphantly" and was "an exciting, visually stimulating, thought provoking and intelligently conceived piece."

His first full-length evening confirmed Bingham as an artist committed to a unique vision. From the beginning of his unexpected career in dance, Bingham had pursued his ideas with passion and perseverance, and he was never afraid to get in there and muck around. "It's just work. You have to do the work," he explains, loathe to romanticize the artistic process. However controversial his aesthetic was at times with his colleagues, Bingham stuck with it. As photographer and occasional publicist Daniel Collins says: "Peter was always the risk-taker. He would try stuff out, and sometimes it would work and sometimes it wouldn't. You never knew what to expect – to this day, he's still got that going for him." Jane Ellison concurs: "Peter's willing to try something that might not work, he's willing to take risks. What I love about Peter is that he has never dropped the 'E' [for Experimental] in EDAM."

Backstage, things were not going so well and the quartet of co-directors was about to be further reduced. By the end of the 1989 season, Peter Ryan and Jennifer Mascall were both gone. Ryan wanted to pursue a more theatrical direction, and eventually settled in Ottawa, while Mascall developed her own company, Mascall Dance. Resident musician Jeff Corness left, too, and began what would be a long and productive collaboration with Karen Jamieson. The dancers scattered. One, Jaci Metivier, remained.

By default, Peter Bingham and Lola MacLaughlin found themselves in an unexpected partnership that lasted only long enough to put together an application for Canada Council funding. By the time the Council received it, EDAM had just one artistic director.

Gift of a Lifetime

Peter and I lived – breathed and slept and ate – dancing. Our physical conversation was all encompassing, all engrossing.
— Jaci Metivier

eemingly out of the blue, Lola MacLaughlin decided that she was leaving EDAM, too. "I just had a change of heart," she says.

> *There was so much conflict putting our Canada Council application together. I remember saying to [arts manager] Marlin Clapson, "Peter and I fought a lot putting this grant together but I'm sure once everything settles down it will be fine." He said, "Well, Lola, crisis time will tell a lot about how people are going to get along."*

Bingham was a team player and truly regretted the group's break-up. However, when sole directorship was thrust upon him, he immediately sat down to re-write the EDAM grant application, insisting the Canada Council allow him to do so although it meant extending the deadline. It was a relief when the Council gave the company a decent grant. Now Bingham had to prove he was worth it.

Dishearteningly, only one dancer from the past season returned. But, although Bingham could not know it yet, over the next few years Jaci Metivier would make a substantial contribution to EDAM and turn out to be the ideal interpreter of his work. Born in Deep River, Ontario, Metivier discovered contact improvisation in 1983 at the age of twenty-one. At the time, she was living on Hornby Island off the coast of British Columbia where Bingham had gone to teach, and her first class with him was exhilarating: "It made me feel more alive than anything I'd ever done." Wanting more, she moved to Vancouver to train at EDAM. Though new to dance, Metivier had worked with the Ottawa Little Theatre, a well-established troupe of community players, from the age of thirteen.

Metivier describes Bingham as responsive and intuitive toward her creative needs as a performer; he describes her as "a natural contact dancer". She had a strong, flexible body, was intelligent and quick-witted, eager and fearless while dancing. Metivier first appeared in the 1986 premiere of Bingham's *Teller of Visions*, and was soon performing in works by other members of EDAM. A personal relationship between Bingham and Metivier blossomed along with her skill in contact and soon they were living together in the basement suite of his West 15th Avenue home.

With Metivier, Bingham made the first of his well-crafted, emotionally honest and popular duets. *Cryptic Heart* premiered December 2, 1989 at Forced Issues, which marks another first – the first evening of dance Bingham mounted as EDAM's sole artistic director. This EDAM studio series had been launched in October 1988, and was an informal opportunity for audiences to watch dance and, afterwards, to mingle with the performers. With his friendly, relaxed manner, Bingham was the perfect host for what became a longstanding series.

Forced Issues

The December 1989 Forced Issues, recorded on videotape, begins with Bingham welcoming the audience and reminding them of the beer for sale in the foyer. He is dressed for a workout in a red t-shirt, faded red sweat pants tucked into black wool socks, and black jazz shoes, with his thick brown hair brushed back. Bingham looks like a dancer, albeit one dressed for rehearsal, but his body language and approach to the audience are that of an ordinary person. In this way, he set a relaxed tone to the evening; laughter and warm applause are heard throughout the recording of the hour and a quarter of dance.

Forced Issues, which typically mixed both improvisation and choreographed works, opened and closed with *Cryptic Heart*. At the start of the evening, this

Jaci Metivier, Peter Bingham, Noam Gagnon and Dana Gingras, EDAM studio/theatre, 1988.

duet was danced to a romantic violin concerto by Edouard Lalo; at the end, the same choreography was set next to the jazzy chaos of the Lunar Adventures quartet, playing live. It was the kind of experiment EDAM had done before, when Barbara Bourget showed a solo three times, to different music and with different costumes, during A Night in the Garden of EDAM. As a choreographer, Bingham remained fascinated with the impact of music on choreography and here he shared that fascination with his audience. The first showing of *Cryptic Heart* was emotionally warmer, while the second had more of an edge, and these differences set audiences, and the choreographer himself, thinking.

The work had begun as an audition solo created for Jaci Metivier before being developed into an intimate duet with Mark Lavelle. Maybe that is why *Cryptic Heart* is as much about independence as about being with someone. A woman, a man, some music: they come together, they fly apart. Bingham knew these dancers well and Metivier believes this fed the creative process:

> *It was not a long creation process because Peter had worked a great deal with both Mark and myself, and we all knew each other inside out. Peter always worked to showcase your strong points and camouflage your weaknesses as a dancer, so it gave him a different palette of movement to choose from for each dancer. He had also been a major teacher/mentor for both Mark and myself, [so] he knew what we knew and to what depth.*

A strength of *Cryptic Heart* was certainly the performers, who had the appearance of being "real people" rather than thoroughbred dancers. This was partly because neither had the thin, hyper-extended body of a dancer who has trained seriously since childhood, and partly because the duet was still being perfected. Thus their performance was a little rough and tumble, with some abrupt transitions and a few rocky partnerings, though this did not detract from the work's effectiveness; instead, it added an impressive realistic edge. The costumes, too, were decidedly casual, and could easily have been worn by someone sitting in the audience: both performers were in cotton pants and t-shirts.

This brief, twelve-minute duet contains what can only be described as one of the great moments in contemporary dance. It comes toward the end, prepared for and marked as a climactic moment by an audacious build-up. Lavelle lies on his back, knees to chest; Metivier balances stretched out across his shins, arching her spine and circling her outstretched arms as if building momentum for flight. What follows, propelled by the thrust of his legs, is her astonishing horizontal roll through the air. This triumphant physical feat showcased their daring, skill and strength.

CRYPTIC HEART

APRIL 11-14 8 PM
Waterfront Theatre
Granville Island

EDAM
performs new dances by
Peter Bingham
and guest choreographer
Serge Bennathan

tickets
$12/$10 regular
$8 advance
call Waterfront Theatre
685-6217
EDAM 876-9559

with the assistance of The Canada Council,
B.C. Cultural Services Branch and the City of Vancouver

Besides the duet, the bill also featured a ten-minute classic ensemble improvisation that does not explore any structured or preconceived ideas; the untitled work is, instead, created fully in the moment. The performers are not, however, unprepared: the group rehearsed together and a certain atmosphere is created by the jazz accompaniment of Lunar Adventures. The audience is treated to a typically open, elegant and inventive Bingham, with an equally open and graceful Metivier, who is eager to direct the action but only when the moment seems right. Dana Gingras, back at EDAM for this show, moves in her characteristically forthright and action-hungry way, determined to devour the moment. Long-time colleagues Mary Craig and Mark Lavelle are both supportive and responsive. All five freely roam the space, searching for interaction.

There were other bits and pieces of improvised and choreographed solos and duets, notably an eight-minute solo created for Bingham by Serge Bennathan called *Arithmetic and Calculus*, set to a quirky, twanging score by Arne Eigenfeldt. French-born Bennathan, the artistic director of Toronto's Dancemakers from 1990 to 2006, was at this time immersed in what he describes as "the fertile ground" of Vancouver dance, also creating work for the Judith Marcuse Dance Company and Ballet British Columbia.

Bingham always dances as a person, not a prince, and Bennathan sensibly presented him as such, while still providing a rigorous framework within which Bingham had to navigate. The work is a curious mixture reflecting both men: Bennathan is recognizable in the sudden bursts of vertical, air-borne energy his choreography is known for; Bingham is evident in his trademark quivering arms and hands. He also retains the Everyman quality with which he typically dances so that, wearing an ordinary white shirt with brown trousers, Bingham looks more like a man dancing than a dancer performing. At one point, fully in character though not choreographed, he takes a moment to tuck his shirt in. It reads as theatre – he does it without any self-consciousness or hurry – and adds a splendidly ordinary moment to the performance.

"EDAM's daring spirit" was the headline for Max Wyman's *Province* review. Wyman, the city's most dedicated dance critic, was doubtless as eager to see what EDAM would look like under Bingham's sole control as the rest of the audience. His review is upbeat and positive, noting that "the eight-part evening was studded with sudden explosions of kinetic daring and surprise." He also refers to the narrative elements and to a new commitment to structure, formal developments Bingham knew were important to his mastery of choreographic craft but that he had not yet pursued fully. Wyman's comments were exhilarating.

Cryptic Heart at the Waterfront

Bingham ran EDAM without a company manager until January 1990, when he was able to hire Paris Simons through a government work/study program. With a manager in place and a successful edition of the Forced Issues series under his belt, Bingham was ready to create his first formal mainstage production, a mixed bill of choreographed works with the umbrella title of *Cryptic Heart*, which premiered on April 11, 1990 at the Waterfront Theatre.

Realizing the dance community was watching closely to see whether he was up to the task of leading EDAM on his own, Bingham felt the need to demonstrate he was as strong a choreographer as an improviser. At this time, he separated improvisation off as more appropriate for Forced Issues, which he saw as the "avant-garde research arm of the company." Contact improvisation, however, remained present in spirit, as Bingham brought to the act of choreography all he had learned from contact about balance, momentum, gravity, energy and responsiveness to a partner.

Beyond wanting to show he had more to offer than his skill as an improviser, Bingham explains, "I wanted to choreograph. I was on my own and there was a sense of freedom, so I felt inspired." There were no fellow artistic directors to worry about or to placate, and what Bingham describes as the "vote of confidence by the funders" suggested at least some of the community was behind him. All this resulted in a period of enormous growth and productivity.

Before Bingham could start choreographing, he had to hire his inaugural group of dancers, giving them a twenty-week contract. They were a disparate bunch with one important thing in common: an expressed interest in working with Bingham, which, at this point in his career, he is frank about needing. Joining the familiar faces of Mary Craig, Mark Lavelle and Jaci Metivier were newcomers Elizabeth Burr and Scott Drysdale, two Simon Fraser University dance program graduates; Susan Elliott from the MainDance Performance Training Intensive; and three recent arrivals to Vancouver: Philippe (Pipo) Damiano, a keen contact improviser from France, and Sylvain Brochu and Katherine Labelle, experienced modern dancers from eastern Canada. Every weekday morning, Brochu and Labelle took turns giving a ninety-minute modern class, followed by an hour of contact with Bingham, and then rehearsals began.

The range of work created with this group of nine, plus one guest artist, is astounding. Bingham was raring to go, eager to explore and determined to succeed. There was the lightly romantic *Spare Time Quartet* and the two-part *Inside Out*, which opened with a taut, flowing solo for guest dancer Allan Dobbs, followed by an exuberant trio for Brochu, Drysdale and Damiano. *Plunge* brought the whole ensemble together, and *Imaga Mortis* continued Bingham's interest in creating unique stage environments, with five large oil paintings by Mona Hamill depicting partially visible female nudes comprising the set. *Cryptic Heart*, the work after which the evening was titled, was polished and refined for this high profile remount. Also on the bill was another showing of Serge Bennathan's solo for Bingham, *Arithmetic and Calculus*.

Spare Time Quartet was surprising in terms of Bingham's aesthetic because a theatrical narrative linked the movement. It is a mating game, set to the sultry *Everybody's Somebody's Fool*, with Dexter Gordon on tenor sax, and features interaction between a woman, Metivier, and three men, Brochu, Damiano and Lavelle. The athletic leaps and catches between various configurations of the men, who wear suits, and the woman, in a red chiffon dress, give the work a contemporary edge. In this change-partners-and-dance romance, love interests are lightly suggested and swiftly changing, but everybody ends up with somebody – somebody other than the person with whom they started. The casual virtuosity and contact-improv-inspired choreography gave *Spare Time Quartet* a distinct Bingham look.

Plunge, on the other hand, showed Bingham in a new light. Bravely, he created a full company work that was his first formal movement study, set to the massive accomplishment of Mahler's adagietto from *Symphony No. 5*, familiar for its use in Luchino Visconti's 1971 film,

Pipo Damiano and Jaci Metivier in *Spare Time Quartet*.
Photo: Chris Randle

Death in Venice. This was a bold leap into beauty and abstraction, something Bingham had not previously attempted, but he was determined to make a work that was easy to view and would create "a bit of peace in this world." *Plunge* was also gently tongue-in-cheek, intended to look like a ballet taking place underwater.

Bingham began by creating the movement without music, setting a spatial score with basic floor patterns, and entrances and exits. During rehearsals, he tried out different recordings. When he put the Mahler to his "rough draft", he recognized how the music helped fulfill his intentions. Only then did he complete the choreography. What stands out in the videotape is the lively unison work by Elizabeth Burr and Susan Elliott: the two young women skip and run together with integrity and verve. Metivier's performance, too, is memorable, balancing soft, fluttering hands and dreamy arms with a steely reserve at her centre. To create a more layered staging, Bingham projected a black and white film of the dancers rolling across a lawn. He also commissioned a Vancouver fashion designer, Pat Robertson, who costumed the group in black or white skirted tunics that, unfortunately, suited the women more than the men. Max Wyman in *The Province* described *Plunge* as "creating an astonishingly

THE DANCE CENTRE PRESENTS A SPLASHY NEW DANCE SERIES

Making Waves

AT THE WATERFRONT

APRIL 10 - 13
8:00 PM
◄EDAM (vancouver)

APRIL 17 - 20
8:00 PM
◄Martha Carter (montreal)
AND
Harvey Meller (vancouver)►

APRIL 24 - 27
8:00 PM
Llory Wilson (seattle)►

MAY 1 - 4
8:00 PM
Lola MacLaughlin (vancouver)►
AND
◄Jennifer Mascall (vancouver)

WATERFRONT THEATRE
GRANVILLE ISLAND

FULL SERIES PASS ONLY $44.
single tickets $16.
tickets at Ticketmaster 280-3311 • info: 872-0432

evocative sense of oceanic motion, a kind of modernist response to [modern dance choreographer] Judith Marcuse's popular *Seascape*."

Even more experimental, and with opposing intentions, was the darkly lit, darkly costumed quartet, *Imaga Mortis*. True to its Latin title, it was filled with images of death and despair, as well as with the sounds of the dancers moaning. Mary Craig remembers that "Peter wanted *Imaga Mortis* to be ugly, to make people uncomfortable." Bingham agrees: "It was not meant to be nice to watch. It's about images of death." The solo for Craig that began the creative process was, Bingham says, "based on her initiating movement from her left shoulder, which was simply a place to start from." As the choreography was being set, the imagery took shape and meaning was revealed. "I realized she was dying. But people didn't get it," he says. "No one liked *Imaga Mortis* except me!" He agrees the subject matter was difficult, especially in the context of a mixed bill of lighter fare, but he was drawn to explore it because "it was about something real."

At the Waterfront, Bingham continued experimenting with *Cryptic Heart*, trying out different music and, also, different costumes. Wyman enthused: "This version, danced in billowy Oriental costumes to the delicate Orientalisms of the Cymbali ensemble, set the two performers like a pasha and his houri in a cloud of rounded voluptuousness." This incarnation would be the audience favourite later in the season at the Canadian Modern Dance Festival in Winnipeg, when Mary Jane MacLennan wrote in the *Winnipeg Free Press*: "The full house of over 200 spectators gave their most exuberant endorsement to dancers Mark Lavelle and Jaci Metivier in Peter Bingham's work *Cryptic Heart*…. Strong, elegant choreography made this work a real dynamo."

Making West Coast Waves

Almost exactly a year after the company's first Waterfront Theatre appearance, Bingham launched The Dance Centre's Making Waves series at the same venue in April 1991. He was followed by Seattle artist Llory Wilson and two double bills: Montreal-based Martha Carter and Vancouver's Harvey Meller; and ex-EDAMites Lola MacLaughlin and Jennifer Mascall. The 240-seat Waterfront Theatre proved hard to fill, although by modern dance standards houses were reasonable, with a total of 347 people seeing the show over EDAM's four-day run from April 10-13. Only the double bill of MacLaughlin and Mascall fared better, with 464 in attendance.

Five of the previous season's dancers returned to work with Bingham: Elizabeth Burr, Pipo Damiano, Scott Drysdale, Susan Elliott and Jaci Metivier, as well as new recruit Jeff Hall, a 1987 dance graduate from Montreal's Concordia University. As part of the company class, Bingham introduced Pilates training with Dianne Miller. Bingham's own classes in contact improvisation were crucial to creating a cohesive group of dancers able to fulfill his work.

Still fired up with the responsibility of being alone at the helm and with the need to establish himself as a choreographer, Bingham continued to work at a fiendish pace, rehearsing three popular works from the previous show and creating three new ones. Again, there were no improvisations. Besides Bingham's six short works, there was one contribution by another artist – *Picnic*, created for the company by Serge Bennathan, set to a softly clicking, clanging score by Arne Eigenfeldt. In February 1991, just before the Making Waves performance, the company presented the seven works on a cross-Canada tour to Halifax, Montreal and Winnipeg.

At the Waterfront Theatre, "Highland", which was the trio section from *Inside Out*, opened the bill. This strong male fling, with its athletic camaraderie and moments of tenderness, was dedicated to Bingham's three brothers. *Spare Time Quartet* and *Cryptic Heart* each had another outing. For this performance of *Cryptic Heart* by Metivier and Hall, Bingham worked to make the transitions between sections smoother, supporting them dramatically through lighting. The build-up to the flip was subtler, too: when Metivier arched across Hall's shins, her arms gently undulated rather than circling propulsively. Deborah Meyers in *Vandance* noted the "frankly erotic" charge to this partnership.

The new choreographies – two solos and an ensemble work – ensured the bill was as varied in content and style as the first Waterfront show had been. The romantic *Tell a Tale*, to songs by Nat King Cole, was a fall-down-and-love-again solo for Burr, while *Senseless* was a driven abstract solo for Elliott. *Never Facing East*, another darkly lit and costumed lament as sombre as *Imaga Mortis*, was a visceral response to the Persian Gulf War. Set to a percussive score by David Macanulty, this twenty-minute closing choreography had the dancers hunched over in despair and moaning aloud.

The press, once again, was fabulous. In *The Province*, Wyman raved over the "dazzling" athleticism of Bingham's choreography, which had "a still point at the centre, a point of control that gives everything that whirls around it logic and strength and integrity." He also appreciated the tinge of "emotional significance" to Bingham's work, which "makes sense in human terms." Deborah Meyers in *Vandance* praised Bingham's "generosity" and "focus", and enjoyed "the dancers' connectedness with each other."

For Max Wyman's preview of the four-week Waterfront series, he had asked Barbara Clausen, then the executive director of The Dance Centre, to characterize the city's modern dance scene. She described it, he reported, as "heavily into experiment and 'messing about with the form. There's also a real sense of crossover among dance, theatre, music – its dominant characteristic is the interweaving of layers … a kind of cross-disciplinary cooking.'"

Clausen, explained Wyman, "believes Vancouver's dance scene is quite distinct from the modernist ferment in Montreal, regarded by many as the country's modern-dance capital. The general tone of work made in Vancouver is softer and less hard-edged, she believes, perhaps a reflection of the West Coast climate and lifestyle."

That climate, which is one of constant rain, casts a subdued light over the city. Evergreen shrubs and trees thrive, and moss threatens to take over the lawns, which remain green all winter when no snow falls, as is often the case. Vancouverites wear colourful rainproof jackets to brighten the grey atmosphere as they trek up the mountains, walk along the beach or even head out for a theatre event. West Coasters are resolutely practical.

A West Coast practicality and no-nonsense approach can be seen in Bingham's choreography, with its athletic flow and down-to-

Scott Drysdale and Jaci Metivier, EDAM studio/theatre, early 1990s.
Photo: Chris Randle

earth portrayal of love and life. Bingham's aesthetic preferences continually reflect the everyday. Costumes are seldom fanciful or outrageous; they tend to be ordinary daywear or, at most, familiar dress-up. Each dancer's posture and stage presence remain true to the body's natural inclinations. At the same time, of course, dance itself is hardly an everyday activity, and even viewed within the often outrageous, high-art tradition of modern theatrical dance, Bingham's choreographic roots are radical, based in Vancouver's counter-culture. Synergy, where he first trained, was never part of the mainstream dance scene and those who studied there often seemed more like members of a longhaired cult than dancers.

Looking at Bingham's early choreographic works from the mid-to-late 1980s, equality between men and women is key in both his character-driven and abstract pieces. This fundamental aspect is perfectly portrayed through the vocabulary of contact improvisation, where the workload is shared equally among men and women. Equality may not be the reality for every individual, but it is crucial to contemporary ideas that society continues to grapple with. Bingham pushed the boundaries of how women and men could be together in dance, and in the life that dance reflects.

Equality was also present in the way Bingham juxtaposed elements of contact improvisation and the more formal techniques of modern dance and ballet, something that developed further in his work over time. Never, however, would he stage relationships that were grand affairs portrayed by an elite corps of dancers. His performers are always people with whom you might sit down and have a beer.

Building from strength to strength, Bingham's sole leadership of EDAM began on a roll. First as an improviser, now as a choreographer, he struck a warm, human note through an apparently straightforward physicality to which audiences and critics could relate. Overall, life as an artist was good. From the moment Bingham first discovered dance, it had been a compelling part of his life. Now, as a full-time artist, dance was tightly interwoven with every facet of his existence. His personal relationship with Jaci Metivier, for instance, was as much about art as about life. For the moment, this was inspiring to both of them.

Jaci Metivier and Peter Bingham in improvisation at EDAM, 1988.   Photo: Chris Randle

Dreamtigers

… as I sleep, some dream beguiles me …
— Jorge Luis Borges, *Dreamtigers*

Peter Bingham had proved that as well as being a brilliant improviser, he was also an exciting choreographer of popular short works. Many of these, like *Spare Time Quartet*, used the language of contact improvisation to inspired effect, as did *Cryptic Heart*, the first of many physically exciting, emotionally resonant duets. In other works, such as *Imaga Mortis*, he began exploring the dark side of human existence. His aim in *Plunge*, in contrast, was for a lighter abstract beauty, drawing on balletic shapes and energy. Ideas and scenarios poured out, and he was intent on expressing them in the best way he could, without concern for stylistic boundaries or rules. It was gratifying that the press, as well as the public, were so responsive to these efforts. Now, Bingham was compelled to go even further by tackling his first full-length, eighty-minute choreography.

First, however, there were practical issues to deal with, such as finding a new manager. It was not hard to convince Gina Sufrin, who was employed as an administrator at The Dance Centre, to take over the business end of things: Sufrin considered it a stroke of good fortune to be asked to manage one of Vancouver's most dynamic companies. "I was very flattered to be asked," she says.

> I knew Peter — not well, but I knew him. He's incredibly charming and a hard man to say no to. I thought it was a good opportunity for me, although I had very little management experience. It seemed like we could develop some kind of partnership.

Then, Bingham had to hire dancers. Returning company members Pipo Damiano, Susan Elliott, Mark Lavelle and Jaci Metivier — all strong in contact improvisation — were joined by Chantal Deeble, a petite, muscular modern dancer. The final member was an unusual choice: Eclilson Matiais de Jesus, recently arrived in Vancouver from Brazil and expert in the martial art form of capoeira. Struck by capoeira's gymnastic display, Bingham also engaged de Jesus to teach a company class, which he did for three months. It was the kind of boundary busting that came naturally to Bingham.

With a group of dancers in whom he was confident, an enthusiastic, personable manager and local press support, Bingham was ready to dive into his most visually and conceptually complex choreography yet. It would be his third

EDAM
at the
Firehall Arts Centre
280 E. Cordova
May 5-9 8PM

choreography:
Peter Bingham
music: Coat Cooke
David Macanulty
Ron Samworth
visual art:
Peter Bingham
Mona Hamill
Chris Randle
lighting:
John Macfarlane

tickets $12/14
689-0926

EDAM gratefully acknowledges the support of the
Canada Council, Canada Employment and
Immigration, Government of B.C. through the
Ministry of Tourism and the Ministry
Responsible for Culture, City of Vancouver
through the Office of Cultural Affairs,
Vancouver Foundation, Alpha Cine Services,
Kodak Canada, New West Press Co. Ltd., Opus
Framing Ltd., Vancouver Step Magazine.

photo: C. Randle design: M. Hamill 1991-2

DREAMTIGERS

major multimedia work, one that would be more formally choreographed and twice as long as either of the first two, 1986's *Teller of Visions* and 1989's *Critical Mass*. Like its predecessors, *Dreamtigers* would be a feast of sound and vision and, at the Vancouver premiere in 1992, it enjoyed a tremendous success. Later, in Ottawa, *Dreamtigers* would have a very different reception.

The Process

Bingham's intention was to allow the choreography, paintings, film and music to follow their own creative impetus, influenced by the same ideas, but realized individually. They would be layered on parallel planes, not woven together, with the film and paintings "as alive and assertive as the performers", as Bingham wrote in a letter to Cathy Levy, then the producer of the Canada Dance Festival. This had been Bingham's instinctive approach in *Teller of Visions* and again in *Critical Mass*, where he had layered image after image – a headless poet, a couple in white, a mad conductor, a quartet of East Indian-costumed dancers, mirrors, water. In these early works, he had not specified what each element meant, either to himself or to others. There were no program notes, no details about the genesis or intention of the piece. He saw his job as bringing images together, making choices through mining his subconscious, and allowing the audience to make their own associations and meanings. The job of the artist, Bingham believes, is to make work, not to explain it, but with *Dreamtigers* he had become more considered in his choices.

This method of layering is a typical postmodern strategy, but combined with Bingham's intuitive approach it also has much in common with the surrealist movement that began in 1920s Europe. The surrealists aimed to bring together seemingly disparate realities, particularly the dream and waking states, in order to create a new super-reality. Feeding this interest in the power of unconscious forces was Sigmund Freud's study of dreams. Automatic writing that mined the unconscious, and collage, where various unconnected elements are brought together, was the basis of the surrealist creative process in literature, visual art, film and photography. André Breton, the "Pope" of surrealism, wrote: "If the depths of our mind contain within it strange forces capable of augmenting those on the surface, or of waging a victorious battle against them, there is every reason to seize them – first to seize them, then, if need be, to submit them to the control of our reason."

Interestingly, the word surrealist was first used to describe a 1917 ballet, *Parade*, a collaboration between choreographer Léonide Massine, composer Erik Satie, poet Jean Cocteau and painter Pablo Picasso. In his program note for the ballet, poet Guillaume Apollinaire describes this collaboration as a "new alliance" of the arts, giving rise to "a kind of surrealism." Dance, with its ability to incorporate a range of artistic voices through such collaborative creation, is an ideal surrealist playground, to which Bingham was instinctively drawn. In fact, the first artist to make an impression on him had been a surrealist, Salvador Dali. Bingham discovered the eccentric painter while at college in the early 1970s, a period when Dali's work, with its dripping clocks and bizarre juxtaposition of images, was extremely popular. This was fuelled by the similarity some viewers found between Dali's paintings and the hallucinations induced by popular recreational drugs like LSD.

Bingham would plumb the depths of his psyche to create *Dreamtigers*, a multi-faceted stream of consciousness loosely inspired by and titled after a prose poem by Jorge Luis Borges, an Argentinean writer considered a forerunner of magic realism. Bingham was fascinated by Borges' *Dreamtigers*, particularly by the poet's description of himself as a boy fervently worshipping the striped royal tiger. As a young artist, Bingham had felt a similar affinity with tigers after he undertook a group ritual based on shamanic tradition designed to discover each individual's inner "power animal". The ritual, led by a drummer, involved participants roaming the interior of the earth in their imagination. Bingham's only encounter with an animal was a sighting of a baboon, and he feared this was going to be his animal spirit, but as the drummer introduced instructions to bring participants out of the meditation, he found himself carried on the back of a white tiger with black stripes.

As well, Bingham was drawn to Borges' presentation of a dream state, particularly by how the poet was haunted by his inability to shape his dreams, which spoke to Bingham of the artist's battle to create. Borges writes:

> *… as I sleep, some dream beguiles me, and suddenly I know I am dreaming. Then I think: This is a dream, a pure diversion of my will; and now that I have unlimited power, I am going to cause a tiger.*

> *Oh, incompetence! Never can my dreams engender the wild beast I long for. The tiger indeed appears, but stuffed or flimsy, or with impure variations of shape, or of an implausible size, or all too fleeting, or with a touch of the dog or the bird.*

Bingham realized that encouraging people to look at his choreography as a dream would help them experience it for what it was: not reality, not a narrative, not a puzzle to be solved, not a symbolic code to be translated, but simply something to be experienced with full psychic involvement. Thinking of the work as a dream created a wide entry point for the audience and it also freed the artist of the restrictions of waking logic.

Referred to as "the triptych project", *Dreamtigers* centred around ten large canvases commissioned from visual artist Mona Hamill, whose paintings had decorated the stage in *Imaga Mortis*. For *Dreamtigers*, Hamill created paintings that were a little brighter than her usual work, and larger: each acrylic on canvas panel was 3.35 metres high by 1.5 metres wide. Hamill worked by throwing paint, creating what at first glance looks like splashes of red, yellow and blue but, on closer viewing, nude female figures are revealed. The panels were used to make four sets of revolving triptychs.

Film created collaboratively by Bingham, Hamill and Chris Randle was projected onto two blank panels. Footage included shots of the paintings as well as of the dancers suspended and whirling in place. During the performance, the images of the dancers were viewed upside down, which gave a mysterious, surreal effect, the bodies weightless and with hair apparently standing on end.

Adding yet another layer was the music. Saxophonist Coat Cooke and guitarist Ron Samworth were joined by drummer David Macanulty, all familiar faces at EDAM. At first, the three composer/musicians improvised with the dancers in the studio; later, they composed to a videotape of the finished choreography. The final score varied from raucous to sultry to meditative, and was what Cooke calls "composed work with improvisation laced through it."

Bingham entered into the project in his usual wholehearted manner, keeping himself open and flexible, maintaining a collaborative atmosphere where everyone could contribute his or her best. He was confident in his dancers, whose different backgrounds – from capoeira to contact to modern – ensured each one came across as an individual, interesting for her or his unique physical dynamic and understanding of movement. This was by no means a cookie-cutter troupe, which suited Bingham's intentions: he wanted a group of real individuals, not a faceless company of elite acrobats. To this end, costumes were a variety of simple white shirts or black tank tops with white or black pants, and black jazz shoes.

Movement was created in the studio, either by demonstrating on his own body or by having the dancers develop certain phrases. Parts of the choreography were tailored to individual strengths, such as de Jesus' cartwheels and backward flips. Throughout, there is a contact-inspired casualness in the many leaps and rolls, with smooth arms sliding out to the side in typical Bingham fashion. At times, someone spins on a long rope hanging centre stage; at the very end, two dancers hang from it and make dizzy circles, round and round. A similar length of hanging rope would figure largely in the personal tragedy that lay ahead.

Vancouver Premiere

The reception at the Vancouver premiere was ecstatic. Tickets sales increased dramatically during the May 5-9, 1992 run at the Firehall Arts Centre. The press turned out in force and the verdict was thumbs way up. The headlines read: "Mysterious movements, superbly crafted" (*The Sun*); "Dreamtigers fascinating multi-media EDAM piece" (*The Province*); "Dancers fly in Bingham's Dreamtigers" (*The Georgia Straight*).

A thoughtful response came from Patrick Cook in *Vandance International* magazine. He began by comparing the casualness of West Coast life with the casualness of *Dreamtigers*, "a work that reads like the colours of an early summer sunset − all purple, yellow and red − over the Strait of Georgia." He described the "haphazard feel" of the beginning, with the multimedia parts not easily fitting together. But then, he said, a "seamless whole" becomes apparent, "creating an excitement-tinged, hypnotic work." He continued:

> *It's difficult to tell why this sliding together eventually happens because, at first, all the different parts of the collaboration seem to suggest something slightly different. Mona Hamill's intense, splatter-painted revolving panels suggest Sri Lanka more than they do, say, Hornby Island. And Cooke, Macanulty, and Samworth's music, from the funk sambas to the polka montages, travels the world for its centre without settling on a particular genre, era or location. Even Bingham's choreography, from the contact improv-inspired falls and jumps to the Montreal-style obsession with hands and arms, is eclectic.*

> *Perhaps these disparate parts come together because, as each works along its own arc of meaning, they all arch towards the same point.*

Cook's insight is crucial to understanding *Dreamtigers*. Rather than "sharp, precise unison" he wrote, Bingham "has allowed the dancers to describe their own arc through space, without trying to jam their movement personalities into one single mold." Cook noted that some − "perhaps those beyond the mountains" − "might complain that this lack of precision in the unison work might be the result of inadequate rehearsing, of dancers not working hard enough to 'get it together'." That is not, however, what *Dreamtigers* is about: "... the world being described is not one of formal lines and sharp direction changes. It is a world of parts juxtaposed with one another, where the players in the dream have personalities, and the landscapes start to move in celluloid." It was a brilliant interpretation of Bingham's work.

Pipo Damiano and Jaci Metivier in *Dreamtigers*, 1992.   Photo: Chris Randle

Ottawa

As you can tell, Cathy, I am very excited about this project and hope for your support. I've been building towards this work since the last Festival, developing an able corps of dancers and my own choreography. Performing in Ottawa would be the perfect opportunity to introduce the new EDAM to the Canadian dance community.

That's how Bingham ends his letter of August 7, 1991 to producer Cathy Levy, clearly eager to make what would be his third appearance at the Canada Dance Festival in Ottawa. The previous two had been modest successes – in 1987, he had performed with the ensemble in a twenty-minute version of *Teller of Visions* as part of the Discovery series in the National Arts Centre Studio, and in 1990, his short solo, *Inside Out*, was performed by Allan Dobbs. For the 1992 festival, Levy would schedule the full-length *Dreamtigers* at the National Arts Centre Theatre on a double bill with legendary modern dancer Margie Gillis. Everyone at EDAM expected the showing to give the company the kind of exposure that would put them on the international stage.

The festival began well. EDAM dancer Jaci Metivier performed her own work as part of a Short Takes program, and Bingham gave an Impromptu Improv with Andrew Harwood, Ahmed Hassan and Steve Paxton, who had been invited to host a daily Choreographer's Discussion. As part of the festival's outdoor programming, EDAM presented *Cryptic Heart* and a company improvisation on June 27 and 28. These performances were hugely successful. Manager Gina Sufrin was proud to be associated with the group and spoke to international presenters with confidence. "There was a lot of buzz," she recalls. "I was chatting up people from Europe who were really interested." The company at this time, she felt, was "a very attractive and charismatic one. There was Jaci and Peter, and Susan and Pipo were an item as well, so there was that kind of chemistry in their improvs. And Eclilson was a blast out of left field – he blew everybody away."

On the 28th, two days before the single mainstage performance of *Dreamtigers*, a special seminar was dedicated to dance and the visual arts, moderated by a staff member of the National Gallery of Canada. Bingham took part with Chris Randle and Mona Hamill; other participants included Paul-André Fortier and Betty Goodwin.

Then Bingham came down with a painful attack of shingles, an acute viral inflammation of the nerve ganglia, and had to find a doctor. He was in a state of extreme physical distress when he received a long-distance telephone call from his family on Quadra Island, off the coast of British Columbia, where his parents and his three brothers had settled. Bruce told him that their younger brother, John, had committed suicide by hanging. It was impossible to process the information, to make sense of this sudden end to his brother's existence. Bingham had known John was unhappy in his personal life and the inevitable thought flashed through his mind: "If only I'd paid more attention." He knew he should fly home immediately to be with his family, but he also knew *Dreamtigers* could not be abandoned.

Suddenly, the images of dancers hanging on ropes which fill *Dreamtigers* in both the film and live sections took on a tragic relevance for Bingham. It felt like he had unconsciously presaged his brother's death and the meaning of the work became filled with unwelcome overtones. The audience would not know this, of course, and the show – with all the hopes for international attention attached to it – had to go on.

At the theatre on June 30th, during the technical run-through, things started to go awry. The company was not used to the strict rules of union technicians, and a work-to-rule situation made the atmosphere tense. Cooke recalls:

> *I moved the music stand and one of the workers came up to me and said, "If you do that again, we'll walk off." [The atmosphere] was that heavy. If we wanted to move the drums, all my percussions and horns, Ron's amp and cords and cables, we'd have to wait for someone to come and move us. And they were working as slowly as possible.*

The lighting plot had to be set and the enormous paintings mounted, all in the allotted half day of stage rehearsal. The technical run was not fully completed. "We got half-way through," says Hamill, "and then we were kicked off the stage." Bingham, despite the work-to-rule, blames himself: "The NAC guys had no tolerance for us. I was the technical director and had I been fully functioning, I think we would have been all right. We just didn't get the performance on the stage quickly enough." A general feeling of anxiety fell over the whole troupe.

Mark Lavelle, Susan Elliott, Pipo Damiano, Jaci Metivier in *Dreamtigers*. Photo: Chris Randle

Margie Gillis' solo show of close to an hour ran first, making for what is typically considered a full evening of dance on its own. After intermission came *Dreamtigers*, which was almost seventy minutes long. Bingham was still scrambling to set up the film projector on stage as the audience entered. During the performance, the lighting cues were off. At one point, says Bingham, "Susan had to do her solo in the only strip of light that was available." Cooke remembers a duet that took place in the dark, with the lights on the other side of the stage: "The dancers didn't know what to do — whether to try and go to the lights or just dance in the dark, and you could see them getting more and more flustered." Some of the choreography had to be changed because the rope was not anchored to a separate grid and the dancers were not able to hang from it with their whole weight. Instead, says Lavelle, "we had to substitute with some lame wandering around the rope." The live music was slower than usual and the sound was too loud.

Bingham, sitting in the back of the auditorium with Hamill and Sufrin, saw the audience begin to leave before the work was over. When the dancers finally took their bows, it was to people's backs. It felt, Bingham said, like watching his brother die. At the end of the ordeal, Bingham confesses he "lost it" and lashed out at the dancers. After the show, says Sufrin, "I had all these presenters avoiding my gaze." Hamill had to face her family, who lived in Ottawa and had come out in force. Worse was yet to come: the public dressing down in the newspapers was vicious.

In *The Globe and Mail*, Robert Everett-Green's review was headlined: "Dancing a sticky web of tedium". He described a "dreadful visitor", the "garrulous bore" who traps the unwary "in sticky webs of talk…. Bingham has redefined the limits of incoherent activity allowable on a major Canadian dance stage." The main fault was "the absence of a structural plan, or of any sound dramaturgical instinct…." So, despite "good ideas and arresting sequences scattered through the piece … they couldn't prevail over context. The piece became its own crucible of inconsequence…."

Renée Laurin, writing for *Le Droit*, was less overwhelmingly negative, mentioning the troupe's originality in movement, and in visual and sound environments. She noted the similarity in acrobatic movement to Montreal's La La La Human Steps, but found that Bingham had pushed the use of gesture further. "The biggest mistake," she wrote (originally in French), was "repeating untiringly the same scenario and the same ideas for more than an hour."

Even with the technical difficulties, it is not easy to understand the complete contrast between the show's reception in Vancouver and Ottawa. It is particularly difficult to put the description by Everett-Green in any kind of critical perspective. Was he over-writing to the demands of his readership or editor? Or did the poor quality of the work merit such invective? Was he just

Eclilson Matiais de Jesus and Susan Elliott in *Dreamtigers*, 1992.   Photo: Chris Randle

tired and in a hurry, and therefore less thoughtful in his writing? The whole episode – with the two radically different experiences of the work in western and eastern Canada – is, quite simply, surreal. "It was a real fall off the mountain," says Sufrin. "It had all been going very well, so we didn't anticipate this disaster, which made it worse."

While posterity can often "rehabilitate" an artist's reputation, as Marcel Duchamp, a pioneer of Dadaism, put it, the verdict of the moment is less easy to reassess in dance because choreography cannot be brought down from the shelf a few years later and looked at again. Thus negative critical opinion can have lasting and damaging effect. In the case of *Dreamtigers*, where the verdict was wildly divergent, critical opinion threatens to cancel out the artwork altogether. The question as to whether *Dreamtigers* was as good or as bad as the highly polarized press made out is impossible to answer.

Back in Vancouver, the company fell apart. "It's hard to know if they lost faith in Peter or just wanted to do something different," says Hamill. "But I think some of the dancers were really quite discouraged." Bingham took the ferry to Quadra Island to spend time with his family, who were struggling to come to terms with John's death.

Even Jaci Metivier broke her ties with EDAM, which she had decided to do before Ottawa, in order to work independently. A few months after the end of their professional relationship, the personal partnership between Bingham and Metivier also ended. It would be years until they danced together again.

Just People Dancing

Art should not be different than life but an act within life. Like all life, with its accidents and chances and variety and disorder and only momentary beauties.
— John Cage

In the familiar surroundings of the EDAM studio, Peter Bingham grappled with the loss of John. His art was one place where the best and the worst that life offered – the light and the dark – could be explored and expressed. Working with Gerry Gradauer, a recent graduate of Simon Fraser University's dance program, Bingham created a tense, sorrowful solo called *Left Behind*.

The title expressed Bingham's feelings as he struggled to come to terms with John's suicide. Though he felt anger at the way John had abandoned his family, especially his three children, it did not diminish his love for his younger brother. Both love and anger propel the direct dramatic movement, set to the disturbing hum of David Macanulty's score.

Left Behind premiered at the Dancing on the Edge Festival in September 1992. The only décor is an electrical cord that hangs centre stage, with a spotlight framed by a large aluminum scoop at the end of it. Gradauer, dressed in jeans, red shirt and work boots, is drawn to the harsh light like a moth to the flame. She circles aimlessly beneath it, then grabs the scoop and sets it swinging. Holding on for dear life, she twirls and falls. She stands still, prays and spits. The spitting is as fervent as the act of prayer: faith and doubt are both part of the human condition. Then she screams, loud and long. Silence comes when her head drops to the side, as if her neck has snapped.

A Mixed Bill For Toronto

It had taken three years of pitching to convince curator Mimi Beck to accept EDAM for her Toronto series, DanceWorks. The show was set for April 1993, less than a year after the disastrous Ottawa performance of *Dreamtigers*. Their appearance at the 300-seat Betty Oliphant Theatre was not well attended, but among the audience were two critics whose comments were informed and appreciative. Penelope Reed Doob, writing in *The Globe and Mail*, captured exactly EDAM's charm when she wrote: "In the varied repertoire created by artistic director Peter Bingham, EDAM's well-trained dancers show remarkable skill and enchanting *sprezzatura*, the nonchalant grace that manifests art by concealing it." Michael Crabb's comments in *The Toronto Star* were equally apt: "The program … showed the gamut of creative possibilities contact improvisation offers. After a brief little doodle of a pure contact duet, EDAM's

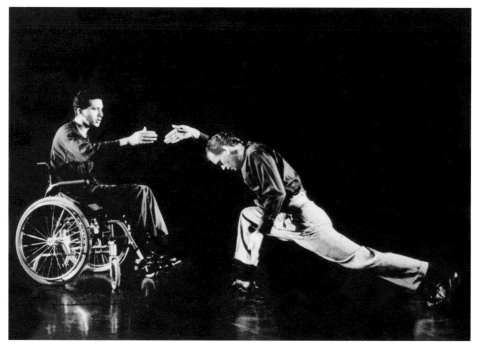

Ahmed Hassan and Peter Bingham at the Firehall Arts Centre, Vancouver, early 1990s.   Photo: Chris Randle

choreographer-director Peter Bingham explored increasingly complex territory with set dances that nevertheless draw on contact's special use of weight and momentum."

The unique atmosphere created by contact improvisation was noted by reviewers, just as it had been when EDAM entered the scene. A new element, also appreciated, was Bingham's choreographic skill. Although his instincts as an improviser still propelled his creative drive, he was more aware of what he wanted to say – of what he could contribute as an artist – and he was discovering how to do this while fully utilizing his unique gifts. For the DanceWorks mixed bill, he performed in an improvised duet and also integrated moments of improvisation within a choreographed duet. Completing the line-up were two choreographed ensembles, including one at the almost full-length running time of forty-five minutes.

Post-*Dreamtigers*, Bingham was happy to start over with a new company that was not part of that painful experience. There were two young men, both over six feet tall: Wilson Blakley, who had been dancing independently in Toronto, and German-born Markus Kuchenbuch. The three women were Gradauer, who had given a compelling performance in *Left Behind*, Australian Rosalind Crisp and Vancouverite Kathleen McDonagh. McDonagh had been working as an independent dancer for about three years, after completing a short pre-professional program at MainDance and a summer intensive at EDAM. Bingham was familiar with her qualities as a dancer and was eager to have the strong young woman join the company. She reminded him, he says, of Jaci Metivier "in power, fluidity, sequential strength. Kathleen has an empathetic body and could do contact right away."

McDonagh was being courted elsewhere and was understandably uncertain about which offer to take. After all, despite her admiration for Bingham's choreography, it was hardly an ideal situation. As McDonagh jokes: "Peter said the piece in Ottawa sucked, the dancers are all leaving, my brother just died, my girlfriend is leaving me – want to join the company?" On the positive side, EDAM was starting over with a brand new team and, also, McDonagh wanted to be as physically challenged as she knew she would be in Bingham's work. So yes, McDonagh said, and she began a long and productive association with EDAM.

The videotape record of the April 13th opening night shows the whole company, including Bingham, on the Betty Oliphant Theatre stage warming up as the audience enters. This immediately dissolved the usual boundaries between spectator and performer, preparation and performance. By making the dancers' warm-up into a public event, Bingham was saying no to smoke and mirrors, and yes to reality. He did not want his dance or his dancers to be perceived as something special and apart from daily life. At one point during the warm-up, Bingham acknowledges an audience member he knows as she takes a seat near the front, greeting her as if they were merely passing on the street. He is not the kind of performer who prepares by escaping into a private place; on the day of a show, for instance, he simply goes about his business, calmly resolving last-minute problems.

The opening warm-up segued gently into a good-natured romp called *You Leave Me Breathless*. Throughout the five-minute duet, Blakley and McDonagh were encouraged to find moments they could make their own. Thus, while the contact improvisation-inspired moves are set, the interaction between them is not. Bingham directed the pair to talk to each other, and their brief exchanges and sounds of breathing are the only accompaniment.

The result is a playful physicality that suggests ordinary human interaction, despite a series of difficult tosses, catches, leaps and turns. The actual physical material was taken from partnering work in *Dreamtigers* – Bingham was

Kathleen McDonagh and Wilson Blakley in *You Leave Me Breathless*, 1993.   Photo: Chris Randle

determined to recycle some of the material that had been so poorly received in Ottawa – but it was transformed in this setting. Here, instead of being one part of a huge surrealistic work, the duet was a polished gem on its own. The movement seemed to sketch an almost domestic relationship between two people, who interact with friendly humour and goodwill.

Friendliness was also at the core of *Present Tense*, an improvisation that took place only on opening night by Bingham and a colleague from EDAM's founding days, musician Ahmed Hassan. Their eleven-minute improvisation did not seem staged; rather, it appeared to be a real encounter between two men. Bingham — arms and legs sliding out, everything smooth and easy — begins by directing himself toward Hassan, who is in a wheelchair because of multiple sclerosis. As he moves away, Hassan, vocalizing with ululating throat sounds and playing the berimbau, directs himself toward Bingham. The two men seem drawn to each other, listening and watching closely, as if they are quite alone and not in a public space. At the end, Bingham lies down in front of the wheelchair, his body open and vulnerable, his head on Hassan's footrest. Hassan responds by bending over and cradling Bingham as best he can. Then, quite unexpectedly, Hassan manages to hoist himself out of the chair and onto the floor next to Bingham, embracing him. The trust between the two men is palpable, creating a moment that is both real and also great theatre.

The first half of the evening concluded with a more formal work, *Paisley*, fifteen minutes of athletic gambolling to Franz Joseph Haydn's *Cello Concerto #2 in D Major*. As with *Plunge*, Bingham did not allow himself to be intimidated or overwhelmed by the classical score; his aim was to illuminate the music as he heard it. Also as in *Plunge*, he began by making the movement first, without knowing what the music would be.

Blakley, Crisp, Gradauer, Kuchenbuch and McDonagh, clad either in red, green or blue pants and matching shirts, form and reform in an easygoing relationship to the lyrical expression of the concerto's first movement, allegro moderato. There is also a brief, foot-stomping game played by the trio of women; this section is dance — pure movement — and yet it is also play — they have the engaged attitude of children in a schoolyard. The dancers' unmannered, contact-based movement is filled with gymnastic tumbles and handstands, and with Bingham-styled port de bras featuring arms and hands that slide and slice, bend and hook. They fulfill the movement smartly, and the sudden twisting and turning of their bodies seems to transform them into brushstrokes — it looks as if they are inscribing patterns in the air. This movement reminded Bingham of the teardrop pattern called "paisley" that was popular in the 1970s, and which provided a title for the work.

Following intermission, a very different atmosphere was created by *Ode to John Angus B*. Bingham was not afraid to include a dark work, as he had with his other mixed bills, and this time there was a personal story — his brother's suicide — to tell. For *Ode to John Angus B*, Bingham reworked more material from *Dreamtigers*, now irrevocably associated with his brother's death. "I realized my brother was the 'dreamtiger', and the material was important to me," he says.

Ode to John Angus B is the closest Bingham would get to creating a full narrative choreography. In it, he attempted to come to terms with John's suicide by presenting his death within a caring family scenario. It is never easy to portray the specifics of character or situation in dance, and it is especially difficult for a son to explore his parents' emotional pain. One strategy by which Bingham copes is to remain as abstract as he can while still telling the tragic tale. To some extent, because a young woman, Gerry Gradauer, danced the role of John, Bingham distanced himself from the real event, yet his family situation is clearly indicated in the scenario. In addition to the main character, there are two dancers in parental roles – Kathleen McDonagh in a flowered dress as the mother and Wilson Blakley in white shirt and dark trousers as the father. Unfortunately, all the performers were about the same age, which did not establish believable cross-generational relationships.

Gerry Gradauer in *Ode to John Angus B*, 1993.　　　　　　Photo: Chris Randle

Gradauer's role as the brother had her on stage throughout, and her small, forlorn figure, clad in jeans and t-shirt, is the strength of the piece. It opens with her sitting cross-legged, obsessively polishing a pair of black boots and watching the parents' lyrical duet. There is a gentle, lost quality to this first section, supported by the sweetly haunting *Three Intermezzi*, Op. 117 by Johannes Brahms, played live on stage by pianist Myron Plett.

In the penultimate scene, Gradauer's fearless performance in Bingham's bare-bones choreography resonates strongly. This section concludes, as in her earlier solo, *Left Behind*, with an obvious depiction of death by hanging.

An odd scene that seems to suggest an afterlife is tacked on as the work's finale. This is a cameo appearance of two ghostly figures (Rosalind Crisp and Markus Kuchenbuch) draped in long folds of fabric, arms gently uplifted. The sentimentality suggests the extent to which Bingham was still grieving over John's death, and it seemed as if he felt the need to escape to the religious tradition of his childhood or to comfort those left behind.

Crossfade

Despite EDAM's success in Toronto, the company members scattered once again and, for various personal reasons, most of them left Vancouver. Only Kathleen McDonagh stayed on. With McDonagh, Bingham created another of his masterly duets, the twenty-minute *Crossfade*, in which he also danced. McDonagh opened herself completely to the creative process and does not recall feeling nervous about the prospect of working so closely with Bingham. Yet, she adds, "how many duets have I done with a choreographer? It was a unique experience." She recalls the process as an enjoyable one where she felt at ease and, importantly, understood Bingham's need to create through a free spirit of play.

Although the work seems to have a narrative lurking within – a kind of loosely stated story of affection – the scenario was discovered and developed organically through movement; it did not come first and it in no way drove the creative process, which had been the case with *Ode to John Angus B*. What did drive it was Bingham's exploration of the particular physicality possible between him and McDonagh, who together have an easy counterbalancing contact style facilitated by their hips being roughly the same height and by a similar flow in movement style.

One element they did not have in common was age: Bingham was forty-two years old and McDonagh, twenty-eight. This relationship gave emotional resonance to the choreography, performed in silence and with an exceptional rapport between the dancers. Max Wyman, writing in *Dance International*, suggested the title, *Crossfade*, might refer to "the spring-autumn look of them together, his scraped head, the face wearing its years, oddly vulnerable on her

Anne Cooper in *A Shadow of Myself*, 1994.   Photo: Chris Randle

lap (though his body is as easy with the air as ever)." Although Bingham can-not remember where the title came from, he insists it was not about their age. "But I don't mind Max's interpretation," he adds. McDonagh, too, does not feel age was a factor in the title or during the creation of the duet.

Wyman devoted a third of his back page column in the Spring 1994 edition of *Dance International* to discussing what he called "a hectic little poem of human intimacy." The way he describes the opening section has nothing to do with praising two dancers dancing; it is more like Wyman is watching a couple of people horsing around together at a park or the beach:

They're kneeling when the lights come up; she's behind him. She nuzzles her head around his outline, tugs him into imbalance and a fall by pulling the shoulder of his garment with her teeth. She kneels, and it's his turn to nuzzle her from behind: he pushes his head up under her right arm and swings her up and over and round, and suddenly she's kneeling again, and now he's lying in her lap.

It's a simple sequence, but it has a sense of magical rightness; watching the way they fall at apparent random into such a satisfying resolution is a matter of mute, primitive delight. Moments like this keep occurring – they fling and push and roll each other in what look like abandoned and spontaneous outbursts, and yet they continue to reach these extraordinary moments of intimate, harmonious repose.

Crossfade turned out to be Bingham's final appearance in a choreographed work. This was not because he was uncomfortable dancing in his forties; rather, he felt he could see his choreography more clearly if he was outside it. Bingham continued to appear on stage in improvisations.

Although McDonagh and Bingham never danced *Crossfade* again, Bingham reworked the material twice. *Just Another Country Tune*, with McDonagh and Stephen O'Connell, was set to country music, and the work had a more sensual look. *The Revengers*, with McDonagh and Susan Elliott, was a playful take on the television detective series, *The Avengers*, and used television theme show music from a detective series Bingham watched as a child. Neither was as outstanding as the original.

At the March 1994 premiere of *Crossfade*, a theatrical solo called *A Shadow of Myself* was also presented. In this twenty-minute work, Bingham had newcomer Anne Cooper portray a listless woman in front of an empty television screen, clutching a remote control. Cooper, who had trained at the Royal Winnipeg Ballet's Professional School, had recently settled in Vancouver and was taking classes with Bingham. *A Shadow of Myself* revealed her as an idiosyncratic performer with a flair for dramatic expression and she became a valued interpreter of Bingham's work. Along with McDonagh, Cooper was part of a pool of dancers working in Vancouver who had a broad grasp of performance aesthetics and, as ballet- and modern-trained dancers, integrated strong technical abilities into Bingham's contact-based choreography. *Crossfade* and *A Shadow of Myself* premiered as part of a mixed bill called Other Issues, a development of Forced Issues into a more formal, professionally presented series.

Also making its debut at Other Issues was the refurbished studio, which had previously been upgraded by removing small risers that ran the length of both sides and by tearing the back wall down and moving it a few feet further north, increasing the floor dimensions to 9.45 metres by 17.68 metres. At that time, the office that had been in the back was moved to the front, across the small foyer at the studio entrance, and the narrow back space became a dressing room. Now, freshly painted and sporting new black curtains and a lighting board, the EDAM studio/theatre was primed for action. It would be the crucible where *Hindsight* came into being.

Hindsight

Hindsight was developed through a self-imposed physical limitation, which was to keep the head on the floor while moving fluently on the ground. The EDAM floor, with its smooth, notoriously slippery surface, was the ideal space for creating such a fantastical work – surprising in Bingham's oeuvre – in which the performers spend much of the time anchored to the earth more intimately, and at times awkwardly, than through the usual force of gravity. This physical motif became key to *Hindsight*'s metaphorical richness.

The dancers were Susan Elliott and newcomer Darren (Daelik) Hackenbrook. Elliott had been among the first group of EDAM dancers in 1990, just after Bingham took on sole directorship, while Daelik (soon to be known by the single name) had just completed the two-year MainDance pre-professional program. When Daelik took his first dance class at the age of twenty-six at EDAM, shortly after moving to Vancouver from Ontario, he was hooked. Besides being inspired by Bingham as both a teacher and performer, other men in the company who impressed him were Pipo Damiano and Mark Lavelle. Daelik, another key member of EDAM, would remain with the company for six seasons.

The twenty-five-minute *Hindsight*, with its atmosphere of memory and regret, premiered at EDAM's Other Issues series in June 1995. It is set to an operatic duet by Hector Berlioz and an aria by Richard Strauss, providing a refined, European background that seems to have little in common with the two small figures on the ground. In separate pools of light, they traverse the stage, rolling restlessly from side to side, or kneeling hunched forward so their heads remain in contact with the floor.

The piece is an elegiac vehicle for the two tousle-headed dancers – Daelik, with his startling bottle blond hair, and Elliott, with her soft black curls. When they are upright, their fluttering arms and grounded movement suggest birds that have lost the ability to fly, or maybe a pair of fallen angels; in either case, intimately connected to the black wings lying at the front of the performing area. Neutrally costumed in loose pants and tops, they could also be contemporary lovers expressing romantic regret. Or maybe they are two halves of the same being struggling for wholeness and flight.

Whether angels or birds or lovers, or something more metaphysical, they remain unreconciled at the end. Daelik, firmly connected to the earth, stands looking out the window on the west wall of the studio. Resigned or content — it is hard to tell which — he closes the shutters. There is darkness until Elliott, dramatically lit, is revealed upstage. She flaps her arms and, using a strict vertical take-off, forces a series of jumps into the air. They go nowhere, though her effort and concentration are intense. The two endure, each in their own way. As angelic metaphors for a spiritual life, they are more subtle and evocative than the ghostly figures that end *Ode to John Angus B.*

Hindsight was introduced in the program by a fragment of poetry composed by Bingham: "… remembering flight from a long time past … broken wings remind them …" Images of flight and of brokenness — of light and dark — fill the work. The tragedy of the last few years, during which life and art had been strangely combined, would never completely leave him. But right now, Bingham enjoyed bringing forth angels, birds and lovers. People loved *Hindsight* and the dancers loved performing it.

OTHER ISSUES

at
EDAM
303 E. 8th Ave

October 20-21,
October 27-28 and November 3-4 at 8pm

new choreography by

Peter Bingham   Frozen Eye   D-Anne Kuby

Advance tickets $10. Tickets $12 at the door. After October 15, advance tickets will be
available Mon.-Fri. 10am-5pm at the Dance Centre, #400-873 Beatty St.   Call 606-6400.

EDAM gratefully acknowledges the support of the Canada Council; the Government of British Columbia through the Ministry of Small
Business, Tourism and Culture; the City of Vancouver, Office of Cultural Affairs, the Vancouver Foundation and the Western Front.   1995

photo: Nicole Rivelli

A Case for Improvisation

Not repeated tonight.
— Conclusion to a review of The Echo Case

T hroughout the 1990s, the EDAM studio/theatre at the Western Front continued to be a popular hot spot for dance, renowned for its intimate improvisations. Only a small audience can squeeze in – fifty seats are set up on risers and an extra half-dozen or more spectators might sprawl in front on the floor – but, for many, one of the joys of an EDAM event is the close relationship between spectator and performer. The audience can see the dancers' expressions and the details of their interactions with each other. The dancers can see the audience and might look at or even speak directly to them. The real world makes itself known when the sounds of passers-by are heard on the street outside, especially if windows are left open on a warm summer night. Following the show, many audience members hang out for a beer, and so do the dancers.

Six months after Peter Bingham turned forty, in November 1991, he gave another memorable improvisation at the EDAM studio. Bingham performed with his company dancers, who included Mark Lavelle and Pipo Damiano, both a decade younger than him. Lavelle, gentlemanly and serious, and Damiano, with his kamikaze fearlessness, had enough experience and drive to challenge Bingham and give him a run for his money. There was no music, just the sounds of the dancers' breath as they threw their bodies into the fray with athletic abandon. "Are you all right?" one of the men asked after a particularly high-flying encounter. It was scary at times, and seemed on the edge of safety and good sense. Yet it was glorious, too, with all the risk-taking and vigour of sport, undertaken with sensitivity and comradeship. It was EDAM at its best.

Bingham was no longer as physically bold and agile as his younger colleagues, but his movement potential remained phenomenal. Moreover, he had the experience to make the most of whatever happened during a performance: if someone offered even an inkling of an idea or movement possibility, he was there for it, ready to respond with an open and non-judgmental attitude. Bingham understands improvisation in the open-ended sense described by American author Ann Cooper Albright: "Improvisation is … a way of relating to movement and experience: a willingness to explore the realm of possibility, not in order to find the correct solution, but simply to find *out*."

Bingham believes part of what you are discovering is your own self. He explains: "In pure contact improvisation, you can connect physically just with the exhilaration of movement invention" but in "open improvisation", which

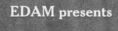

EDAM presents

The Echo Case

June 24-25 8pm

Peter Bingham
Marc Boivin
Andrew Harwood
Coat Cooke
Ron Samworth
Robert Meister

EDAM Studio Theatre
303 East 8th Ave. Vancouver, BC
Advance tickets $15
Tickets $18 at the door

Reservations **604-876-9559**

www.edamdance.org

Photos: Chris Randle - Design: Depicture Graphics - 2005

BRITISH
COLUMBIA
ARTS COUNCIL

EDAM gratefully acknowledges the support of the Dance Section, Canada Council, the Government of British Columbia through the BC Arts Council and the Gaming Branch, the City of Vancouver, Vancouver Foundation, the Leon and Thea Koerner Foundation and the Western Front.

can include any kind of movement or theatrical element, "you have to dig down and find out what's there to share." Thus your main resource is your own psyche: "Who you are that day is who you have to perform." Through that performing, as Steve Paxton has written, you are given "a chance to glance at yourself sideways as you move through time and space and to learn about your own behavior." According to Bingham:

> You investigate yourself in a way that is really no different than what Jung or any of the great philosophers did.... It's about authenticity and self-expression, and is essentially a spiritual quest. To know who you are, and to be able to express it without self-consciousness, you have to understand your spirit — your energy. That's what we have to give as dancers.

Despite his lofty goals, Bingham's approach is resolutely practical. Even if you are not in the best mood or in the best of shape, he says, "an audience will make you feel up to performing one way or another." This is not about toadying to the masses; rather, it reflects absolute respect for his job as an artist, which Bingham believes is basically about relating honestly to those who come out to see him dance.

On the last weekend in March 1994, Bingham engaged in another legendary improvisation when he partnered Jaci Metivier during an hour-long ensemble performance. Metivier, prior to moving with her husband to Salmon Arm in the British Columbia Interior, was working as an independent dancer and choreographer. Though she and Bingham had not danced together for a couple of years, their intimacy was as satisfying as ever. As always, each fully matched the other's eagerness and joy in dancing.

"It was total exhilaration," Metivier says of their improvisations in general. So it was for many watching. Dancer Kathleen McDonagh praises "Peter and Jaci's great rhythm together" and the way "you could see and sense the communication between them." Gina Sufrin, EDAM's former manager, found the pair "so beautiful to watch — and what was wonderful was the humour and affection that informed the movement."

Metivier, though several inches shorter than Bingham, and with a slender frame, was sturdy, strong and technically skilled. It seemed as if she could lift Bingham almost as easily as he could lift her, and both were as quick to support as to be supported, to resist as to yield, to instigate as to develop. It gave their male/female dynamics a satisfying equality and was important to their success as a duo.

This gender equality is integral to contact improvisation. British author Ramsay Burt, however, finds that contact favours a "risky and/or organic male style of dancing." In contact, he complains, "Male dancers rarely take on movement qualities and conventions that are in the range associated with feminine behaviour. Female dancers, however, get to dance material or movement qualities conventionally associated with masculinity."

This is not so with Bingham. One of the remarkable aspects of this master of improvisation is his readiness to yield and support, and to wait and accept periods of quiet pacing and development – attributes more often associated with female improvisers. In his dancing, Bingham does not value the role of the active instigator any more than he does the responsive follower, and he embodies both comfortably and with style. A hallmark of Bingham's improvisation is his generosity toward fellow performers – female and male – always respecting their individuality while also fully expressing himself.

The Echo Case

In The Echo Case, Bingham's highly regarded annual improvisations with Andrew Harwood and Marc Boivin, audiences have the rare opportunity to see three men dancing together. Beyond that, the trio's intense empathy breaks the stereotype of men as objective, unemotional forces. Refreshingly, their on-stage touch and tangle is highly sensual although not overtly sexual. Bingham says, "All the dances I have, with men or women, are sensual. Being physical *is* sensual." However, he adds, the performance is just that – a performance – and not biographical material reflecting his personal relationships. "There's a lot of steaminess that goes on between Marc and Andrew and I, but I would never take it literally."

For those unfamiliar with the conventions of the form, these improvisations can be challenging to "read". Burt notes that, in ordinary life, "this kind of physical proximity between two men would ordinarily be interpreted as either sexual or confrontational – getting 'too' close may trigger off homophobic fears." As Burt points out, in contact improvisation just having men close together pushes the usual boundaries of conventional male behaviour.

Bingham and Harwood were old friends when their annual improvised performances began in 1992. They brought decades of experience to improvising, which both discovered at Synergy. Then, with Fulcrum, they pioneered contact improvisation across Canada. Boivin, over ten years younger and an integral part of Montreal's contemporary dance scene, first joined the duo as a member of EDAM's Summer Intensive faculty. In 1994, during his second year teaching technique, he participated in Bingham and Harwood's classes, and joined them in that summer's performances.

This first experience of improvising in front of an audience was not easy, particularly with the element of contact involved. Boivin explains: "Contact

Peter Bingham, Marc Boivin, Andrew Harwood in The Echo Case, 2006.   Photo: Chris Randle

improvisation was not my world and I had some preconceived judgements about the form being too open to really create something solid." Now, Boivin calls it "a huge gift" to have been introduced to improvising on stage with Bingham and Harwood.

The three men are so comfortable and familiar with each other that watching The Echo Case in the small EDAM studio is like sitting in your living room with friends. The dance flows like easy conversation and the audience is close enough to catch every nuance. While the trio seems relaxed and spontaneous, they never lose sight of technical considerations like pacing and timing, aware of the bigger picture while still expressing themselves. For instance, the improvisations always finish uncannily close to the expected sixty minutes. According to Bingham:

> *We're very time conscious because that's a big part of dancing. In the early days of improvising, I'd think I was really into something, yet later, when I looked at the video, it had lasted maybe ten seconds. You have to really readjust your sense of time.*

Working spatially is another important parameter, as Bingham explains:

> *Improvising is like instant choreography. A lot of the time when I'm dancing I'm thinking spatially – I know what the lights are doing, I know where I*

am in relationship to other dancers, if it's a duet I know where the dance is moving to and how it's moving.

Being aware of the audience, feeling their energy and whether they are with you or not in a particular development, is also necessary.

I enjoy the extra energy of an audience and I don't think I let it get in the way. The difficulty with performing improvisation is how much you transform when you have an audience in front of you, and the challenge is not to transform at all. Not to let that audience energy get you out of practice. You have to find yourself in front of people and be comfortable with that.

For Bingham, then, dance is about relationship: with the audience, with the space and with fellow performers, all the while remaining centred in himself. In a teaching document distributed to students during the 2003 EDAM Summer Intensive, Boivin describes this multiple focus in terms of inward and outward listening: "Inward listening refers to images, inspiration, physical sensations, and intellectual references. Outward listening refers to the space, others, everything that is present and a part of creation." All three Echo Case improvisers have what Boivin considers the necessary ability to be both passionately involved and witnessing with perspective at the same time.

From the beginning, musicians Coat Cooke and Ron Samworth, and lighting designer Robert Meister, were integral to the improvising team. The closeness between the group is suggested by Meister's insider's description in *The Dance Current* magazine of the dancers' unique relationships to his lighting choices, which also hints at their different styles and personalities:

Andrew is always a mystery to me. I sometimes think that he couldn't care less where the lights are or what kind of set is out there, but then something I do with the lights or the video will catch his interest and he incorporates that into his dance.... Peter is always right in the hot spot. It's spooky sometimes. I think of it as the choreographer in him. He knows where the light is and by standing in that exact spot, he invites me to enhance what he's doing with light. Marc seeks out the dark areas. He exists in the "shadowlands" and it is not my place to seek him out with my light.

Despite their individuality, during improvisations the dancers come together in a fascinating, often hugely entertaining way as a team. Boivin, with his chaste, angelic manner, often seems bemused by the real world situations he finds himself in with the others. It is as if he understands the abstract world of movement better than the concrete one of human interaction, but he is good-natured and does his best. Harwood is the trickster who alternates between austerity and absurdity. He uses physical and vocal humour to provoke, addressing his fellow performers and sometimes the audience in comic or ironic fashion. The most conceptual, he pursues ideas with gusto. Bingham likes to try things out, pushing himself into shapes or spinning in his loose, low-key way. Elegant yet unmannered, Peter Bingham is the guy next door who can fix your leaking tap and waltz you around the living room afterwards.

The series title, The Echo Case, was coined for a 1999 tour to Edmonton, Winnipeg, Toronto and Halifax. Judging from the press reports, the tour was a great success and audiences had a good time. Pamela Anthony in the *Edmonton Journal* noted: "The natural unfolding of hilarious narratives, the quick-witted riffs, the sly sense of slapstick and sheer comedic rhythm were tremendously enjoyable."

In Halifax, Janet French ended her *Gazette* review:

> *Most importantly, the performance was a lot of fun, both for the performers and the audience. It is exciting to see professional performers that have taken a step away from the pretentiousness of the mainstream dancing world to create performances that are both unique and playful.*

In Halifax's *Chronicle-Herald*, Stephen Pedersen was equally inspired and made some insightful technical observations:

> *... the dancers demonstrated a fluidity and a flexibility that is more the property of things that flow, roll, stream, compact and burst open – things like rivers, breezes, ribbons, balls, trees, flowers or things that tangle like rope and rain-forest vines.... Each dancer ... integrated his own personal imagery and style into that of the others and of the dance itself, in a remarkable display of sensitivity – not only to each other, but to larger forces of weight, momentum, balance and poise.*

Finally, Rebecca Todd, writing in Toronto's *Eye Weekly* newspaper, made an apt comparison between The Echo Case's best moments and a hockey game:

> *Good improvisation can give performance the excitement of a spectator sport. When inspired conjunctions of sound, gesture and light create breathtaking images that can only happen by accident – and when all the performers are fully listening to each other – we feel as privileged to be there as hockey fans present at a historic play.*

In contrast, the Vancouver press paid little attention. Generally, newspaper coverage of dance in the city during this period was minimal. Even at the best of times, studio performances are considered low profile and thus are unlikely to be given precious newspaper space, while improvisation is often dismissed as spur-of-the-moment doodling not worthy of serious attention.

A good improvisation does not come out of nowhere, but from a solid foundation of training and practice. This is something Bingham has supported in the Vancouver community in an extraordinarily committed fashion throughout his artistic directorship by offering classes, workshops and performance opportunities. He also understands the importance of professional development for his own artistic growth and, during the 1990s, he organized the arrival of key international players at the EDAM studio, all artists he was inspired by.

Relationships with colleagues from the United States go back to the 1970s, when Steve Paxton, the originator of contact improvisation, and Nancy Stark Smith, a leading American exponent of the form and the co-founder of the *Contact Quarterly* journal, visited Vancouver. One of the first things Bingham did once he was in charge at EDAM was to arrange for Paxton to return for a month-long residency.

Bingham reconnected with Smith when both happened to visit Paxton's Vermont home, Madbrook Farm, at the same time. This resulted in Smith being in residence at EDAM in 1991, and then, over two weeks in August 1994, she attended EDAM's Vancouver International Improvisation Symposium. Other prominent American improvisers among the symposium-goers were Lisa Nelson, Karen Nelson, Simone Forti, K.J. Holmes, Chris Aiken, Ray Chung and Julie Carr, a co-founder of the New York Improvisation Festival (where Bingham performed from 1992 to 1994). Paxton attended but left early due to a death in the family.

Three working groups were formed, with Bingham part of the contact group and also attending the sessions led by Forti, a pioneer in improvisation with a fascination for movement and words. Forti had participants explore three different locations: the Western Front, the Vancouver Art Gallery and Brandywine Falls, in order to develop "land portraits", in which the history and geography of a place inform an individual's improvisation. After each outing, the artists spent an hour alone writing before meeting in the studio, where they read their work aloud and danced.

Forti had begun to develop a dance/narrative form in the mid-1980s, and it was her interest in using the voice that attracted Bingham to her sessions. According to Forti:

I started speaking while moving, with words and movement springing spontaneously from a common source. This practice has been a way for me to know what's on my mind. What's on my mind before I think it through, while it is still a wild feeling in my bones.

In the contact group, Bingham interacted with seasoned contact improvisers Aiken, Bliss, Carr, Chung and Smith. "We'd have our rehearsal," recalls Smith, "and then we'd get in Peter's pick-up truck and go out to the beach. We were on a perpetual high working together; it was really a wonderful summer." Crammed together in the truck, "we joked about calling ourselves Group Sex – and this became Group Six, because there were six of us."

Group Six performed together for two and a half years, exploring the connection between composition and contact improvisation. A typical Group Six practice session began with everyone entering the space and warming up before finding a partner for contact work. Then the group would have a more formal practice of something decided on the day before, such as working on solos, on moving in and out of contact, or with a unit bigger than two or three people. Afterwards, they would de-brief. This was followed by an open set, and a longer discussion about what did and did not work, leading to an idea to focus on for the next day's practice. Smith explains:

In performance, every time we would get together we'd bring more refined practices to bear and they would start to be layers within our open scores – layers of reference to one another. But open is a misnomer. I interviewed Anna Halprin once ... and she felt nothing was open because you bring to it all your associations. As soon as you have any history together you're drawing off that very strongly. I know that was true with Group Six.

Over the next few years, each member produced a Group Six event, though not everybody could always attend. All six were present for their final performance in January 1997 in San Francisco at the ODC/SF Performance Gallery Theater. Smith tells the story of how Group Six folded:

In San Francisco, we realized we had come full circle – we had each produced something, though we hadn't set out to do that. So we took a walk in a park on top of a mountain ridge to talk about what to do next. I brought my I Ching sticks and we each did the sticks to create one line of the hexagram. When we read the hexagram [and then a second one], they confirmed our feelings that we had reached fruition and needed to let [Group Six] go. It was great to leave on a high note.

The first hexagram read "Development (Gradual Progress)"; the second, "Splitting Apart."

In November 1998, Bingham invited Smith, Aiken and Chung to EDAM's second Improvisation Symposium. Three Vancouverites well trained in contact at EDAM also took part: Susan Elliott, Anne Cooper and Kathleen McDonagh, plus Chantal Deeble, who had been with EDAM during *Dreamtigers*.

Two groups were formed for the weekend performances that closed the symposium. The first, fondly referred to as "the old-timers", was made up of forty-seven-year-old Bingham, the American visitors, and musicians Coat Cooke and Ron Samworth. The second group was the Vancouver gang, experienced artists who were a decade or so younger, joined by musicians Dylan van der Schyff and André Lachance. The abandon and bravado of the younger artists was matched by the inventiveness and style of the older ones.

Bingham speaks philosophically about dancing his age: "One of the things I love about improvisation is that when you're young, you can dance the young body and when you're older, you can dance the older body." He has never let convention dictate what he can and cannot do – in his view, the mere fact of age is hardly reason for a dancer to be still.

Remember Me From Then

… this single moment/which never stops opening, never stops revealing …
— Octavio Paz, *Sun stone*

When *Remember Me From Then*, a collaboration between Peter Bingham and Ballet British Columbia's artistic director, John Alleyne, premiered at the Queen Elizabeth Theatre in 1996, the audience numbered in the thousands. A performance mounted at EDAM's tiny studio might draw one hundred people over a two-night run. A show running three or four nights at the Firehall Arts Centre or the Vancouver East Cultural Centre might attract two or three hundred more. The Queen Elizabeth Theatre seats almost 3,000, and the show ran for three nights to good houses. As Bingham stood on the enormous stage taking opening night bows with Alleyne and the dancers, he revelled in the experience.

Besides giving him access to a large audience, *Remember Me From Then* offered the chance to go deeper into the meaning of his movement vocabulary by placing it next to a very different one. Together, Bingham and Alleyne agreed to bring the 1970s-born, renegade form of contact improvisation into the same room as the centuries-old tradition of ballet and from that create no less than an inspired work of art. *Remember Me From Then* would stretch the bounds of each artist's aesthetics and beliefs.

In this collaboration, Bingham developed meaning by creating new movement in the studio, particularly arm and gestural phrases, as well as by developing movement words and phrases from his previous choreographic works; these are what form Bingham's lexicon and allow him to create without having to discover a new vocabulary each time. It was partially a practical decision. Bingham recalls: "When we began the ballet collaboration, I had three weeks to make a work with John for the Queen Elizabeth stage, and I went in with everything I had going. Since none of [the ballet crowd] knew my work, I could put my best stuff on that stage." The same movements, the same moments, had yet more to reveal.

During rehearsals at the Ballet B.C. studio, Bingham explored the way in which phrases from different works could be arranged to follow one another, noting how this affected the dynamics of the movement. What would a section from an early work, *Cryptic Heart*, look like in this context? How could a move from the idiosyncratic *Hindsight* contribute to the whole? What would dedicated ballet dancers bring to a sequence made for his contact-based quartet, *Magnet*? Then Alleyne came in and set the material, adding

John Alleyne.

choreography of his own, bringing dancers on and off with finesse, arranging groupings and dividing the twenty-three minutes into three major sections.

The project with EDAM fit in well with Ballet British Columbia's mandate to present "ballet of our time". The small, ten-year-old company had already performed pieces by ballet's notorious revisionist, William Forsythe, as well as by modern dance choreographers David Earle, Christopher House and Serge Bennathan. In 1995, Ballet B.C. had shared an evening with House's Toronto Dance Theatre. Pairing up with a radical contact improvisation-based company, one with strong local roots and a reputation for experiment, was the perfect, and daring, next step.

The initial idea for a collaboration arose when Bingham happened to sit across the aisle from Alleyne on their return flight from a Canada Council meeting in Ottawa. Bingham mentioned to Donna Spencer, a Vancouver presenter who runs the Firehall Arts Centre, how well the two men had got along, and Spencer jumped in with the suggestion that if they worked together on a project, she would be happy to present it. Alleyne was keen, as long as he could also present it as part of Ballet B.C.'s annual season at the Queen Elizabeth Theatre.

With hindsight, bringing Bingham and Alleyne together creatively was a brilliant thought, although it must have seemed an unlikely project – the two men and their companies have almost nothing in common. While Bingham had studied some ballet, he was hardly an initiate in the world of tutus and pointe shoes, and only occasionally attended ballet performances. Alleyne, a graduate of the National Ballet School, had danced with the National Ballet of Canada and with Stuttgart Ballet before becoming artistic director of Ballet British Columbia in 1992. While he was aware of contact improvisation and its influence on dance in general, Alleyne had no first-hand experience of it.

One thing Bingham and Alleyne did share was their enjoyment of the open process of collaborating. In Bingham's case, he craves the camaraderie and energy created through such a relationship. For Alleyne, co-creation is a form of research and development, a way to access fresh ideas. His 1993 collaborative work, *The Archaeology of Karl…A Romantic Adventure*, involved the company dancers' individual interpretations of the life and times of Ludwig van Beethoven, whose string quartets were the basis for Timothy Sullivan's score. In 1995's *Can You Believe She Actually Said*, the dancers spoke text they had written themselves. The same year, Alleyne co-created *The Don Juan Variations* with theatre director Roy Surette, using text from the 17th-century play, *El Burlador de Sevilla*. With the present project, the research was more fundamental. Here, the focus was on putting new steps with a contact base together with familiar ballet ones.

During this period of co-creation with Bingham, Alleyne was already thinking about the full-length choreography he was planning for 2000, *The Faerie Queen*, based on Shakespeare's *A Midsummer Night's Dream*. Alleyne's description of the mix of fantasy and reality in Shakespeare's play as being "a collision between two worlds" could equally describe the project with Bingham. Indeed, Alleyne felt that, as in Shakespeare's play, a magical setting was needed that would allow logic to be dispensed with, a place where ballet and contact improvisation could meet and gracefully collide. Alleyne explains, "We created an isolated location where you could have a snowstorm, where creatures and fairies could come out of the mist." A forest glade was suggested by set designer Nicola Kozakiewicz's craggy tree branches, which hang from the flies centre stage. Adding an air of cool mystery, dry ice is used at the start of the piece and snowflakes fall midway through and again at the end. Costuming, too, contributes to the creation of a fantastical atmosphere: although Kate Nelson put the men and women in the same well-cut trousers, bustiers and jackets, with soft shoes, one EDAM dancer wears a long, white tutu in the middle section, giving her an otherworldly look. Adding to this romantic setting is Sullivan's lush orchestral score, *Double Concerto*.

In such a setting, Alleyne could give his imagination free reign and make sense of the earthy quality of Bingham's contact improvisation-based vocabulary, with its rolls and tumbles, and peasant squats so unlike any ballet plié. In the spirit of collaboration, Bingham accepted this element of fantasy as something needed to accommodate ballet audiences, but it was foreign to his understanding of dance and he would not direct his own attention to it.

Besides the two very different choreographers, there were two very different teams of dancers. The Ballet B.C. roster included Isabelle Itri, John Ottmann, Sylvain Senez, Gail Skrela and Wen Wei Wang; on the EDAM side were Anne Cooper, Susan Elliott, Kathleen McDonagh and Alexandra Cyril,

EDAM's newest company member and a 1992 graduate of the Professional Program of Winnipeg's Contemporary Dancers.

In general terms, the modern dance/ballet dichotomy had been breaking down for decades as individuals were drawn to wider creative experiences or as scarce jobs on either side became available. Ballet B.C.'s Senez and Wang had danced with Judith Marcuse's contemporary troupe, and in 1993 Ottmann had begun freelancing during the off-season with modern dance choreographers. The previous year, Skrela and Wang were two of five ballet dancers in *The Protecting Veil* by modern dance choreographer Lola MacLaughlin. More and more, choreographers demanded a full spectrum of technical possibilities from their casts and most dancers cross-trained to some extent. The EDAM dancers, for instance, all had ballet training, and occasionally took company class with Ballet B.C. before rehearsals of *Remember Me From Then*. Cooper, who had trained at the Royal Winnipeg Ballet's Professional School, had even danced on the Queen Elizabeth stage as a graduate student in the company's *Nutcracker*. She recalls times when she felt caught between two realities, neither fully one kind of dancer nor the other:

> *It was kind of neat and somewhat bizarre to be back in the ballet world. I had a mini-identity crisis! I use classical technique a lot — it's still there, but unless you're doing turns and leaps every day, the pathways through, and the strength, becomes different. And I'm not as richly ingrained in contact as somebody who started with that.*

Cooper feels the challenge for the EDAM dancers was to smooth the movement to the required finish and to perfect some of the technical ballet steps. On the ballet side, Wang describes the profound differences in the way the two choreographers wanted them to move by saying of Bingham's aesthetic: "The colour is very different from ballet." Wang feels some of the choreography for his duet with Isabelle Itri was changed to accommodate their ballet-based technique, though Bingham was too gentlemanly to actually state this. In partnering work in general, the Ballet B.C. men were not used to being lifted and supported by the women, and the women were not used to receiving weight. Another challenge for the ballet dancers was handling the large amount of floor work, particularly the numerous rolls, comfortably and without bruising.

Senez, one of Ballet B.C.'s most charismatic dancers, admits:

> Remember Me From Then *was a challenging piece and physically exhausting because we were out of our own habits. It was like a different language and required extra energy. There was ten percent more effort and*

Excerpt from program for *Remember Me From Then*, 1996.

thought needed for us to do it. But we're professional dancers, and we're used to working with different choreographers. Having the EDAM dancers there we could learn a lot by watching, and also by communicating with each other during rehearsals.

By the time of the premiere on March 28, 1996, Senez and his partner, Anne Cooper, were fully in synch and facilitated each other's moves cleanly and simply. He was able to perch on Cooper's back just as she did on his and the pair breezed through unison movement with the same fresh force. From elegant cabrioles – all speed and lightness – to body surfing and taking weight – organic and supportive – they were well matched.

Remember Me From Then opened a mixed bill, followed by the premiere of Crystal Pite's domestic ballet, *Moving Day*, in which one dancer performs in a bathrobe, her face covered in a beauty mask. Two 1990 works completed the evening: Alleyne's *Split House Geometric* and Mark Godden's *Rapsodie espagnole*, the only piece in pointe shoes.

In this strong line-up, Bingham and Alleyne's collaboration more than held its own, presenting a fascinating portrayal of both freedom and form. Itri and Wang, for instance, were concerned with line and shape during their duets, moving efficiently and seriously. The relationship between them was a traditional balletic one where the man facilitates the woman, allowing Itri the luxury of supported poses and pirouettes. In contrast, the friendly duets with Cooper and Senez had a freer flow and energy, and they performed the same steps. Yet the two couples were perfectly at home on the same stage and both offered their own delights.

This blurring of aesthetic boundaries was evident throughout the choreography, and there were numerous duos of all persuasions: besides those noted above, there was a playful pairing of EDAM's Alex Cyril and Kathleen McDonagh, and a cross-company one between Susan Elliott and John Ottmann. Trios and quartets form and reform, and at times it was difficult, and perhaps irrelevant, to know whether one was watching a ballet, a modern dance or a cross-company grouping.

In its next incarnation less than a month later at the Dancing on the Edge Festival, *Remember Me From Then* was doubled in length to forty-five minutes and mounted at the Firehall Arts Centre. Bingham and Alleyne switched roles – Alleyne made more of the movement and Bingham was more concerned with staging and structure, which this time included one substantial section of improvisation.

The ballet dancers had some experience improvising, though not to the extent of their modern dance colleagues. Alleyne often asked dancers to improvise during his creative process and, in performance, Wen Wei Wang recalls improvisatory moments in William Forsythe's *The Vile Parody of Address*, which was in the company's repertoire. During one solo, explains Wang, another solo takes place at the same time in its own space, and the tempo for the dancing comes not from the Bach score but from the other dancer's body. Usually, Wang would have to either slow down or add more steps to ensure he finished at the right time.

In the ten-minute improvised section during this extended version of *Remember Me From Then*, the dancers had phrases they could start and finish at any time, also choosing whether to dance in unison or not. The need to make decisions meant they remained highly connected to each other and, in the intimate Firehall theatre, the audience could see them relating through eye contact, which made the dance about human as well as physical relationships.

Anne Cooper explores the differences between choreographed ballet and improvised dance:

> *In ballet, it's very important for the lifts to be extremely smooth, so nobody notices where they take off from or where they land. It's the kind of aesthetic where you don't see the mechanics or the physics involved, or any of the effort. Improv can have a raw quality, but a rough moment that's not perfect can lead to the next moment being even smoother than if it was choreographed.*

In the end, the remarkable accomplishment of *Remember Me From Then* is the creation of a cohesive work of art based on the very different belief systems of these two forms of dance. Contact improvisation and ballet come together in an arresting flow of movement that seems inevitable. The quality of free and easy movement gently pressing against formal restrictions gives the work its philosophical heart. True to the inclusiveness of the 1990s, the hierarchy is dismantled and a place is found for everyone.

The title, *Remember Me From Then*, was created during a brainstorming session late in the process. Both choreographers freely wrote down words and phrases, putting together a combination of these that had resonance and style; the intention was not to indicate a specific meaning or "reading", but to evoke a certain atmosphere. Both men recall that Bingham was thinking of his grandmother, Nora, who had first taught him to dance, but that is as far as either can go in terms of assigning a specific inspiration for their choice. When pressed, Bingham admits that the fairy tale setting of *Remember Me From Then* suggested childhood in general to him. The past, however, was on his mind for another reason: his mother was undergoing treatment for stomach cancer and concern for her, and memories of his childhood, flooded his thoughts.

During rehearsals and performances for Dancing on the Edge, with preparations for EDAM's Annual Summer Intensive in progress, Etelka Bingham's condition worsened. Immersed in projects, Bingham was unable to leave the city to visit his mother on Quadra Island. Although she clearly could not travel to Vancouver, Etelka was very much a presence during the creation of a new solo, *After the Wake*. Most of the dance takes place on the ground within a rectangle of light that transforms into a cross, to a mix of Bach, Beethoven, contemporary music and ocean sounds. The subtle Christian symbols – the light, the cross – interact intimately with the sounds of nature, which for Bingham must have evoked Etelka's island home. At the work's quiet centre is the dancer, Daelik, who, in a suit and with long blond hair, is reminiscent of the well-mannered rebel, Peter Bingham, from the 1970s.

On June 18, Bingham began teaching at the EDAM Summer Intensive. The first weekend, June 21-22, he gave a studio performance with colleagues Marc Boivin and Andrew Harwood. The morning of June 28, with Daelik's solo set to premiere that evening as part of EDAM's Other Issues series, Bingham was called by his family, who urged him to come see Etelka before it was too late. He agreed to leave the next morning, knowing he had a full day at the Intensive ahead of him and then, that night, the premiere.

Early on June 29, Bingham journeyed to Quadra Island. He arrived midmorning and went directly to his mother, who was barely conscious. Then he and his brother Bruce built her coffin. After that, he went to see her again.

Etelka looked uncomfortable and he put his left hand on the top of her head and the right on her sacrum. She died that moment. Peter felt her spirit leave through his left hand.

Etelka Bingham was cremated in the coffin built by her sons, after which Peter returned to Vancouver to continue his responsibilities with the Summer Intensive. The following weekend he made the journey back to Quadra Island for a church service held in Etelka's memory.

Another person was gone from his life. This time, although Bingham mourned deeply, his creative impulse was not given over so completely to the cold fact of death. Having lost his grandmother, his brother and now his mother, death was more familiar. As well, Etelka Bingham was eighty-three when she passed away so, unlike John's suicide, the end of her life was less shocking. As a trained nurse, Etelka was competent at managing her pain, and her stoic attitude and religious faith helped make the situation bearable.

Born Naked, Died Blonde

... I keep the television on all the time. And I keep the windows open. I want my paintings to be reflections of life, and life can't be stopped.

— Robert Rauschenberg

Peter Bingham's next major work was an inspired statement devoted to the full spectrum of his artistic beliefs. *Born Naked, Died Blonde: Our Roots Exposed*, which premiered in November 1996, was an encyclopedia of his choreographic strategies, a tour de force celebrating his creative will. It is as if, through working with John Alleyne on *Remember Me From Then* and butting up against the rarefied world of ballet, Bingham had discovered exactly what mattered to him.

The artistic process was a messy one and at times beyond the creative team's understanding, even that of the choreographer himself, who was simply following his instincts and could offer no reassuring rationale during rehearsals. This left the dancers on edge – their artistry was also on the line because they would be the ones in front of an audience bringing the dance to life. Part of the challenge was the sheer number of dancers and musicians involved, along with the intricate mix of choreography and improvisation with composed and improvised music, all of which brought increased demands and tensions for everyone. No one really knew what *Born Naked, Died Blonde* was about until it came together on opening night. "The work process was ugly," Bingham reluctantly admits. Loyal as ever to his team, that is all he will directly say.

Bingham did not deliberately withhold information: he creates from gut instinct and in his most successful work, the content is realized during the hands-on period of creation, not through prior contemplation. "I totally enjoy discussing ideas but I don't translate those ideas into making dances," Bingham says. This means the creative process is, at its most fecund, a time of discovery. In *Born Naked, Died Blonde*, the meaning arrived subtly within the parameters of the dance being constructed – hammered and chiselled into being, as it were, from the choreographer's unconscious. At no point did Bingham translate the dance into words, not even toward the end for a program note. He dances the meaning; that is his art. As Georgia O'Keefe wrote from her point of view as a painter: "The meaning of a word – to me – is not as exact as the meaning of color. Colors and shapes make a more definite statement than words." For Bingham, movement, shape, relationship, energy – the building blocks of his choreography – say what needs to be said.

The project began simply. Bingham and his collaborators, jazz composers Coat Cooke and Ron Samworth, co-directors of the NOW Orchestra,

Kathleen McDonagh in *Solace*, 1994.

Photo: Chris Randle

intended to look to their artistic pasts and celebrate their beginnings; hence the subtitle, *Our Roots Exposed*. Saxophonist Cooke and guitarist Samworth had improvised for EDAM performances since 1989 and together composed a major score for *Dreamtigers*. Thus the three men's shared roots included both composed and improvised music and dance. For Bingham, honouring his roots in contact improvisation was paramount.

Bingham's technical approach, which Cooke and Samworth followed in constructing the music, is described in a letter the composers wrote to a provincial music commissioning jury. They explain Bingham's intention to choreograph "cells or sections of movement" that will establish parameters within which "the dancers retain some freedom to make movement and timing choices." This was not, of course, a new strategy for Bingham, who describes this more fluid approach as "performing a concept". He considers it closer to choreography than to improvisation because the movement is worked out in rehearsal, as was the case with *Born Naked, Died Blonde*: "We practiced together over and over again to recognize what worked and what didn't work."

Even when a choreographer aims for absolute precision, this is difficult to achieve. Dancers, being human, bring interpretive skills to the most precise vision, which creates flux from performance to performance, to say nothing of unintentional changes caused by errors in memory or execution. As well, venues change, which introduces varied spatial dimensions and requires technical accommodation. Bingham does not agonize about giving up absolute control over what happens on stage: time and space are understood as fluid and open, and his intentions are fulfilled when the dancers and the dance remain correspondingly fluid and open.

This openness might be seen to betray the expectation that the artist's role is to present specific meaning – a grand truth – through whatever means and sacrifice necessary. Yet even the great ballet choreographer George Balanchine showed a degree of openness while choreographing and staging his work. We see this in reports given by his dancers in Francis Mason's *I Remember Balanchine*. According to Patricia McBride:

> [Balanchine] always went for the natural way. This would happen a lot
> when he choreographed. He would not make you fight your natural instincts.
> If you fell a natural way, he would incorporate that into the choreography. It
> wasn't like someone saying, "I am going to choreograph this great work." He
> hadn't really gone that far in thinking what he was going to do.

Another dancer, Marian Horosko, describes how Balanchine handled the need for her to fill more time on stage in *The Nutcracker* when, due to technical difficulties, the growing Christmas tree took longer than planned to reach its full height. Just before the performance, he told her to "do something" to fill in the extra time. So she improvised some stage business and "Balanchine just nodded when I reached the wings. It was all right. We were family."

Bingham's present group of dancers, an ensemble of proficient individuals who were conversant with his technique and could fulfill the range of his aesthetic, were also "family". Returning company members Anne Cooper, Alex Cyril, Susan Elliott and Kathleen McDonagh knew Bingham, his work and each other very well. The two apprentices, Daelik and Chris Wright, had recently performed in Bingham's quartet, *Magnet*. Although he was confident in the group's abilities, Bingham wanted to enhance their skills in contact improvisation, since this was the vocabulary on which the choreography would be based. Bingham arranged to work with the dancers for the month of July, honing their technical abilities and ensuring they were used to dancing together.

Composers Cooke and Samworth also attended some of the July technique sessions in order to immerse themselves in Bingham's aesthetic. In August, Cooke, Samworth and Bingham met a number of times to work specifically on the music. Decisions were made about solos in terms of pairing musicians with dancers and they agreed that the main organizing principle would be an arc from high to low energy. Starting at a peak and ending quietly is a daring and unusual way to structure a theatrical work. According to Bingham, one assessor from the Canada Council for the Arts found it incomprehensible, chastising him for letting the energy drop. Yet this arc became crucial to enabling Bingham to bring his inchoate ideas to fruition.

In September, Bingham and his six performers were back in rehearsal, working every weekday until the November premiere. Cooke and Samworth, as well as various combinations of the ten-member NOW Orchestra, often joined them. Having to co-ordinate the musical team as well as the dancers added to the difficulty of scheduling. Last-minute changes were often made to accommodate the musicians, which would leave certain dancers with un-planned free time. The dancers began feeling they were not getting enough rehearsal hours, and this became a major concern. The presence of musicians during rehearsals also meant the studio was too crowded. Adding to the chaos was Wright's departure due to injury.

Conflicting agendas and needs from choreographer, composers, dancers and musicians struggled to be resolved, and the atmosphere was tense and often unpleasant. It was not clear where the creative process was leading and Daelik remembers missing the calm inspiration that had impressed him during rehearsals for *Hindsight*. At one point, in reference to the title, Bingham made a suggestion that Daelik says horrified him and his colleagues: "Peter said maybe all the dancers should be blonde. I was the only blonde and the next day I came in with red hair. He said, 'I can't believe you did that!' Then we said, 'If we're going to go blonde, the musicians have to be naked.'"

Part of the difficulty lay in the amount of improvising Bingham was asking the dancers to do in performance. Although she enjoys improvising, Susan El-liott recalls feeling concerned over her solo. "I wanted some boundaries and I wanted Peter's physicality," she says. "I'm a dancer, and I love being given steps." Arriving at the right balance, one that satisfied the choreographer and the dancer, was not easy, but in the end Elliott feels she got the best of both worlds "because I had steps from Peter and I also had the freedom to play."

Finally, in order to deal with the negative attitude of one individual, Bingham cancelled a rehearsal shortly after it started. Doing this, he says, "pissed everybody off" because it cut into their rehearsal time, which they were already concerned was not long enough. Today, Bingham adds, "if I get diva behaviour I deal with it right away" but back then he was slow to gain control of the situation. He felt as

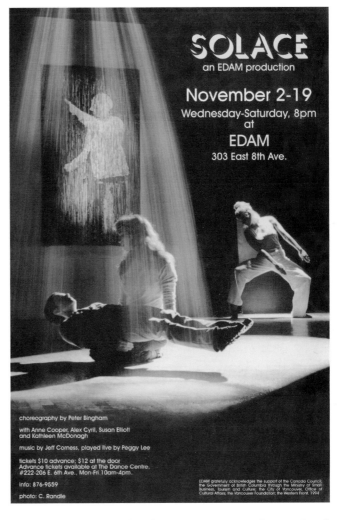

SOLACE
an EDAM production

November 2-19
Wednesday-Saturday, 8pm
at
EDAM
303 East 8th Ave.

choreography by Peter Bingham

with Anne Cooper, Alex Cyril, Susan Elliott
and Kathleen McDonagh

music by Jeff Corness, played live by Peggy Lee

tickets $10 advance; $12 at the door
Advance tickets available at The Dance Centre,
#222-206 E. 6th Ave., Mon-Fri 10am-4pm.

info: 876-9559

photo: C. Randle

EDAM gratefully acknowledges the support of the Canada Council;
the Government of British Columbia through the Ministry of Small
Business, Tourism and Culture; the City of Vancouver, Office of
Cultural Affairs; the Vancouver Foundation; the Western Front. 1994

though everyone lacked confidence in what he was creating; determined to realize his vision, Bingham often wondered, "How the hell do I get this to work?"

From the musical side, the NOW Orchestra had its own problems, as many of the musicians were not used to working with dancers. Cooke felt some of them lost focus when they were not actually playing their instruments and he wanted them more engaged throughout. He explains:

Dancers and musicians have a different way of rehearsing. For dancers, it's intense and repetitive, but musicians practice alone in their room. We're used to getting together, having one rehearsal and being able to do whatever's brought to us.

In an improvising group, the focus [needs to be] more like dance, and both Ron and I brought that aesthetic to it. Improvising is more about knowing who you're playing with and what their tendencies and interests are, how to support them and how to be supported by them. So the process as improvisers is more over the long term.

In the chaos of creating this fast-moving puzzle, the end seemed far from sight, and dancer Kathleen McDonagh recalls feeling empathy for Bingham's position: "Peter was walking around with a stopwatch making timings galore. I really felt for him!" Yet, as the allotted rehearsal period neared completion, and with her solo still to be rehearsed, she began getting nervous along with everybody else and admits to succumbing to the general feeling of anxiety. Once they did start work on her solo, which would end *Born Naked, Died Blonde*, further tension arose over the subject matter. Although Bingham never discussed content with her, McDonagh felt her solo was evoking something much darker than the rest of the piece.

It did not help when, on one of the first days rehearsing the solo, the NOW Orchestra joined them. McDonagh found the situation uncomfortable: "I was doing it fresh off the mark, so it was a little scary having them there." The overall tensions meant the group dynamics were not great and, she explains, "I was feeling unsupported by my gang of dancers, just because of their own frustration." The trajectory and emotional weight of her solo was challenging, and McDonagh was driven to clarify the choreographer's intentions. She needed to know that her intuition regarding the tragic overtones was sound and that she was heading in the right direction. So, in the studio with everyone present, she confronted Bingham.

What McDonagh was sourcing were memories of her older sister's suicide. She wanted to have this out in the open and to know whether the choreographer was behind her. She knew Bingham was familiar with her family tragedy because it had happened during the first week of rehearsals for his 1994 choreography, *Solace*. At that time, after taking a week off, McDonagh returned to the studio despite her emotional turmoil.

During rehearsals of *Born Naked, Died Blonde*, McDonagh was also recalling the Bingham family tragedy, the suicide of John, told in *Ode to John Angus B*, in which she had a major role. Even before that, McDonagh had performed a short duet with Bingham, *Etelka's Lament*. This had been performed in the Firehall Arts Centre courtyard during the 1992 Dancing on the Edge festival, when both their mothers were in the audience. For Etelka Bingham, the duet offered comfort; for McDonagh and her family, it proved to be an eerie foreshadowing.

This professional and personal history forged a bond between the two artists that McDonagh felt was surfacing during the creative process for *Born*

Naked, Died Blonde. Bingham would not give specific instructions to direct her grieving solo but, yes, he agreed, she was going in the right direction. Death could not have been too far from Bingham's thoughts; besides the experience of a sibling's suicide that he shared with McDonagh, there was the recent loss of his mother. "We were undergoing a mutual creation process," is as much as Bingham can say. Given another dancer or even the same dancer at another stage of her life, a different solo would certainly have resulted.

Over the eight-week rehearsal process, life and death quietly infused the trajectory of *Born Naked, Died Blonde.* The technical framework Bingham had started with – the slow descent to quiet, low energy – came to fruition. By the time of the premiere, the work went confidently from light, bright and unselfconscious energy to a dark, sombre note that is not threatening or overwhelming, but is quietly mournful, a statement from someone who has learned to cope with the harder facts of existence, and who has struck a truce with them.

On the opening night of November 6, 1996, the cosy Firehall Arts Centre stage was bursting at the seams with fifteen artists crowded onto it – five dancers and ten musicians, with the latter spilling over into the seating area. There was a sold out audience. *Born Naked, Died Blonde* begins with the sounds of the NOW Orchestra's happily dissonant music, which seems to propel the dancers onto the performing area, running and tumbling, looking like a group of ordinary young people having a good time. Costume designer Ainslie Cyopik dressed them in quietly styled pants and tops that could have been worn home on the bus after the show without attracting attention. There were no instructions regarding makeup and hair, so the dancers remain comfortably themselves – real people.

The first section is choreographed, but not completely. The dancers need to be on their marks to offer a back to support another dancer's roll or to catch a flying body as it hurtles toward them, but there are also relaxed moments of waiting and of interaction. At other times, the type of energy is specified but not the exact movement. Or the choreography is an instruction, such as "stop the others from jumping", which creates a practical, task-like focus. Sometimes the movement is set but the timing comes from interaction between the performers. Rarely are the dancers in strict unison: It is more important to Bingham's aesthetic that the choreography is performed with the same intention but is individually realized, so there is easy camaraderie rather than mechanical or military precision.

Within the constantly shifting rules of the game, the dancers are showcased in solos that are a mix of choreography, choreographic structure and structured

born NAKED died BLONDE

our roots exposed

at the Firehall Arts Centre

Wed., Nov. 6   8pm $8
Thurs., Nov. 7   8pm $8
Fri., Nov. 8   8pm $15
Sat., Nov. 9 8pm $15

Tickets:
Firehall Arts Centre 689-0926
Group Rates (10 or more)
call EDAM 876-9559

A bold new work from EDAM Dance & the NOW Orchestra

improvisation. The first two solos, by Anne Cooper and Susan Elliott, are like fireworks. Cooper improvises a path away from the ensemble to her choreographed solo, which begins with an outpouring of flung dissonance, her limbs insistently thrusting outwards, and then develops into a sultry languor. Daelik watches, seated nearby, the staging reminiscent of *Cryptic Heart*.

Elliott's solo, about halfway through, moves from choreography to an improvised, fast-stepping response to Dylan van der Schyff's improvised drums. Although the steps and music remained basically the same over the four nights, the flow became stronger with each performance. The only structure during the improvised section is a spatial score, partly to ensure Elliott reaches the right spot for her choreographed jump into Cooper's arms.

Alex Cyril's choreographed solo, to silence, is quiet and flowing; Daelik's solo is quiet and weighted, in tune with the spare sounds of Paul Blaney's bass. The score for Daelik's choreographic structure directs its overall development and sets strict parameters for the type of movement. At one point, to allow his arms to be seen in port de bras, Bingham had Daelik take off his shirt, which left him in a sleeveless undershirt. It looked, in performance, like a relaxed moment of natural behaviour.

The work's penultimate section, preceding McDonagh's solo, begins the emotional descent with a series of movements that take the dancers to the ground in dramatic falls. The scene begins with one dancer standing, eyes shut, at the front of the stage. Her face is vulnerable, softened by the closed eyes. Another dancer approaches, whispers in her ear and together they collapse to the ground. Soon, the entire group is falling, over and over again, first one, then another and another. Each dancer surrenders to gravity, sightless, relying on a partner to guide them safely to the ground, alternating between being the one to fall and the one to support. The luxurious falls release generously into space, some taking place in a close embrace or ending in one. The partner could be a lover, a mother, a friend or just a physical force that eases the way.

"It was great to perform," says McDonagh of this section. "There's a certain sense of vulnerability when you're standing waiting for your partner to approach, and you don't know which fall is coming until they tell you [by whispering one of the designated names]. You know you're in a bigger image, too. There's a rhythm being built."

McDonagh's role is to try and keep people upright. But she can't keep up with all the falling bodies and eventually a dancer falls and does not get up. Soon, the whole group lies collapsed on the ground. Her inability to change the course of events leads McDonagh into her improvised solo, for which there were no physical parameters. "The pathway was emotional," says Bingham. McDonagh had improvised as a member of EDAM before, but never so fully, and her fear of this fed into the dramatic finale; by the time it came to the performance, her emotions were part and parcel of the whole. She did have musical parameters, and could relate to the other dancers, who lay as if sleeping or dead on the floor. During her jittery solo, McDonagh says, "I was really feeling wind in my chest and my throat. I think that's where you hold grief – I was opening it up and getting it out, and letting that motivate and generate movement." Solemn and disturbed, yet also centred and enduring, this is the statement that ends the work.

Born Naked, Died Blonde read full and fast, which is how, back in 1987, Bingham said he liked his dances to read. Now, however, the choreography was clearly defined, filled with multi-dimensional physical shapes and relationships, yet still containing room for the performers to manoeuvre with some element of freedom. The improvised sections were tightly scored, and everything was based in a thorough knowledge of contact improvisation.

Throughout, considerable team effort was required, demanding close concentration between members of the group. This is something choreographer Chick Snipper, who until the end of 2006 was the artistic director of DanSta-Bat, considers crucial in Bingham's ensemble work:

> *In Peter's group work, when the dancers are connected, when they have to pay attention to one another, that's the theatre of it. They're not pretending to pay attention – you can really feel them working off one another's rhythm and energies. Even though they may not be looking at each other, there's a sense of ensemble that is the piece of theatre.*

Born Naked, Died Blonde was a masterly mix of freedom and form as Bingham juggled a variety of ways to stage dance. The generosity toward the performers, and the responsibility they were given, were huge. In many ways, *Born Naked, Died Blonde* is about not being able to distinguish the dancer from the dance because, through structured improvisation and open choreography, the dancer must create within the parameters set by the choreographer, who is sometimes acting more like a theatre director. In theatre, there is a script, which the actor interprets. The script for *Born Naked, Died Blonde* is the kind of interpretive vehicle that bears repeated casts and interpretations, as when a shorter version was remounted on a group of apprentices at the EDAM studio/theatre in October 2004. Their interpretations, particularly of the solos, were fully in line with the original performances yet also true to each dancer's individual talents.

Disappointingly, there were no press reviews at the premiere beyond a brief mention. Carefully crafted, deeply felt, *Born Naked, Died Blonde* was a triumphant culmination of Bingham's artistic explorations and deserved public notice.

A Simple Act of Balance

I just dance. I just put my feet in the air and move them around.
— Fred Astaire

In the years leading up to the millennium, Peter Bingham continued to make dance. In 1997, after major achievements like *Remember Me From Then* and *Born Naked, Died Blonde*, Bingham premiered another brilliant miniature, *woman walking (away)*. This expressionist solo was created for Mary-Louise Albert, a veteran Vancouver-based modern dancer who was nearing the end of her stage career. To mark the occasion of her final performances, and to allow her to go out with a bang, Albert commissioned work from experienced choreographers who she felt would challenge her – Bingham, Allen Kaeja, Joe Laughlin and Tedd Senmon Robinson. In *woman walking (away)*, the fiercely focussed quality of Albert's physicality resulted in a dramatic work with a gripping, staccato flow. The choreographer and the interpreter received enthusiastic reviews from both Vancouver and Toronto critics.

Despite these successes, there were no significant funding increases, no in-depth media coverage. No prizes, no assurances. There was, however, a fair amount of travel, both across Canada and in the United States, to teach and perform. During one cross-border trip, Bingham became romantically involved with Gill Wright Miller, an associate professor in the dance and women's studies departments at Denison University in Ohio. Their long-distance relationship, with shared vacations travelling the Oregon coast and to Vancouver Island, would continue for a few years.

Relationships are important to Bingham in both life and dance, with his numerous friendships and occasional love affairs mostly taking place within the dance world. Colleagues are looked on as friends and he likes meeting them over a meal. In spring and summer, that often means driving to his favourite beachside café for a salmon burger and a few beers.

"My art," Bingham says, "is a way of expressing my interest in people, whether I'm making solos, duets or group pieces." Mona Hamill, the company manager since 1993, agrees: "Peter genuinely likes people and doesn't like to work alone. Through conversation, he gets interested in something and then it generally just goes from there. He enjoys talking with everyone – the dancers, people he improvises with, other choreographers, other artistic directors, even administrators."

Hamill appreciates Bingham's loyalty to her as an individual. She is, for instance, a serious amateur tennis player, and Bingham supports her need to

Mary-Louise Albert in *woman walking (away)*, 1997.

Photo: Chris Randle

work part time to accommodate athletic commitments. She also enjoys chatting with Bingham about whatever fiction or non-fiction she happens to be reading, and feels satisfaction at the number of times their conversations have contributed to his work. Take her fascination with Latin American poetry: it was Hamill who drew Bingham's attention to Jorge Luis Borges' *Dreamtigers*, and she reinforced his decision to use *Sun stone* by Octavio Paz, whom she had been reading for years. As well, more than once Hamill's paintings were part of Bingham's set design or, as with *woman walking (away)*, were key inspirations. In that work, the title and central image came from four large canvases by Hamill, each of which showed a woman walking away.

One of Bingham's longest-standing working friendships is with Chris Randle who, apart from a few years spent in Montreal, has never stopped photographing and videotaping the events at EDAM. Randle also works for others in the Vancouver dance community, and has made a name as one of the country's top dance photographers.

Randle was introduced to the field through photographing Bingham during the early days with Fulcrum, explaining: "It was a way of hanging out together." His black and white photos from that time, and even to the present day, have the same easy energy as the contact improvisation that was his introduction to dance. Like Bingham, Randle is an off-the-cuff kind of guy, preferring to shoot during performances or rehearsals rather than in a photographer's studio. Currently, he runs his art practice from the top floor in Bingham's house, where he also rents space to live. He says of their friendship:

> *I go to Peter's shows, he looks at my photos, but we don't spend a lot of time dissecting things. We just hang out together, and talk about sports, travel, music or women. A lot of people say we're like an old married couple. God forbid there should ever be anything like sex in it – there's no desire, neither of us have ever gone that route. But we argue sometimes and natter like an old married couple. And we indulge in whisky together some nights.*

Compatible working relationships are crucial to Bingham's art, and he is relieved he only had to fire a dancer once, although one or two left under a cloud, which still troubles him. Bingham relates personally to the individuals on his team and values a positive atmosphere. "We laugh a lot," he says, "and we have fun." Not always – sometimes a dance phrase is worked over and over again. This is part of the process, and he feels dancers need to deal with boredom just as they do with fatigue, so they remain professionally involved and are a positive influence. The experience of *Born Naked, Died Blonde* reinforced the importance of good communication between him and the dancers, and he believes the intimacy of his best duets, such as *Cryptic Heart* and *Crossfade*, could not have been created in an uncooperative environment.

E D A M

Red-Handed

MARCH 16-18 & 23-25, 2000 8 PM

CHOREOGRAPHY:	PETER BINGHAM
PERFORMERS:	DELIA BRETT, ANNE COOPER, DAELIK, CHANTAL DEEBLE, JACKIE NEL, OLIVIA THORVALDSON, ALVIN ERASGA TOLENTINO, CHANTI (APPRENTICE)
COMPOSERS:	COAT COOKE, RON SAMWORTH
MUSICIANS:	COAT COOKE, RON SAMWORTH, DYLAN VAN DER SCHYFF, CHRIS KELLY
COSTUMES:	JOANNE LAMBERTON
LIGHTING:	PETER BINGHAM
TECHNICAL DIRECTOR:	JAMES PROUDFOOT

FIREHALL ARTS CENTRE
280 E. CORDOVA STREET • BOX OFFICE: 689-0926
TICKETS: $18/20; $30 FOR KOKORO DANCE/EDAM COMBINATION
SPECIAL ADVANCE TICKET PRICES/GROUP DISCOUNTS AVAILABLE. CALL 872-6266

EDAM GRATEFULLY ACKNOWLEDGES THE SUPPORT OF THE DANCE SECTION OF THE CANADA COUNCIL FOR THE ARTS, THE PROVINCE OF BRITISH COLUMBIA THROUGH THE BRITISH COLUMBIA ARTS COUNCIL, THE CITY OF VANCOUVER, VANCOUVER FOUNDATION QMFM ARTIFACT, THE BC GAMING COMMISSION, AND THE WESTERN FRONT

     PHOTO: CHRIS RANDLE

Red-Handed

For Bingham, the millennium began with a double bill called Red-Handed, presented at the Firehall Arts Centre for six nights between March 16-25, 2000. When Bingham commenced work on this mainstage presentation, he had just started seeing a naturopathic physician, feeling despair over ongoing problems with his knees, sacrum and neck, which were so painful he was thinking about giving up dancing. An investigation with his naturopath of the link between mental and physical states inspired what was intended to be the evening's major work, *The Brain Waves, the Heart Bleeds, and the Body Parts*. Yet this seventy-five-minute piece for eight dancers would barely hold its own next to the masterly ten-minute duet called *The Intimates* that opened the evening.

The awkwardly titled *The Brain Waves, the Heart Bleeds, and the Body Parts* is a meditative journey for which Bingham wrote his first and last program note, which ran a full page. In it he states, "As an aging dancer, it has been increasingly difficult to keep my body healthy and dancing." He thanks his naturopath, who "has gone to extraordinary lengths to help me continue dancing, differentiating between the natural aging process and injury." Naturopathic medicine believes in the body's ability to heal itself as an individual moves toward mental, physical and spiritual health, and the intention was to portray that integrated state in the choreography.

Despite the work's glowing review in *The Vancouver Sun*, Bingham was not happy with the results. *The Brain Waves* loses its way early on, with a long solo dominating and slowing down the first part. Another problem might have been that while the dancers were skilled, not everyone was proficient in contact. Bingham prefers not to explore that possibility, more comfortable blaming the fact that he had an agenda regarding the content, which he feels side-tracked him. Daelik supports this conjecture from his point of view as one of the dancers when he describes the creative process as confusing, and lacking the organic method of working that he considers is Bingham's strength.

Joanne Lamberton's costumes eschewed Bingham's usual casual touch; instead, there were lace-up corsets and, for one male dancer, revealing mesh pants made of velvet. Also unusually, Bingham designed a large set, a sculpture built with pipes and shaped into a ribcage, which ran from ceiling to floor and filled the stage from front to back. As well, he tackled the lighting design himself; today, he says the stage was too dark.

A major problem was the commissioned score, composed by Coat Cooke and Ron Samworth, which was not part of the rehearsal process until a couple of days before the premiere. According to Cooke, the score was ready but there was no money to have it played in rehearsal with the four musicians; the budget only covered the performances. Unfortunately, when the choreographer finally heard the music, he felt it did not support the movement. "As a piece of music, it was great," Bingham says, "but it was not what the choreography needed." There was no time to make changes and, in any case, Cooke considered the score complete.

As rehearsals for this extravagant undertaking dragged on, Bingham had the company explore an idea that had been kicking around in his head for some time: How can two basically still bodies find and maintain physical balance? Daelik speculates about why Bingham introduced this material:

> It might have been part of Peter's attempt to get the dancers who weren't strong with contact used to feeling each other's weight, because it was mostly about sensing skeletal structure – giving and supporting weight in interesting positions. As an exercise it was useful for the company, but then he saw the interesting part of it could be used for something else and that's maybe when he decided to do The Intimates.

Bingham describes the additional rehearsals with Daelik and Delia Brett as a needed break from the frustrations dogging *The Brain Waves*. He was already familiar with the qualities of the two dancers – Daelik, who was in his fifth season with EDAM, and Brett, in her second – but, at the first rehearsal, he noted how they worked as a team. Daelik and Brett had met as students in the MainDance Performance Training Intensive, and Bingham knew they were good friends, which helped ensure the relaxed atmosphere he wanted in both rehearsal and performance. He told them the choreography should be "really comfortable", with the boundaries developed organically – discovered through physical limits and not intellectual decisions. He was thinking about the way rocks are painstakingly balanced to form sculptures. Bingham says:

> By trial and error, we developed balances, and had about twice as many as we used. Some of them turned out to be quite hard on the dancers but they liked doing the piece. They had to stretch their skills – I don't think people realize that repeatability in contact is incredibly virtuosic.

The Intimates was rehearsed to a Beethoven piano sonata, but when the work premiered informally at a Vancouver Symphony Orchestra fundraiser, an unexpected change proved fortuitous. For practical reasons, the symphony asked Bingham to find another piece of music that did not feature a pianist. He suggested J.S. Bach's calm, measured *Air on a G String*. "We adjusted our timing, and cut a bit [of the choreography] here and added a bit there.

The original idea was just to use Bach for the symphony performance but it worked so well, we never changed it back," he says.

When *The Intimates* formally premiered as the opening piece on the Red-Handed double bill, it upstaged *The Brain Waves, the Heart Bleeds, and the Body Parts*. The duet's flow and grace, as Brett balances on Daelik's shoulder or he rests on her back, matches the sureness and integrity of the classical score. Besides the supportive, intimate poses on which the work is built, there are ordinary moments, too, as when Daelik's fingers trace a pattern on the palm of Brett's hand.

The duet showcased the choreographer's skill in using physical qualities of weight, momentum and balance to create dramatic human encounters. It also allowed the performers to display their skill in partnering and interpretation, as they quietly embody this sensuous portrayal of intimacy. Jaci Metivier, who performed in the earlier, equally sensuous duet, *Cryptic Heart*, aptly describes *The Intimates* as being "smooth as old wine." There is not a false moment throughout. *The Vancouver Sun*'s Michael Scott praised what came across as "real physical intimacy between the two performers." Daelik calls it "the best work I've ever been in. It made me feel the same way that *Hindsight* did – I felt really proud to dance in it."

Daelik and Delia Brett in *The Intimates*, 2000.   Photo: Chris Randle

Although built on the straightforward physicality of two bodies in constant balance with each other, *The Intimates* was read by audiences as a romantic metaphor about equality in a relationship. The intimate balancing act of the dance was seen to represent the way a man and a woman can be together in life and love. "We have a quite beautiful and nicely balanced relationship," might be the simplistic verbal equivalent of the intricate choreography. Louise Phillips in *The Vancouver Courier* saw the work as "a tiny, perfect balancing act about the weights we bear in relationships."

Watching *The Intimates*, experiencing the dancers' technical skill and the choreographer's sure timing and sense of transition, the state of balance permeates the spectator's consciousness, evoking an instinctual understanding of what that means in a relationship.

Philosopher Mark Johnson sheds some light on how this understanding happened in his pursuit of the meaning of balance in his book, *The Body in the Mind: The Bodily Basis of Meaning, Imagination, and Reason*. Johnson believes our experience of being embodied affects how we conceptualize in every area of life, and argues this is how we make sense of reality. He writes:

> *The experience of balance is so pervasive and so absolutely basic for our co-herent experience of our world, and for our survival in it, that we are seldom ever aware of its presence. We almost never reflect on the nature and meaning of balance, and yet without it our physical reality would be utterly chaotic, like the wildly spinning world of a very intoxicated person. The structure of balance is one of the key threads that holds our physical experience together as a relatively coherent and meaningful whole.*

Throughout our lives, we experience everyday acts of balancing, such as walking upright without falling, and we strive for balance in our bodily functions and states, like eating enough to make us full but not bloated. Johnson convincingly describes how it is through this pervasive physical experience that we understand existence. For instance, the idea of justice is often symbolized by an image of scales, and when we talk about our psychological state, we might describe ourselves as emotionally balanced or unbalanced.

As an artist, it is not Bingham's job to explain things intellectually. Instead, in *The Intimates*, he beautifully showcased the physical act of balance, allowing audiences to intuit meaning and leaving them deeply touched.

Vuelta

willow of crystal, a poplar of water,
a pillar of fountain by the wind drawn over,
tree that is firmly rooted and that dances,
turning course of a river that goes curving,
advances and retreats, goes roundabout,
arriving forever:
— Octavio Paz, *Sun stone*

These are the opening lines of *Sun stone* by Nobel prize-winning writer Octavio Paz. They are the same lines with which the poem ends, with that final colon suggesting the entire text could follow. The idea of eternal return is important to the poem; turning and returning are also important choreographic elements. Hence *Vuelta*, a Spanish word meaning turn or return, was on many counts a relevant title for Peter Bingham's second co-created choreography.

Bingham's partner for this collaboration was Tom Stroud, then the artistic director of Winnipeg's Contemporary Dancers. The two men knew each other well, as Stroud had brought Bingham to Winnipeg to work with his company a number of times. They shared much in common, such as their age and the fact that both had discovered the performing arts in their early twenties. Both had trained at Vancouver's Synergy, and Stroud was familiar with contact improvisation through his involvement with a company called TIDE (Toronto Independent Dance Enterprise). The two men's approach to choreography, however, was very different. Hamilton, Ontario-born Stroud trained as an actor before studying dance at Simon Fraser University, and theatre remains central to his work, which is usually text-based.

The groundwork was laid in advance. Bingham and Stroud brought each other out to teach workshops in their respective cities so that the dancers – three from Vancouver and two from Winnipeg – would be familiar with both their aesthetics before the project began. In Vancouver at the EDAM studio, when Stroud offered sessions working with text and sourcing emotions, among the participants were *Vuelta* cast members Delia Brett, Anne Cooper and Ron Stewart. Gabriela Rehak and Dan Wild, who completed the team, were present when Bingham taught improvisation, including contact, at the Winnipeg studio.

Following Stroud's lead, they decided to make a text-based work. Bingham had used text before but always as a background element; this time, it would be central. Stroud's first suggestion was *Hamlet*, which had inspired his work, *The Garden*. Bingham, only superficially familiar with Shakespeare and

remembering his affinity for Jorge Luis Borges, suggested something Latin American. Stroud came up with Paz's *Sun stone*, which had been part of the soundtrack for his most recent production, *El Río*.

At first, Bingham found the long cyclical poem challenging, but he was soon drawn in by Paz's provocative images and surreal sense of logic. "For me, surrealism is like coming home," he says. He appreciated the fact that *Sun stone* does not follow a linear narrative; rather, through a constant flow of disparate, often shocking images, it makes sense by juxtaposition.

Neither Bingham nor Stroud wanted to dissect the poem by illuminating every idea and explaining every reference it contains; both work more instinctively. In fact, during the creative process, the text operated almost as music, offering structure and tone rather than specific meaning. As they wrote in a program note: "… dancing with the poem, the 'relentless water by my side', became the foundation of our exploration."

Without it ever being a conscious decision, once the choreography was complete a change in emphasis was evident: now it was the dance that operated almost as music, offering structure and tone, in order for the poem – which is heard live or through recordings almost in its entirety – to be clearly experienced. This reversal respectfully placed the almost fifty-year-old poem centre stage.

Although Bingham and Stroud would be the ones to birth and direct *Vuelta*, the aim was not to present their personal interpretations of Paz's poem. Instead, the pair set about discovering *Sun stone*'s meaning with the five performers, who, during seven weeks of rehearsal, were involved in intense group improvisations in close relationship to the poem's rich language and rhythm. In this way, the usual private reading of poetry became a multi-voice exploration. Bingham explains, "We all centered on the poem – Tom, me, the dancers, Tony [Gort, the sound designer] and James [Proudfoot, the lighting designer]."

Bingham does not usually improvise to generate choreographic ideas but the strategy turned out to be a goldmine. For someone who seldom engages in the private act of reading, it meant the poem became approachable, its intricacies explored in the supportive atmosphere of shared creativity. As well, it gave the choreographers time to become accustomed to each other and to discover how to bring themselves to the collaboration.

First, a brief period of improvisation was based on general physical exploration. One technique used here was something Bingham calls streaming, from stream of consciousness, which involves individuals following their impulses – Bingham describes it as "following the mind in the body". The aim is to move for ten or fifteen minutes at a time without judgment. Then, specific parameters were given: to follow an impulse in a particular direction, say, or to work in pairs. Music was played, to see how it affected the improvisation, and then the poem was read aloud. This developed into group improvisations using *Sun stone* as the score. "We needed to let the poem shape us," explains Stroud. "You don't so much work on the text as let it work on you."

Over and over again, Bingham, Stroud and the dancers read *Sun stone* aloud, and pages of the poem were strewn around the EDAM studio floor at the end of each day. New meanings emerged as old ones were abandoned. Different phrases stood out and demanded to be heard; emotions, pacing and intentions were continually altered. The only constant was the fact that it took about an hour to read the complete poem, whose depictions of light and dark, beauty and horror, the fullness of the moment and the barrenness of time, slowly became very real and familiar.

At the core of the interpretations were the dancers' instinctual responses to what they heard in the moment. In some ways, they could relate to *Sun stone* as though it were dance, the art form in which they were so knowledgeable. Poetry and choreography have much in common, including the use of intense images and powerful rhythms, and in the fact that both create a heightened reality. The dancers knew how to do justice to the poem by being fully open and present to nuance and meaning: the same full presence is the basic skill needed to make convincing dance.

Paz, too, understood the need to be present in the moment. In *Sun stone*, he warns of the dangers of "the moment [that] scatters itself in many things", which prevents the poem's narrator from being able "to go on, to go beyond". He also describes the other, creative kind of time: "the integrated time when nothing happens/ but the event…." Paz writes about this in the context of "two people shaken by dizziness and enlaced … fallen among the grass …": lovers, like poets and dancers, know the compelling present.

Although improvising proved such a rich experience, eventually decisions needed to be made about finalizing the work. Stroud feels that if they had been planning a studio performance, *Vuelta* would have been left as an improvisation because "the level of commitment from the performers was quite extraordinary." However, both choreographers felt their mainstage presentation warranted a more formal work of art. Stroud recalls:

> One day we went for dinner and we made the choice not to improvise [in performance]. Then I looked at the calendar and said, "If I was doing my own show, I'd be a lot farther along." I think Peter felt the same way. It was just a recognition that the process was going slowly and we were both waiting for the other person to move it forward. So we hit the go button and then we tended to task out — Peter worked on movement ideas he had, and I did some work with Danny [Wild] and Delia [Brett] to shape the text.

Some sections of the finished work were left as structured improvisations. One of these, Bingham explains, was Brett's main solo:

> We looked and looked at her solo, and eventually realized there was no point in choreographing it. Delia uses movement ideas she developed — we just approved those choices, or said, "Don't go there, and make your phrases longer, you're thinking too much." Tom and I helped her succeed in the improvisation through our direction.

Some improvisations that occurred during the rehearsals were used in the final piece, fine-tuned through detailed direction to create coherent meaning and structure. Wild's impassioned recitation of a major excerpt from *Sun stone*, directed by Stroud, is one of these. "It's something Danny did in improvisation," says Stroud, "but technique and repeatability are about articulating and shaping. In performance, the emotional arc was the same each evening, even to the line."

This was new territory for Bingham and he was impressed with Stroud's skill at recognizing the essential dramatic core. "It was hard sometimes because the dancers wanted to let things shift and move according to the feeling of the moment, but Tom was really smart about saying, 'No, now you've lost it.'" Stroud's theatre experience meant he was familiar with the way an actor improvises to develop a character, which a director then shapes and guides. This detailed direction would inform the highly structured improvisations Bingham co-created in later projects with Wen Wei Wang and Crystal Pite, where the same intentions and theme were manifested each night.

The choreographed sections Bingham contributed to *Vuelta* included both new movement and earlier material that he reworked. One new duet, with Gabriela Rehak and Dan Wild, began simply as an exploration of momentum and swing. Gradually, the choreography's rhythm of intensity and release, as well as the emotional approach of the dancers, resulted in a frankly sexual duet. Since the poem celebrates the heightened state of existence inspired by sexuality, this was an apt interpretation and their duet subtly evoked the rhythms of lovemaking.

Another section of new movement became a recurring motif. In it, the group runs in a loose formation toward the front, stage right corner, and kick their legs softly upward: they are like a river running a rocky course, directed this way and that by natural forces, not at all like trained dancers controlling the height and line of an extended leg. In many ways, this harkens back to the imagistic movement Bingham pursued with his work group in the 1970s. The difference is that as well as being familiar with Bingham's contact-based aesthetic, these dancers are highly trained in terms of more traditional theatrical dance.

The material that Bingham re-used came from a duet and an ensemble. The latter was created during one of the classes he gave in Winnipeg at the Contemporary Dancers' studio. Bingham worked with a geometric notion in which each dancer imagined herself sitting at the centre of a small square, moving around the stage by rocking and tipping over while holding her seated position and keeping her orientation in the square. The resulting stage effect was flowing and easy.

This section would open *Vuelta*, which begins in darkness with the sound of dripping water. When the lights come up, the dancers are sitting cross-legged on the floor, gently rocking, bathed in a golden glow. The first lines of the poem are heard in a voice over as the group rolls together and apart, creating different formations, much like a landscape changes over time. The scene is restful and easy, allowing space for the lush densities of the poem to be clearly heard.

The recycled duet, *Gridlock*, had premiered at the EDAM studio in May 2002. When he began rehearsals for the fifteen-minute piece, Bingham was already thinking about *Sun stone* and the collaboration with Stroud. Images from the poem of warm, sensuous bodies versus cold stone and relentless time became the kernel of truth for the work. The choreography succinctly combines the contrasting forces of time and timelessness as Delia Brett flows like a river around Anne Cooper's frozen body. A kiss lets loose an eruptive force, and Cooper explodes into a frenzy of shaking and eventual collapse.

During the initial rehearsal with the two women, Bingham remembers reading *Sun stone* aloud for the first time. As he did so, he walked in a circle around the pair, who were warming up with contact work. Reading aloud in public is not something Bingham is normally comfortable doing, but the startling imagery carried him forward. As the torrent of words and ideas exploded into the quiet studio, the full force of Paz's passionate logic was overwhelming.

***

When the hour-long *Vuelta* premiered at the Vancouver East Cultural Centre on September 7, 2002, it received an enthusiastic audience response, but only a single local review. This was from Gail Johnson, a staff writer for *The Georgia Straight*, who described *Vuelta* as "a beautiful partner to Paz's sensual words." Bingham and Stroud, she wrote, are "two modern-dance stalwarts" who "helped Paz's masterpiece live on."

Encouraged by the work's tremendous popular appeal, and recognizing the level of structure and imagery the work attained, Bingham hoped *Vuelta* would be accepted for Ottawa's prestigious Canada Dance Festival, but this was not to happen. Instead, after some development, it was remounted in Winnipeg in May 2003, when the *Winnipeg Free Press* called it "a wonderful moment" in that city's dance history. At a second run in Vancouver during the 2003 Dancing on the Edge Festival, there were close to full houses.

Apparently, again quoting Octavio Paz, an artist's career also

> *… goes curving,*
> *advances and retreats, goes roundabout,*
> *arriving forever:*

Deserving Isadora

Rather abide at the centre of your being; for the more you leave it,
the less you learn.

— Lao-tzu

As a dancer, Peter Bingham remains loyal to his earliest relationships while also moving forward into new territory with an impressive range of partners. In the century's first few years, he improvised at the EDAM studio with longstanding colleague Susan Elliott and, for the first time, with independent dance artist Helen Walkley, both based in Vancouver; twice with Montreal's Lin Snelling; and with Nancy Stark Smith and Ray Chung from the United States. Chung, who integrates contact, martial arts, bodywork and Authentic Movement into his improvisational practice, visited EDAM four times, most recently in January 2007. Bingham also continues his annual summer performances with Andrew Harwood and Marc Boivin.

In May 2001, two weeks before Bingham turned fifty, he and Chris Aiken premiered The Tuning Effect in Minneapolis, Minnesota. The hour-long forum, in the tradition of The Echo Case, featured improvised dance, music and lighting. Aiken, who is on faculty in the dance department at Pennsylvania's Ursinus College, is a natural partner for Bingham. Contact improvisation is fundamental to both their artistic identities and, though shorter, lighter and a decade younger than Bingham, Aiken moves with the same casual grace and sense of curiosity. The Tuning Effect was reprised for the 2003 Vancouver International Dance Festival.

Thirst

A more surprising partnership was with Wen Wei Wang, who has had a radically different career trajectory than Bingham. He trained from a young age in Chinese classical and folk dance, as well as in ballet, before joining the Langzhou Regional Dance Company. After immigrating from China to Canada in 1991, Wang danced with Judith Marcuse's contemporary company and then spent seven years with Ballet British Columbia, when he was one of the dancers in *Remember Me From Then*. Wang launched his company, Wen Wei Dance, in 2003.

With Wang, Bingham would create another formal work, *Thirst*, which premiered May 15, 2003 at the EDAM studio/theatre. Unlike *Vuelta*, or the ballet-and-contact-styled *Remember Me From Then*, the new work was fully improvised, but rigorously prepared for and structured. The two artists set firm parameters within which to navigate: a spatial score laid out where they would be at particular times; some sections were cued by movement, such as when Bingham lies down in a certain spot on the floor; and there were a number of musical cues. They also devised an overarching theme to guide them throughout.

These structural elements meant, in fact, that the work was essentially re-created at each performance. This was not new territory – Bingham had been exploring structure and intention through mixing improvisation and choreography since he and Peter Ryan had co-created *Laughter is a Serious Affair* in 1985. But the level at which Bingham, now a senior dance artist, and Wang worked was unprecedented.

Though Wang had improvised on stage before, for instance in solo work in his own choreography, he had little experience of contact improvisation, so to level the playing field it was excluded from their movement palette. This led to the decision not to touch or have any direct partnering at all. Avoiding contact was difficult, especially when their arms would twist and entwine, and their bodies quite naturally moved closer. By fulfilling the physical idea of not touching, the improvisation became about resisting closeness and remaining in a state of desire, or thirst. As so often with Bingham's work, a physical boundary led to metaphorical resonance.

In *Thirst*, Wang combined fleet, aerial qualities with a remarkable ground-edness, fluid and free, spinning tightly, with lively port de bras that engaged

Chris Aiken and Peter Bingham in The Tuning Effect.   Photo: Chris Randle

his whole spine. Bingham, in contrast, used his whole body to calmly weave and sway. Between them, the roles of leader and follower were equally shared, characteristic of Bingham's best duets. Their satisfying relationship gave the work heart as, whether directly watching or indirectly sensing, there was always empathetic awareness of what the other was doing.

Thirst was remounted at EDAM in October 2005 and, the following month, a full-length version opened The Dance Centre's five-day Dance in Vancouver showcase at Scotiabank Dance Centre. Despite the longer running time and larger space, its focussed, meditative course was not compromised and there were only

Peter Bingham and Wen Wei Wang in *Thirst*, 2006.
Photo: Chris Randle

two short sections of allegro movement. The increased length was used to build tension; nothing was rushed. Though more serious and even austere, the work retained its warmth because of the closeness between the men.

When Toronto's Dancemakers presented Bingham and Wang in the hour-long *Thirst* at the end of November, *The Globe and Mail*'s veteran dance writer, Paula Citron, described "two superbly trained bodies moving with optimum control through space" and "two mature artists at the peak of their powers." She also noted a "never-ending fund of choreographic ideas", concluding: "The effect is like a dream, a fantasy, a surreal encounter. In fact, *Thirst* is an oasis of tranquility where the hurly-burly of today's mean times gives way to the healing power of art."

The words are reminiscent of Stephen Godfrey's 1978 review of a Toronto performance by Fulcrum, the renegade trio of Bingham, Andrew Harwood and Helen Clarke. Writing in *The Globe and Mail* twenty-seven years earlier, Godfrey had described the evening as "one of the most serene theatrical

experiences imaginable," creating "the most tranquil mood on Yonge Street...."
These reviews suggest that, over the many decades of his professional career,
Peter Bingham has remained true to something central to his art and to
himself.

Wen Wei Wang feels Bingham approached him as a collaborator because
"somehow, dancing in his work at Ballet B.C., we connected. We're not like
close friends, but we understand each other." The telephone call came out of
the blue: "One day he phoned me, and said, 'I want you to dance in my piece
... It'll be about twenty minutes long.'" They met for lunch at a small Chinese
restaurant, and Bingham's confidence in Wang's ability to improvise convinced
Wang to accept the offer. He also remembered how enjoyable working with
Bingham had been when he was a dancer with Ballet British Columbia:

> *During rehearsals of* Remember Me From Then, *I could see Peter was
> happy to work with me. A lot of the time, a choreographer tells you, "No, no,
> no, no!" But Peter didn't do that. Also, I see a similar quality in our move-
> ment – an Oriental [quality] – because we have the same understanding of
> how to move our bodies.*

Though the polished, technical surface of Wang's choreographic mix of
Chinese, ballet and modern dance is quite unlike Bingham's more natural approach, at a fundamental level the sensual, spirited embodiment of the men's
dancing, with its understanding of weight and sinuous port de bras, is indeed
strikingly similar. On stage together, there was even a physical resemblance
despite Wang being almost fifteen years younger and from a different ethnic
background – in matching clothes (black pants and white tank tops), with
closely shaven heads, they looked like brothers.

Another thing in common was that neither came from a European tradition
of theatrical dance. Bingham's aesthetic roots are in the United States, where
contact improvisation was born, while Wang's are in China. Their cross-cultural
partnership is typical of Vancouver, where multiculturalism has resulted in a
dance scene known for bringing together forms like Chinese dance, bharata
natyam and martial arts in ballet- or modern-based contemporary theatrical
choreography.

This wide-ranging mix reflects the fact that Vancouver's cultural landscape
is no longer dominated by a European, primarily British influence; it has
evolved a broader base with a strong Asian presence. Sushi restaurants dot the
city and take-out Thai food is easy to find. Chinatown, a bustling centre just
outside the downtown core, is no longer a suspect "foreign" territory and,

since opening in 1986, Chinatown's Dr. Sun Yat-Sen Classical Chinese Garden has offered a popular alternative to the much older cultivated gardens at Queen Elizabeth Park. A South Asian cultural district has developed and is as busy and bustling as the long established Little Italy.

First Nations culture, which all but disappeared from public view under Canada's colonial history, is also making an increasing impact. In 1991, *Gawa Gyani*, a collaboration between modern dance artist Karen Jamieson and Northwest Coast First Nations artists, premiered to considerable acclaim at the University of British Columbia's Museum of Anthropology. In 2007, First Nations artists contributed choreography and design for a Pacific Northwest-styled version of Mozart's *The Magic Flute*, presented by the Vancouver Opera.

When The Dance Centre mounted a show in September 2005 during the Chinese Mid-Autumn Moon Festival, Chinese-Canadian artists were featured. Wang fit the bill and *binary* – a structured improvisation he performed with Peter Bingham – made a satisfying finale to the evening.

Deserving Isadora

The Dance Centre was founded in 1986 as a non-profit member service organization. Their most significant undertaking has been the championing of a shared space for dance, one that would increase the profile of the art form and be a rallying point for artists. In 2001, the seven storey, six studio Scotiabank Dance Centre opened in downtown Vancouver. From offices on the sixth floor, The Dance Centre, under executive director Mirna Zagar's leadership, manages the building, and supports artists through residencies, research-oriented DanceLabs and performance opportunities, and by facilitating international connections.

Another Dance Centre initiative is the Isadora Award, a juried competition founded in 1999. In 2004, when awards in three separate categories were handed out, Peter Bingham was one of the recipients. At the awards ceremony on International Dance Day, April 29, he accepted his handsome glass sculpture with some chagrin. He was not being honoured for Excellence in Performance (awarded to Anne Cooper) or in Choreography (awarded to Chick Snipper). His Isadora Award was for Excellence in Teaching.

It rankled him that the dance community chose to recognize his pedagogical skills rather than his performance or choreographic expertise. Giving him this award seemed to emphasize Bingham's place in dance as an educational one, while he considers his teaching to be driven by his needs as a choreographer: "I train dancers to do my work." Within the dance community, however, his contribution is appreciated in a wider context. Brian Webb, the producer of the Canada Dance Festival since 2002, says: "Peter is an important dance artist in the Canadian context for his whole practice and the way that

Mary Filer (award designer), Anne Cooper, Peter Bingham and Chick Snipper at The Isadora Awards, Vancouver, 2005.

plays inside the community." Chick Snipper, who has known Bingham since she moved to Vancouver in 1983, echoes these sentiments: "Peter's body of work as an artist has as much to do with his teaching, his school, his philosophy, his support of dancers, as it does his choreography. That's something to be proud of."

Bingham's Isadora Award testifies to his success in passing on his unique skills. Snipper says:

> I only like working with dancers who've trained in contact, even though I use very little in my work, because they understand sequencing, shifts of weight inside their own body, release, flow and dynamic changes of direction – all things that interest me as a choreographer. The dancers who can take my work and make it look really great are those who've trained with Peter.

Snipper describes Bingham as "a master teacher ... who's turning out master teachers as well." He is also "a mentor through and through," she believes, explaining:

> Peter will say things – he'll come to see my work and then say one thing about something he saw and it will completely turn my head around. Years

ago Peter asked me how I choreograph. I said ninety-nine percent comes from my own body, but when it gets onto the dancers' bodies, it's not mine, it's theirs. I don't want it to look like me; if I want it to look like me, I'll do it. They need to honour where my impulses are coming from and then flesh it out. Peter said to me, "You know, the great creators don't have issues around ownership." I didn't think I did, but somehow his words became a guiding principle for the next year.

Susan Elliott talks about the ripple effect Bingham has had on the dance community through sharing the form with generations of dancers, including herself. Elliott, one of Canada's top modern dancers, spent three formative years as a member of EDAM. She recalls: "We did class every morning – contact three times a week and then Pilates and ballet. It was incredible training." While she found her introduction to contact challenging, it was necessary in order to be able to do Bingham's work. Now, Elliott understands first-hand how it benefits every kind of dancer, particularly in providing valuable partnering skills and the ability to work comfortably on the floor, which is so much a part of postmodern dance. She still enjoys taking Bingham's classes, and believes contact "is incredibly beneficial in how it teaches a dancer to work from inside the body, which provides a layer and a texture to dancing that other forms don't."

When Bingham began teaching in the 1970s, it was a way to find others to practice with. It was tough going at first, and he remembers some days when the only student who would show up was the loyal Lee Masters. "By guaranteeing she would be there every week," Bingham says, "Lee turned me into a teacher. She would try and get other people to come, and sometimes there were two or three more. It was like that probably for a year and a half before my classes mushroomed into twenty, twenty-five people." Later, when EDAM formed as a collective, the contact classes by Bingham and Peter Ryan gave the group something unique to offer, and helped to develop a following for the company.

Since he became EDAM's sole director, Bingham has run an annual Summer Intensive, taught from 1993 by the same trio: Bingham and his long-time improvising partner Andrew Harwood, who both teach contact improvisation as well as a more general form of improvisation, and independent dancer Marc Boivin, who offers a comprehensive modern technique class. Contact is situated firmly within the intensive but is supported by, and in its turn supports, a wider understanding of theatrical dance. Bingham has also taught regularly at the University of Winnipeg and, in the United States, at Ohio's Denison University, the University of Minnesota, and Ursinus College in Pennsylvania.

Today, with decades of experience behind him, Bingham has considerable skill to offer. He knows the many ways a body can release into the floor, and

EDAM SUMMER
INTENSIVE
2003

June 2-20

The EDAM SUMMER INTENSIVE 2003 is intended for experienced dancers wanting to expand their skills and knowledge through an intensive period of research, practice and performance. The workshop will use a multi-faceted approach to training based on the correlation between the techniques of contemporary dance, contact and improvisation. Classes will be offered on a daily basis at an advanced level in each of these techniques.

In a series of evening classes, instructors will provide an environment to facilitate the investigation of improvisation as performance. Workshop participants will take part as both performers and audience, drawing upon their stage experience to focus on issues of commitment and composition, craft and perception.

This workshop includes two formal performances: The Echo Case show, featuring improvisation by the workshop's instructors and lighting designer Robert Meister and a second show featuring performances by workshop participants.

The cost of the EDAM SUMMER INTENSIVE 2003 is $650 plus GST (total: $695.50). Once an applicant is accepted into the program, a deposit of $200 (cheque or money order) will be required to confirm registration. The balance of the fee is due on the first day of the Intensive.

This workshop is intended for professional and pre-professional dancers. Interested applicants are requested to submit a CV (e-mail only - send to edamdance@bigfoot.com) and a letter of reference (including the phone number of the person writing the letter). To ensure your participation, submit your application for consideration by April 1st, 2003; all applicants will be contacted by April 15th.

Throughout the intensive, participants must be available Monday-Friday 9:30am-9pm.

Each participant must come prepared to present a 3 minute solo on opening day, either improvised or choreographed.

EDAM 303 East 8th Avenue
Vancouver, BC
V5T 1S1
Phone: 604-876-9559
e-mail: edamdance@bigfoot.com
www.edamdance.org

EDAM gratefully acknowledges the support of the Dance Section, Canada Council; the Province of British Columbia through the BC Arts Council; the City of Vancouver; Vancouver Foundation; the Leon and Thea Koerner Foundation; the BC Gaming Commission and the Western Front.

Photos: Chris Randle. Design: Marlo Adam. Capiture Graphics.

he understands the inside out of lifting and supporting a partner. For instance, he explains, "when I'm dancing, I'll actually move my partner into a place where they can support me." He teaches how to become aware of the nuances of listening through the skin, the muscles and the bones, and how to extend this sensitivity to a partner by also listening closely to his or her body. "You can keep your centre attached to your partner's centre so that you're using eight limbs instead of four."

In terms of improvising, Bingham explains, "I do a lot of work on recognizing what's going on in the big picture – the whole room – and not losing your own dancing in the process. It's easy to get lost in your body and lost in the duet you're doing, and forget the fact that you're only a small part of a whole group."

Performance skills include the need for intense focus even when an individual is just standing and watching: "You're getting your energy back but, if you also watch intently what's happening on stage, you're still contributing."

And after the show is over? Following a student performance, the group "hunkers". This means the students "sit down with their notebooks and write for ten or fifteen minutes. You don't often get a chance to do this when you're performing all the time, but it helps develop a way to deal with finishing your performance instead of just dropping into celebration or pain."

At the core of his teaching, beneath the practical skill building, is the intelligent relationship between mind and body. Bingham says:

> Mostly, I teach the art of investigating. Investigating dancing with another person with the body, not in the body. I develop exercises to get students thinking about ways to work with their body – not thinking about it up here in the head, but getting their minds activated into their body, so they're making choices more instinctively. That way, their thinking doesn't get in the way of what they're doing physically. When you can trust your body, you can let it do the dancing, and then your mind, your eyes or your voice can connect to the detail. It's about how to make sure you're not ruled by your body, though you're also not in charge of it – you're actually in a state of balance between these things.

Bingham does not worry about differentiating in his teaching between contact improvisation and improvisation, and moves freely between the two. Something he refers to as the "contact mind" can be called upon in many different situations:

> When you're soloing, you can have a contact mind through your relationship with the floor. Or you can have it with your partner even if they're far away.

You might work at maintaining an exact distance between you, which is no different than physically leaning on them; conceptually, it's the same thing.

An improviser through and through, he does not plan his classes ahead of time: "Because the technique I teach is improvisation, I try to keep my classes improvised, too. It's the same as being in the moment in improvisation – I walk in, see who's in the room and start with whatever level they're at."

Of course, partnering skills are a great part of what students learn from Bingham simply by dancing with him during classes. One of his American students, who travelled north to Canada for the 2003 EDAM Summer Intensive, described the nonchalant way Bingham can facilitate the most exciting partnering: "You'd be standing next to Peter and something would happen. Suddenly you'd be flying – but in a safe way!"

Monica Strehlke, Peter Bingham and Jennifer Clarke in rehearsal for *Energetic Bodies*.

This Particular Place

A room of his own.
— Adapted from Virginia Woolf

The small studio nestled quietly in the northwest corner of the Western Front, where Peter Bingham has worked since EDAM was founded in 1982, remains his laboratory, as well as his primary canvas; it is where he teaches, creates and most often performs. Besides presenting his own work there, Bingham is generous with its accessibility and offers opportunities to colleagues looking for a low-key performance space and to dancers making their first choreographic experiments. The studio, which is a handy few minutes from his home by car or a ten-minute bicycle ride, has served Bingham and the dance community well on a number of levels.

What is widely known among performers, but is not obvious to audiences, is how the studio's physical parameters influence the dance he creates there. While everyone can see how Bingham often uses the west side windows and the two doors on either side of the north wall as part of his set, there is another less easily observable parameter with far-reaching implications: the extremely slippery floor. According to Susan Elliott:

> *The EDAM studio has the ideal floor for contact. Because it's slippery, it facilitates sliding and rolling, and being able to move with another person on your body as you're doing these things. It does mean, though, that transferring work that's been made at EDAM is challenging. One of the hardest things to deal with as a dancer is to adapt work that Peter has made on that floor for a sticky marley surface.*

Bingham knows well the impact and value of the space on his dancing, and he became one of five co-owners of the Western Front in the late 1990s in order to protect EDAM's tenancy. The floor is important for its encouragement of slip and slide in terms of his creative needs, and he appreciates the intimate theatrical possibilities offered by the well-equipped studio. Brian Webb considers the studio to be the ideal frame for Bingham's friendly aesthetic. Jane Ellison, talking about Bingham's early studio performances, says, "I really loved their intimacy. There was never a sense of Peter being on stage, you were just in the studio with him." It is easy to see how the sense of warm sharing that remains a part of Bingham's performance was nourished in this space.

As well, the floor plays a role in keeping Bingham dancing for so long. At the EDAM studio he can turn easily, without putting pressure on his damaged knee, whereas a typical marley surface requires a firm push into the floor, which would force stressful torque through his legs.

Chick Snipper points out that it is not just "happenstance" that Bingham is in this "beautiful position" of having his own space: "This is where Peter's wisdom, foresight, good luck and dedication come in. He has a place where he can experiment and the important thing as an artist is to be able to try things out."

Vanishing Point

Crystal Pite is a classically trained ballet and modern dance artist who took some of Bingham's morning classes at the EDAM studio during their collaboration on a work called *Vanishing Point*, which premiered March 9, 2005 at the EDAM studio/theatre. Pite describes the sessions with Bingham:

> [They were] a really important part of the process for me. For Peter, too, I think – he felt what we were doing in our rehearsals needed to be addressed and explored in those classes. A lot of the time he would say, "This is something Crystal and I have been working on," and then he would describe and demonstrate it, and the whole class would do it. The classes were an extension of – and another environment for – our process.

About the studio's slippery floor, Pite says:

> The way you're able to use the floor to turn and slide is different than what I'm normally able to do. It brought out things in my dancing I hadn't been able to access. [Working on this surface] allowed me to dance more like Peter, or to understand more the way he moves, because he moves very much in reaction to that floor. It's a small detail but it has a major effect.

These practical insights into the importance of the floor established a very real common ground between her and Bingham. As with his earlier ballet-trained collaborators, Wen Wei Wang and John Alleyne, Pite has no formal training in contact improvisation and might seem another unlikely partner. Pite began her career as a dancer with Ballet British Columbia before spending five years with William Forsythe's renowned Ballett Frankfurt. On her return to Canada in 2001, she had a three-year contract as choreographer-in-residence at BJM Danse (Les Ballets Jazz de Montréal), where her daringly funny *The Stolen Show* was instrumental in helping the company update its image and reputation. In 2001, Pite founded her own company, Kidd Pivot.

Peter Bingham and Crystal Pite in *Vanishing Point*, 2005.   Photo: Chris Randle

Yet, as dancers, Bingham and Pite do share some of the same qualities, although Pite admits: "It's something I don't understand fully, but there's a release quality through the knees and a kind of suspension through the spine, plus a flow pattern we have that's quite similar." Bingham is also hard put to explain what they share, but notes the same contained flow and the way they both like to work quickly with the feet.

It was their different needs in terms of structure that led to what Pite characterizes as "a very happy" struggle during the rehearsal process. She explains:

> I do enjoy a certain amount of risk but Peter and I have very different points at which we're willing to leave things up to chance. For example, I always had tons of pieces of paper, and was always making maps, and writing down times and modalities and parameters, and taping up paper on the wall and laying it around the floor. Peter was less interested in that and more interested in going with whatever came to him in the moment. Which of course he's very good at.

In *Vanishing Point*, as in *Thirst*, all the movement sequences were improvised, though once again each section had a clear intention and focus. From the audience's point of view, the piece looked basically the same each night but, according to Pite:

There was no set choreography or even any choreographic phrases from which we worked. The dancing would have been different [at each performance], but energetically it would have had the same kind of build because we were structured by music. And we had certain tasks — we had the videos to work to and we had sequences of events, like when a certain part of the music started it was time to go into our skimming duet, where we had no contact but improvised in very close proximity, trying to dance in each other's negative space, and to show the space between our bodies. Then I would head out toward the door, and we'd start the video for the door sequence.

Vanishing Point was far less structured than Pite would normally be comfortable with but, by working in "Peter's space", she feels she developed a strong connection to his aesthetic. Also, Pite began to see the studio — the place where Bingham took his first dance class and which has been home base since EDAM was founded — almost as an extension of him. For her, their collaboration became partly about his physical relationship to that space, and the studio itself would be crucial to the staging of the work: a substantial amount of action was built around the two upstage doors and the back room; the upstage wall was an important backdrop; and the proximity to the audience made quiet verbal exchanges possible.

Pite has attended many of Bingham's shows over the years and recognizes that "Peter's done everything there is to do in that space already and he's kind of over it." Nonetheless, she says,

In terms of the content of the piece, and specifically in terms of the emotional content, I felt I wanted to look at the time and place of Peter in that space, to capture the moment in time of him being there. I mean, yes, he's been there for over twenty years, but it's still just this little blink of time that he actually exists, and for me it was about trying to grasp that.

One day early on in the process, Bingham brought Mona Hamill's painting of a steep, centuries old, European street into the studio and suggested they use it as a set piece; he had spotted the canvas, which incorporates a vanishing point, in the back room where Hamill had set up a workplace. Bingham's intuition proved apt and the painting tied well into Pite's thoughts about time, place and perspective. She liked the way it expanded the borders of the room where Bingham had spent so many years creating, rehearsing and teaching, especially when she discovered he had never been to Europe; this brought Europe to him.

In the final scene, the studio is imaginatively transformed into the small European town suggested by Hamill's painting, but for the most part *Vanishing Point* is set very much in the present time and place. The piece begins with the pair gently warming up, discussing whether to start the piece formally or informally. They converse easily, and Pite tells the audience that she and Bingham have been dancing for the same length of time: both started dance classes in September 1975. That was when Bingham discovered Synergy and Pite, who was only four years old, began attending a dance school in Victoria, on Vancouver Island.

During a later scene, they exchange banter: "I can't see changing a diaper in this position," says Bingham, arms raised stiffly above his head and thrust back into the space behind him. "I can't see me robbing a bank in this position," adds Pite from the same awkward pose, and, later, "I can't see how we're going to save the world in this position." "I can't see much from this position," concludes Bingham. The real question might be about the role of art and the artist, but the work does not speak so directly.

The camaraderie between these accomplished artists, who chat to each other, to their filmed images and to the audience, was extraordinary, but their deepest communication was physical. In *Vanishing Point*, Bingham flows and spins with his signature elegance, while Pite moves with her usual intense waves of broken grace. At the end, the lighting casts dark shadows, a church bell tolls and a sad Scottish folk song is heard as the two lean toward each other in close conjunction and step delicately upstage, their feet tangling softly. It is one of the few times they actually touch; mostly, they dance side by side or take turns with solo work. While the lights slowly dim, there is an almost tangible communication between them: nothing so obvious as words or gestures, more a sweet animal awareness.

Bingham enjoyed a triumphant return to the Canada Dance Festival when he and Pite were invited to perform *Vanishing Point*. Ottawa's small Nouvelle Scène theatre, where they recreated the intimate Western Front studio, was full, and the air was electric throughout their performance, for which they received a standing ovation. Susan Macpherson, from her perspective as a senior modern dance artist based in Toronto, called *Vanishing Point* "the highlight of the 2006 Canada Dance Festival", describing the work as "funny, eloquent, poignant, thought-provoking, whimsical, endearing … and … brilliant." In an act of inspired showmanship and artistic integrity, Bingham and Pite made the philosophical musings of their dance seem as familiar and cosy as a favourite television show.

Peter Bingham.

Photo: Daniel Collins

A Man Dancing

Peter Bingham ... a contact improvisation legend from Vancouver....
— Deborah Jowitt, *The Village Voice*

Peter Bingham's identity as a dancer is the driving force behind everything he does. Even now, in his mid-fifties, Bingham continues to perform as an improviser long past the time when dance artists usually retire from the rigours of the stage. New adventures continually open up, such as his first trip to Europe. This was in the fall of 2006 to teach and to perform an improvisation in Italy with Charlotte Zerbey of Company Blu Danza. At this point in his life, Bingham explains, improvising for an hour in performance "is the most intense meditation you can imagine ... It's the most alive I ever feel."

In performance, Bingham is as graceful as ever, and still moves with extraordinary ease. The long, thin body has gained the inevitable solidity time quietly builds, but Bingham is trim and muscular, his skin usually brown from the sun, his dark, grey-tinged hair shaved close to the scalp, minimizing the smooth crown. After years of taking ibuprofen at the end of a performance to ensure he woke up the next morning without aches and pains, he now relies on his naturopathic doctor to keep him pain-free. Bingham had not visited a medical doctor for close to a decade until, during a naturopathic appointment in 2005, it was recommended he do so; a tumour was found but has since been declared benign. During recovery from surgery, he choreographed lying supported on a garden couch.

The fact that Bingham's first love is contact improvisation helps him to continue as a performer because this dance form does not favour precisely styled, light movement that always strives upward. In ballet, the downward motion of a plié will be as much about pulling up through the spine and the top of the head as it is about bending the knees and pushing down. Martha Graham, from the modern dance world, said: "My dancers fall *so they may rise.*" Bingham may fall in order to rise or he may fall in order to be on the ground. Moreover, as Bingham explains,

> *It's never just falling down. I would call it varied descents. I can let go and release into the floor in many ways. My body has travelled all those falling pathways. It understands them. I'm in control; I can change direction in the middle. I'm conscious all the way through.*

This state of consciousness is important to Bingham, and is something he learned in the early days from Steve Paxton. Writing in *Contact Quarterly* magazine, Paxton explains why full consciousness is crucial:

A blackout lasting fractions of a second during a roll is not acceptable as full consciousness of the roll, and the gap will remain embedded in the movement as part of the overall feeling of the movement. If consciousness stays open during these critical moments, it will have an experience of them, and will enlarge its concept to match the new experience. This expanded picture becomes the new ground for moving.

Bingham has spent his career developing full bodily consciousness, which is evident in the high state of alert physicality and presence he brings to his dance. The lively young man who enjoyed himself on stage and shared his pleasure with audiences has evolved into a knowledgeable, finely tuned performer with a wide repertoire of possibilities, and his expertise as a partner is legendary.

Bingham's partnering skills are key to his successful artistic practice because it is not only to other dancers that Bingham connects – it is also to audiences, to funders, to a whole range of individuals. His natural sense of camaraderie ensures there is never a shortage of colleagues and friends. He is a shy man, but not a solitary one, and dance is not a solitary act for him. After all, Bingham discovered dance by whirling around the living room with his grandmother. As a young man, he was an enthusiastic club dancer, the kind for whom people cleared the floor. At Synergy, when he first experienced dance as an art form, he learned the value of creating in community through improvising, something that was reinforced shortly after when he began practicing contact improvisation. So it is not surprising that connecting with others and expressing himself spontaneously remain critical to his dance.

One relationship Bingham has lacked is with a mentor. Bingham considers Paxton and Nancy Stark Smith to have been instrumental in his growth as an artist, but there has been no one closer to home – somebody who has seen all his work and is supportive of his vision and goals. What he has had is a loyal team behind him on both the administrative and creative sides, and with their support he continues to keep the EDAM studio hopping.

If being a dancer signifies the essence of Peter Bingham, his choreography is the formal expression of that essence. Looking back over his body of work, it is clear that the best of his creations contain the same sense of connection to others, and to space and time, that defines his own performance. Chick Snipper says of his contact-based choreography:

Do you know how complex that is at the psychological and emotional level? The dancers are lifting one another, they're sensing one another's timing, they're intimate – truly intimate – and that can be so challenging psychologically. Peter is managing that, and he's shuffling the dynamic and trying to get what he wants to happen. He's been doing it for years, so he's doing something right because people go back and work with him.

Snipper attributes Bingham's particular gift for making solos and duets to the fact that these more intimate forms are close to his psyche: "He understands, at a very profound level, the role of solos and the role of duets in life and in art." It is perhaps through the duet form that Bingham most consist-ently and effectively expresses himself, as in choreographed gems like *Cryptic Heart, Cross-fade* and *The Intimates*, as well as in structured improvisations like *Thirst* and *Vanishing Point.* Snipper agrees: "Peter really understands the nature of the

Peter Bingham and dog Jesse, 2000.

intimate duet. That's what he does when he's dancing with you and that's what he does with his work. It's also what he does in his personal life." Referencing his love life, she adds, "though maybe not for the long term."

The long-term relationship at which Bingham has excelled for more than thirty years is with dance. That is one affair that has lasted and thrived, though it has been as difficult and demanding as any great passion is. Dance has given him a clear and certain place in the world – something to do and to believe in; a calling, if you will – through which he has made an enormous impact on the Canadian cultural landscape.

Bingham continues to work, as he always has. There are no plans to stop, no thoughts of retiring. The act of creation is not easy to leave behind – why should anyone want to renounce a lifetime of hard-won knowledge and finely tuned skills? By following a philosophy of improvisational liveliness in life as in art, he remains ready for whatever opportunities arise.

So the next project continues to drive Bingham forward, whisking him out of the past and into the here and now of dance. That is where riches lie. Peter Bingham is a master of the present moment, as all great dancers are.

Forced Issues

NOVEMBER 23-24
JANUARY 25-26
MAY 3-4
A STUDIO SERIES
PUSHING
THE
BOUNDARIES
OF
DANCE
AND MUSIC

8 PM
EDAM
303 E. 8th
$6 at
the door

info
876-9559

AM gratefully acknowledges the financial support of Canada Council, Canada Employment
d Immigration, Government of British Columbia, City of Vancouver. 1990-91

Peter Bingham and Crystal Pite in *Vanishing Point*, 2005.

EDAM
presents
in association with
VANCOUVER INTERNATIONAL
DANCE vidf.ca
FESTIVAL
MARCH 1 - APRIL 2006

SLIP
SLIP
SLIP
SLIP

March
16–18
7 pm

Choreography
by
Peter Bingham

Performance
by
Delia Brett
Anne Cooper
Ali Robson
Monica Strehlke

Lighting
by
James Proudfoot

Roundhouse
Community Centre
181 Roundhouse Mews
Box Office : 604-662-4966

info@edamdance.org
www.edamdance.org

EDAM gratefully acknowledges the support of the Dance Section, Canada Council,
Government of British Columbia, through the BC Arts Council and the Gaming Branch,
The City of Vancouver, The Vancouver Foundation, and the Western Front.

BRITISH COLUMBIA ARTS COUNCIL   Canada Council for the Arts / Conseil des Arts du Canada   BRITISH COLUMBIA   VANCOUVER FOUNDATION

Chris Randle / 06

Steve Paxton and Helen Clarke in an improvisation at Western Front Lodge.

Photo: Chris Randle

Monica Strehlke and Jennifer McLeish Lewis in rehearsal for a remount of *Born Naked, Died Blonde*. Photo: Chris Randle

Peter Bingham in The Echo Case.   Photo: Chris Randle

List of Works by Peter Bingham

NOTE: For collaborations, the name of the co-choreographer or co-improviser follows the title.

2007
one thing after another
Point of no return with Ray Chung

2006
In the between
No give aways with Charlotte Zerbey
Quell with Lin Snelling
Signs of the time
silence before the bridge
Swerve with Ray Chung

2005
binary with Wen Wei Wang
Slip
Vanishing Point with Crystal Pite

2004
Baseline with Nancy Stark Smith
Interface with Lin Snelling and Helen Walkley
Murmurs

2003
Moment's Notice with Ray Chung
Thirst with Wen Wei Wang

2002
An Evening in Performance with Lin Snelling
Gridlock
Sinking Suzy Fong
Vuelta with Tom Stroud

2001
Body Narrative with Ray Chung and Susan Elliott
Heaven can wait … I'm busy right now

2001 (cont.)
Instinct Ensemble with Chris Aiken and Sandy Mathern Smith
Spinal Accord
Spiral Discord

2000
The Brain Waves, the Heart Bleeds, and the Body Parts
The Intimates
Free Trade with Chris Aiken
Free Trade with Chris Aiken and Andrew Harwood

1999
Hardfelt

1998
RELATIVITY: Men Creating Momentum with Chris Aiken
  and Andrew Harwood
Seeking Silent Ground
Through Someone Else's Eyes

1997
Bloom
Second Sight: broken wings remind them
woman walking (away)

1996
After the Wake
An Informal Evening of Dance Improvisation with Chris Aiken
Born Naked, Died Blonde: our roots exposed
Remember Me From Then with John Alleyne

1995
Hindsight
Magnet

1994
A Shadow of Myself
Crossfade
Hand Held (videodance directed by Hank Bull)
It always happens that way with peaceable people. One day they run amok.
  (quote from Henry Miller's *Tropic of Capricorn*)
Just Another Country Tune

1994 (cont.)
Solace
The Revengers

1993
Ode to John Angus B
Paisley
Present Tense with Ahmed Hassan
You Leave Me Breathless

1992
Dreamtigers
Etelka's Lament
Left Behind

1991
Never Facing East (ensemble)

1990
Highland
Imaga Mortis
Inside Out
Never Facing East (solo)
Plunge
Senseless
Spare Time Quartet
Tell a Tale

1989
Burnout
Critical Mass
Cryptic Heart

1988
Fear Thought
Perhaps if I Crawled

1986
Teller of Visions

1985
Chatterbox
Laughter is a Serious Affair with Peter Ryan

1985 (cont.)
Stuck on You with Lola MacLaughlin
Turbo Pascal with Barbara Bourget, Jay Hirabayashi, Lola MacLaughlin,
  Jennifer Mascall, Peter Ryan and Connie Schrader
XYZ with Peter Ryan

1984
Sui Generis with Peter Ryan

1983
All Flames are Waiting to Kill All Moths with Helen Clarke
  and Jennifer Mascall
Coming Out of Construction with Peter Ryan
Orbits with Jay Hirabayashi and Peter Ryan
Ray De Us (later *Radius*)
Reflect
Run Raw: Theme and Deviation with Barbara Bourget, Jay Hirabayashi,
  Lola MacLaughlin, Jennifer Mascall and Peter Ryan
Violators Will Be Towed Away
Wangarata Crawl

1977
Four Men Dancing with Andrew Harwood, Michael Linehan and Peter Ryan
Four on the Floor with Helen Clarke, Jane Ellison and Andrew Harwood
if two and two still = two all the rest is easy with Helen Clarke

List of Improvisation Ensembles

2001–2004
The Tuning Effect with Chris Aiken, Peter Bingham
and André Gribou (pianist)

1994–1997
Group Six with Chris Aiken, Peter Bingham, Jeff Bliss, Julie Carr,
Ray Chung and Nancy Stark Smith

1992–ongoing
The Echo Case with Peter Bingham, Marc Boivin, Andrew Harwood,
Coat Cooke (musician), Ron Samworth (musician) and Robert Meister
(lighting designer)

1977–1978
Fulcrum with Peter Bingham, Helen Clarke and Andrew Harwood

Source Notes

During the research for this book, I conducted over a dozen formal interviews with Peter Bingham between October 2001 and October 2005. I also interviewed him twice in August 2000 for my View From Vancouver column in *Dance International* magazine. The quotations found throughout are drawn from this material.

As well, I spoke with numerous other players in Peter Bingham's life story, some more than once. These interviews took place between the same 2001–2005 period, either in person, on the telephone or via email. These interviews are noted below.

Waltzing With Grandma

All quotations from Montague Bingham are from author interviews.

A Radical Time and Place

All quotations from Father Jim Roberts, Bruce Fraser, Linda Rubin, Daniel Collins and Jane Ellison are from author interviews.

"Here we are ...", Baba Ram Dass (a.k.a. Richard Alpert), *Be Here Now*, San Cristobal, New Mexico: Lama Foundation, 1971, p. 31, original in caps.

"In her jeans and sandals, leotard and bolero ...", Terry French, *The Province*, May 2, 1970.

"modern ballet company", Western Dance Theatre brochure, Norbert Vesak Portfolio, Dance Collection Danse.

"barely adequate for the job", Max Wyman, *The Vancouver Sun*, May 26, 1970.

"edges were ragged ...", James Barber, *The Province*, May 26, 1970.

"cheeky, bouncy eagerness ...", Max Wyman, *The Vancouver Sun*, undated.

"selected staff of experienced instructors", West Vancouver Studio of Dance and the Allied Arts brochure, Norbert Vesak Portfolio, Dance Collection Danse.

"a lumpy, uneven presentation", Max Wyman, *The Vancouver Sun*, February 13, 1971.

"based on the premise that ...", "Synergy Studios Open", *Westender*, September 30, 1971.

"The first room you enter ...", Peter Clements, *The Georgia Straight*, Spring, 1972.

"depressed and disappointed", Max Wyman, *The Vancouver Sun*, January 29, 1972.

"fun", James Barber, *The Province*, January 29, 1972.

"very sloshy, very obvious....", James Barber, *The Province*, undated, Linda Rubin archives.

First Contact

All quotations from Michael Linehan, Linda Rubin, Andrew Harwood and Peter Ryan are from author interviews, unless otherwise noted.

"Sometimes, I think that ...", Elizabeth Zimmer, *YVR* magazine, March 1978.

"an avant-garde dancer named Steve Paxton", Elizabeth Zimmer, *The Vancouver Courier*, November 25, 1976.

"homespun ...", Peter Ryan quoted in *Sharing the Dance: Contact Improvisation and American Culture*, Cynthia J. Novack, Wisconsin: The University of Wisconsin Press, 1990, pp. 209-210.

"viewed the experience of ...", Cynthia J. Novack, *Sharing the Dance*, op. cit., p. 11.

"Contact improvisation is a ...", poster for *The Dance Dojo*, Michael Linehan personal archives.

"An evening of ...", poster for *Four Men Dancing*, Michael Linehan personal archives.

"After an opening meditation ...", Elizabeth Zimmer, typed photocopy of article for *Contact Quarterly*, undated, Michael Linehan personal archives.

"Fulcrum aims for ...", poster for Fulcrum, EDAM company archives.

"began with an obviously rehearsed ...", Elizabeth Zimmer, *YVR*, March 1978.

"Contact improvisation is no ...", *The Vancouver Sun*, February 6, 1978.

"Fulcrum ... is not only one of ...", Stephen Godfrey, *The Globe and Mail*, October 19, 1978.

"One misses the variations in ...", Stephen Godfrey, *The Globe and Mail*, May 24, 1980.

Listing in Voice Choices, *The Village Voice*, April 1978, Michael Linehan personal archives.

"Any chance you may relocate ...", Jennifer Dunning, letter to Michael Linehan, May 8, 1978, Michael Linehan personal archives.

Making EDAM

All quotations from Barbara Clausen, Daniel Collins, Karen Jamieson, Jennifer Mascall, Lola MacLaughlin, Jay Hirabayashi, Lee Masters, Peter Ryan and Mark Lavelle are from author interviews.

"a blending of dance, drama and ...", Meredith Yearsley, *Vandance*, Summer 1982.

"a tour de force of ...", Selma Landen Odom, *Dance Magazine*, November 1982.

"a silent, intense working-together ...", Max Wyman, *The Province*, May 1982.

"Most of us had worked together ...", Barbara Bourget, Letter to the Canada Council, September 8, 1983, Jay Hirabayashi personal archives.

"We intend our organization ...", ibid.

"sense of explosive energy ...", Max Wyman, *The Province*, February 25, 1983.

"We intend to utilize ...", Canada Council funding application, September 10, 1982, EDAM company archives.

"*Run Raw* begins with a variation ...", Susan Mertens, *The Vancouver Sun*, undated clipping, EDAM company archives.

"There's an Olympian nobility ...", Max Wyman, *The Province*, May 31, 1983.

"drove themselves literally ...", Max Wyman, *The Province*, June 8, 1983.

"... the work accomplished a number ...", Canada Council Explorations Project, Final Report, September 1983, Athletic Aesthetics in Dance, EDAM company archives.

Coming and Going in the Garden of EDAM

All quotations from Jennifer Mascall, Jane Ellison, Sheenah Andrews, Peter Ryan, Lola MacLaughlin and Jay Hirabayashi are from author interviews.

"'pioneer' false front façade....", Keith Wallace, Ed. *Whispered Art History: Twenty Years at the Western Front*, Vancouver: Arsenal Pulp Press, 1993, pp. 1–2.

"Willoughby Sharp, a performance artist ...", Peg Campbell, "Cineworks Beginnings (A Personal Chronology)" in *Cineworks 2000: Twenty Years of Independent Filmmaking in British Columbia*, ed. Justin MacGregor, Vancouver: Cineworks Independent Filmmakers Society, p. 9.

"fabulously successful", *The Newfoundland Herald*, Philip Hicks, March 17, 1984.

"the most absorbing works ...", *The London Gazette*, Shelley Long, February 28, 1984.

"This is a group of ...", Linda Rimsay, *Daily News*, undated clipping in EDAM company archives.

"... the policy of the Canada Council ...", Peter Ryan, *Dance Connection*, September/October 1995, p. 22.

"It is a pleasure ...", Deborah Meyers, *Vandance*, Autumn 1984, p. 24.

"high degree of general ...", Charles Pope, *The Ottawa Citizen*, March 15, 1985.

"EDAM is perhaps the country's most …", Deirdre Kelly, *The Globe and Mail*, undated clipping in EDAM archives.

"the look of contact improvisation …", William Littler, *The Toronto Star*, March 11, 1985.

"a relatively low tolerance level …", Jay Hirabayashi, letter of resignation, May 9, 1984, Jay Hirabayashi personal archives.

"the kind that I'm really sick of …", Jay Hirabayashi, letter to EDAM, May 14, 1984, Jay Hirabayashi personal archives.

"I do not think that EDAM …", Jay Hirabayashi, letter to Jennifer Mascall and Ahmed Hassan, May 16, 1984, Jay Hirabayashi personal archives.

"there was a marvelous feeling of unity …", Agnes Stevens, *The Vancouver Courier*, May 30, 1984.

"found some of it surprisingly …", Max Wyman, *The Province*, May 27, 1984.

"Peter Bingham … trapped …", Alanna Matthew, undated clipping in EDAM company archives.

"a rapid-fire rhythmical talk …", Agnes Stevens, *The Vancouver Courier*, September 1984, EDAM company archives.

"strongly danced", Agnes Stevens, *The Vancouver Courier*, September 1984, EDAM company archives.

"[Peter Bingham] is an impassive and rigid …", Deborah Meyers, *Vandance*, Autumn 1984.

"The initial three minute section …", Jay Hirabayashi, CV, 1999, Jay Hirabayashi personal archives.

"… just how skilled these individuals …", Max Wyman, *The Province*, undated clipping, EDAM archives.

"great sense of comic timing", Agnes Stevens, *The Vancouver Courier*, undated clipping, EDAM company archives.

"made vital by their all-risks-accepted …", *The Vancouver Sun*, unsigned review, September 8, 1984.

"demonstrate the complexities of laughter …", Colleen Fee, *Vanguard*, published by the Vancouver Art Gallery, December 1987/January 1988.

"an indictment of television …", Susan Mertens, *The Vancouver Sun*, June 29, 1985.

"to the interests of efficiency and control", Jennifer Mascall, Lola MacLaughlin and Peter Ryan, "EDAM as a Cooperative: A Statement of Position", Jay Hirabayashi personal archives.

"EDAM has never been a cooperative….", Jay Hirabayashi, Letter, July 21, 1985, Jay Hirabayashi personal archives.

"My proposal …", Jay Hirabayashi, Proposal to EDAM Board of Directors, Jay Hirabayashi personal archives.

"hypnotic, pristine form of improvisation …", Stephen Godfrey, *The Globe and Mail*, February 8, 1986.

"The value of EDAM's influence …", Jamil Brownson, *Dance in Canada*, Summer 1986.

"stress having polished works …", Barbara Bourget and Jay Hirabayashi, Letter to Monique Michaud at the Canada Council for the Arts, May 12, 1986, Jay Hirabayashi personal archives.

And Then There Were Four

All videos referred to are part of the EDAM company archives.

All quotations from Jennifer Mascall, Daniel Collins and Jane Ellison are from author interviews.

"You let yourself go …", Patricia Ludwick, *Peter Pan in Neverland: The Adventures of Peter Pan and Wendy*, video recording of EDAM and Tamahnous Theatre 1986 co-production.

"a multi-media performance collage …", flyer, EDAM archives.

"Even more mind-boggling …", Renée Doruyter, *The Province*, November 16, 1986.

"a novel-sized book", Agnes Stevens, *The Vancouver Courier*, November 19, 1986.

"served up enough self-indulgent …", Michael Scott, *The Vancouver Sun*, January 16, 1988.

"shorter, faster-moving …", Agnes Stevens, *The Vancouver Courier*, January 20, 1988.

"… the visual chaos …", Raewyn Whyte, *The Georgia Straight*, January 22-29, 1988.

"a potpourri of modern …", Gordon Armstrong, CHQM Radio, May 10, 1985, written transcript, EDAM company archives.

"multi-media choreographic trend", Alanna Matthew, *Vandance*, Spring 1989.

"far-out, groovy new headspaces", Susan Inman, *Dance Update*, Vol. 2, No. 3, 1989, Vancouver: The Dance Centre.

"blazed triumphantly", Olivia Zanger, *The Ubyssey*, February 3, 1989, Vancouver: University of British Columbia.

Gift of a Lifetime

All videos referred to are part of the EDAM company archives.

All quotations from Jaci Metivier, Lola MacLaughlin, Chris Randle, Serge Bennathan and Mary Craig are from author interviews unless otherwise noted.

"EDAM's daring spirit", *The Province* headline, December 3, 1989.

"the eight-part evening was …", Max Wyman, *The Province*, December 3, 1989.

"creating an astonishingly …", Max Wyman, *The Province*, April 16, 1990.

"This version, danced in …", ibid.

"The full house of over 200 …", Mary Jane MacLennan, *Winnipeg Free Press*, May 28, 1990.

"frankly erotic", Deborah Meyers, *Vandance*, Summer 1991.

"dazzling", Max Wyman, *The Province*, April 11, 1991.

"generosity", Deborah Meyers, *Vandance*, Summer 1991.

"heavily into experiment …", Max Wyman, *The Province*, April 5, 1991.

Dreamtigers

All videos referred to are part of the EDAM company archives.

All quotations from Gina Sufrin, Coat Cooke, Mona Hamill and Mark Lavelle are from author interviews.

All quotations from Jorge Luis Borges are from *Dreamtigers*, translated by Mildred Boyer and Harold Morland, Copyright © 1964, renewed 1992. By permission of the University of Texas Press.

"as alive and assertive …", letter to Cathy Levy, Canada Dance Festival producer, August 7, 1991, EDAM company archives.

"If the depths of our mind …", *Manifestoes of Surrealism*, by André Breton, Ann Arbor: University of Michigan Press, 1972, p. 10.

"new alliance", Guillaume Apollinaire, from program for *Parade*, found in *Modernism: An Anthology of Sources and Documents*, Vassiliki Kolocotroni, Jane Goldman and Olga Taxidou, eds., Chicago: University of Chicago Press, 1998, p. 211.

"Mysterious movements …", *The Sun*, May 7, 1992.

"Dreamtigers fascinating multi-media …", *The Province*, May 7, 1992.

"Dancers fly in …", *The Georgia Straight*, May 15-22, 1992.

"a work that reads like the colours …", Patrick Cook, *Vandance International*, Summer 1992.

"As you can tell …", Peter Bingham, letter to Cathy Levy, Canada Dance Festival producer, August 7, 1991.

"Dancing a sticky web of tedium", Robert Everett-Green, *The Globe and Mail*, June 2, 1992.

"The biggest mistake …", Renée Laurin, *Le Droit*, original in French, translated by Jessie Pepper, undated clipping in EDAM company archives.

"rehabilitate", Marcel Duchamp quoted in *Surrealists on Art*, edited by Lucy R. Lippard, Englewood Cliffs, N.J.: Prentice-Hall, Inc. 1970, p. 113.

Just People Dancing

All videos referred to are part of the EDAM company archives.

All quotations from Kathleen McDonagh are from author interviews.

"Art should not be different …", John Cage quoted in *Legacies of Twentieth-Century Dance*, Lynn Garafola, Middletown, Connecticut: Wesleyan University Press, 2005, p. 249.

"In the varied repertoire …", Penelope Reed Doob, *The Globe and Mail*, April 15, 1993.

"The program … showed …", Michael Crabb, *The Toronto Star*, April 16, 1993.

"the spring-autumn look of …", Max Wyman, "Notebook", *Dance International*, Spring, 1994.

"They're kneeling when …", ibid.

A Case for Improvisation

All videos referred to are part of the EDAM company archives.

All quotations from Jaci Metivier, Kathleen McDonagh, Gina Sufrin, Marc Boivin and Nancy Stark Smith are from author interviews.

"Not repeated tonight", Pamela Anthony, *The Edmonton Journal*, February 27, 1999.

"Improvisation is … a way of …", Ann Cooper Albright and David Gere, excerpt from *Taken By Surprise: A Dance Improvisation Reader* © 1988 by Wesleyan University Press and reprinted by permission of Wesleyan University Press, p. 259.

"a chance to glance at …", Steve Paxton quoted in *Sharing the Dance: Contact Improvisation and American Culture*, Cynthia J. Novack, Wisconsin: The University of Wisconsin Press, 1990, p. 190.

"a risky and/or organic …", Ramsay Burt, *The Male Dancer: Bodies, Spectacles, Sexuality*, London and New York: Routledge, 1995, p. 154.

"this kind of physical proximity …", ibid., p. 154.

"Inward listening refers to …", Marc Boivin, EDAM Summer Intensive 2003: Technical training and interpretation seminar, p. 21.

"Andrew is a mystery to me …", Robert Meister, *The Dance Current*, October 2004.

"The natural unfolding of …", Pamela Anthony, *Edmonton Journal*, February 27, 1999.

"Most importantly, the performance …", Janet French, *Gazette*, March 25, 1999.

"… the dancers demonstrated a …", Stephen Pedersen, *Chronicle-Herald*, March 23, 1999.

"Good improvisation can give …", Rebecca Todd, *Eye Weekly*, March 11, 1999.

"I started speaking while …", Simone Forti, "Animate Dancing", *Taken by Surprise*, op. cit., p. 57.

Remember Me From Then

All quotations from John Alleyne, Anne Cooper, Wen Wei Wang and Sylvain Senez are from author interviews.

"… this single moment …", Octavio Paz, *Sun stone* in *Selected Poems, Octavio Paz*, ed. Eliot Weinberger, New York: New Directions Publishing Corp., 1984.

Born Naked, Died Blonde

All quotations from Daelik, Susan Elliott, Coat Cooke, Kathleen McDonagh and Chick Snipper are from author interviews.

"… I keep the television on …", Robert Rauschenberg, *Rauschenberg*, New York: Vintage Books, Random House, 1987, p. 72.

"The meaning of a word …", Georgia O'Keefe, "Reflecting on Why I Am an Artist", *Women, Creativity, and the Arts: Critical and Autobiographical Perspectives*, eds. Diana Apostolos-Cappadena and Lucinda Ebersole, New York: Continuum, 1995, p. 141.

"cells or sections …", Ron Samworth and Coat Cooke, letter to Ms. Brydon, Colleagues, and Members of the Jury, part of application to the BC Music Commissioning Awards Program, April 26, 1996, EDAM company archives.

"[Balanchine] always went for the natural …", Patricia McBride, *I Remember Balanchine: Recollections of the Ballet Master by Those Who Knew Him*, Francis Mason, New York: Anchor Books, Doubleday, 1992, p. 441.

"do something", Marian Horosko, ibid., p. 369.

A Simple Act of Balance

All quotations from Mona Hamill, Chris Randle, Daelik and Jaci Metivier are from author interviews.

"I just dance …", Fred Astaire, author's notebook.

"real physical intimacy …", Michael Scott, *The Vancouver Sun*, March 25, 2000.

"a tiny, perfect …", Louise Phillips, *The Vancouver Courier*, March 22, 2000.

"The experience of balance …", Mark Johnson, *The Body in the Mind: The Bodily Basis of Meaning, Imagination, and Reason*, Chicago: The University of Chicago Press, 1987, p. 74.

Vuelta

All quotations from Tom Stroud are from author interviews.

"willow of crystal …", Octavio Paz, *Sun stone* in *Selected Poems, Octavio Paz*, ed. Eliot Weinberger, New York: New Directions Publishing Corp., 1984.

"the moment [that] scatters …", ibid.

"a beautiful partner …", Gail Johnson, *The Georgia Straight*, September 12-19, 2002.

"a wonderful moment", Garth Buchholz, *The Winnipeg Free Press*, May 1, 2003.

"… goes curving …", Octavio Paz, *Sun stone*, op. cit.

Deserving Isadora

All quotations from Wen Wei Wang, Brian Webb, Chick Snipper and Susan Elliott are from author interviews.

"Rather abide …", Lao-Tzu, author's notebook.

"two superbly trained bodies …", Paula Citron, *The Globe and Mail*, November 26, 2005.

"one of the most serene …", *The Globe and Mail*, October 19, 1978.

"You'd be standing next to Peter …", Sarah Baumert, interview with author, June 2003.

This Particular Place

All quotations from Susan Elliott, Jane Ellison, Crystal Pite and Chick Snipper are from author interviews.

"A room of his own", adapted by the author from the title of a book by Virginia Woolf, *A Room of One's Own*, 1929.

"funny, eloquent, poignant …", Susan Macpherson, email to author, October 15, 2006.

A Man Dancing

"Peter Bingham … a contact improvisation …", Deborah Jowitt, *The Village Voice*, December 12-18, 2001.

"My dancers fall …", Martha Graham, "A Modern Dancer's Primer for Action," *The Dance Anthology*, ed. Cobbett Steinberg, New York: New American Library, 1980, p. 52, italics in original.

"A blackout lasting fractions …", Steve Paxton, "Drafting Interior Techniques", *Taken by Surprise*, op. cit., p. 177. Originally in *Contact Quarterly* 18, no. 1, Winter-Spring 1993, pp. 61-66.

Index

A

After the Wake 131, 178
Aiken, Chris 122, 123, 124, 157, 158, 178, 180
Albert, Mary-Louise 143, 144
Alleyne, John vii, 125, 126, 127, 129, 130, 133, 168, 178, 190
All Flames are Waiting to Kill All Moths 44, 180
Ankle On (Steve Paxton) 66
Arithmetic and Calculus (Serge Bennathan) 83, 84
Armstrong, Kay 2, 13
Around Nine 26, 29, 30

B

Bach to the Future 67
Ballet British Columbia 83, 125, 126, 127, 128, 157, 160, 168
Ballet B.C.: *See* Ballet British Columbia
Bamboula (Leonard Gibson) 2
Bennathan, Serge vii, 83, 84, 88, 126, 187
Bingham, Bruce 1, 5, 7, 8, 9, 10, 98, 131
Bingham, Dan 1, 5, 6, 7, 9, 10
Bingham, Etelka 1, 2, 3, 4, 5, 6, 7, 8, 9, 131, 132, 138
Bingham, John 3, 4, 5, 7, 10, 36, 37, 98, 102, 103, 107, 108, 109, 132, 138
Bingham, Montague vii, 1, 2, 3, 4, 5, 6, 7, 8, 9, 10, 181
Bingham, Nora 3, 4, 5, 6, 7, 8, 131
Blakley, Wilson 104, 105, 106, 107, 108
Boivin, Marc vii, 118, 119, 120, 131, 157, 163, 180, 189, 190
Borges, Jorge Luis 91, 94, 145, 152, 188
Born Naked, Died Blonde 133, 135, 138, 139, 142, 143, 145, 178
Bourget, Barbara 38, 41, 43, 44, 47, 48, 49, 57, 58, 59, 61, 64, 65, 67, 68, 74, 81, 180, 183, 186

Brain Waves, the Heart Bleeds, and the Body Parts, The (*The Brain Waves*) 147, 148, 149, 178
Brett, Delia 148, 149, 151, 154, 155
Brochu, Sylvain 84
Broken Up (Jennifer Mascall) 36, 41
Burnout 75, 76, 78, 179
Burr, Elizabeth 84, 85, 87, 88

C

Canada Dance Festival 73, 93, 97, 156, 161, 171, 188
Chatterbox 64, 69, 70, 179
Chung, Ray 122, 123, 124, 157, 177, 180
Clarke, Helen vii, 21, 22, 26, 29, 30, 31, 34, 35, 36, 44, 45, 159, 180
Clausen, Barbara vii, 37, 40, 88, 183
Cole, Gisa 18, 34
Collins, Daniel vii, 20, 21, 23, 37, 78, 181, 183, 186
Coming Out of Chaos (Karen Jamieson) 36, 38, 39, 40, 41, 43
Cooke, Coat vii, 75, 95, 96, 98, 100, 120, 124, 133, 134, 135, 136, 137, 147, 148, 180, 188, 190, 191
Cooper, Anne vii, 110, 111, 124, 127, 128, 129, 130, 135, 141, 151, 155, 161, 162, 190
Corness, Jeff 71, 76, 77, 78
Craig, Mary vii, 21, 67, 71, 76, 77, 83, 84, 87, 187
Crisp, Rosalind 105, 107, 109
Critical Mass 76, 77, 78, 93, 179
Crossfade 109, 111, 145, 175, 178
Cryptic Heart 80, 81, 83, 84, 87, 88, 91, 98, 125, 141, 145, 149, 175, 179
Cyril, Alexandra (Alex) 127, 130, 135, 141

D

Daelik vii, 112, 113, 131, 136, 141, 147, 148, 149, 190, 191

Damiano, Philippe (Pipo) 84, 87, 91, 97, 99, 112, 115

Dance, Stuff and Nonsense (Barbara Bourget, Jay Hirabayashi and Lola MacLaughlin) 64, 74

Deeble, Chantal 91, 124

de Jesus, Eclilson Matiais 91, 95, 101

Dobbs, Allan 84, 97

Dreamtigers 91, 92, 93, 94, 95, 96, 97, 98, 99, 100, 101, 102, 103, 104, 105, 107, 124, 134, 145, 179, 188

Drysdale, Scott 84, 87

E

Echo Case, The 115, 118, 119, 120, 121, 157, 180

EDAM (Experimental Dance and Music) x, xi, 21, 37, 40, 41, 42, 43, 44, 46, 47, 48, 49, 51, 53, 54, 55, 56, 57, 58, 59, 60, 61, 62, 63, 64, 65, 66, 67, 68, 69, 70, 71, 73, 74, 78, 79, 80, 81, 82, 83, 87, 90, 95, 96, 97, 98, 102, 103, 104, 105, 106, 109, 112, 115, 117, 118, 119, 120, 122, 124, 125, 126, 127, 128, 129, 130, 131, 134, 141, 142, 145, 148, 151, 153, 155, 157, 159, 163, 166, 167, 168, 170, 174, 183, 184, 185, 186, 187, 188, 189, 190, 191

Elliott, Susan vii, 84, 85, 87, 88, 91, 99, 101, 111, 112, 113, 124, 127, 130, 135, 136, 137, 141, 157, 163, 167, 177, 190, 192

Ellison, Jane vii, 21, 23, 24, 40, 51, 52, 55, 78, 167, 180, 181, 184, 186, 192

Etelka's Lament 138, 179

Étude (Kay Armstrong) 2

F

Florin, Peggy vii, 34, 43

Forti, Simone 122, 190

Fulcrum 30, 31, 32, 33, 34, 35, 37, 69, 118, 145, 159, 180, 183

G

Gagnon, Noam 76, 80

Gilbert, Gerry 52, 63, 64, 77

Gingras, Dana 76, 77, 80, 82

Gradauer, Gerry 103, 104, 107, 108, 109

Gridlock 155, 177

Group Six 123, 180

H

Hall, Jeff 87, 88

Hamill, Mona vii, 84, 95, 96, 98, 99, 100, 102, 143, 145, 170, 188, 191

Harwood, Andrew (de Lotbinière) vii, 21, 22, 26, 27, 29, 30, 32, 33, 34, 35, 97, 118, 119, 120, 131, 157, 159, 163, 178, 180, 182

Hassan, Ahmed 37, 40, 41, 42, 43, 44, 47, 58, 59, 60, 63, 65, 97, 104, 107, 179, 185

Highland 88, 179

Hindsight 112, 113, 125, 136, 149, 178

Hirabayashi, Jay vii, 36, 41, 42, 43, 44, 45, 46, 47, 48, 49, 51, 57, 58, 59, 60, 61, 62, 65, 66, 67, 68, 180, 183, 184, 185, 186

Hunter, Terry 34, 38, 40

I

if two and two still = two all the rest is easy 22, 180

Imaga Mortis 84, 86, 87, 88, 91, 95, 179

Inside Out 84, 88, 97, 179

Intimates, The 147, 148, 149, 150, 175, 178

Itri, Isabelle 128, 129

J

Jag Ville Görna Telefonera (Steve Paxton) 60, 61

Jamieson, Karen vii, 34, 37, 38, 39, 40, 42, 43, 47, 66, 73, 78, 161, 183

Just Another Country Tune 111, 178

K

Kuchenbuch, Markus 104, 107, 109

L

Labelle, Katherine 84

Laughter is a Serious Affair 62, 64, 66, 158, 179

Lavelle, Mark vii, 46, 75, 76, 77, 81, 83, 84,
    87, 91, 99, 100, 112, 115, 183, 188
Left Behind 103, 105, 109, 179
Léger, Monique vii, 46, 47, 71
Lewis, Maria 34
Linehan, Michael (Seamus) vii, 21, 25, 27,
    28, 29, 30, 33, 34, 75, 180, 182, 183
Lloyd, Gweneth 3

M

Macanulty, David 88, 95, 96, 103
MacLaughlin, Lola vii, 37, 40, 41, 42, 43, 44,
    47, 48, 55, 57, 58, 60, 61, 65, 66, 68,
    69, 73, 78, 79, 87, 128, 180, 183, 184,
    186, 187
Magnet 125, 136, 178
Marcuse, Judith 34, 66, 83, 86, 128, 157
Mascall, Jennifer vii, 32, 36, 38, 39, 40, 41,
    42, 43, 44, 47, 48, 51, 53, 58, 59, 60, 61,
    64, 65, 66, 67, 68, 69, 71, 73, 74, 78, 87,
    180, 183, 184, 185, 186
Masters, Lee vii, 46, 71, 163, 183
McDonagh, Kathleen vii, 105, 106, 107,
    108, 109, 110, 111, 117, 124, 127, 130,
    134, 135, 138, 139, 141, 142, 189, 190
Meister, Robert 62, 71, 120, 180, 190
Metivier, Jaci vii, 71, 74, 75, 76, 77, 78, 79,
    80, 81, 82, 84, 85, 87, 88, 90, 91, 97, 99,
    102, 105, 117, 149, 187, 189, 191
Miller, Dianne 43, 87
Movement Piece No. 1 (Linda Rubin) 15

N

Never Facing East 88, 179
*Neverland: The Adventures of Peter Pan and
    Wendy* (*Neverland*) 69, 74, 186
Night in the Garden of EDAM, A 59, 81

O

Ode to John Angus B 107, 108, 109, 113,
    138, 179
Orbits 46, 180
Ottmann, John 127, 128, 130

P

Paisley 107, 179

Parenthesis (Norbert Vesak) 14
Paxton, Steve 25, 26, 28, 34, 52, 60, 61, 66,
    97, 117, 122, 173, 174, 182, 189, 192
Paz, Octavio 125, 145, 151, 152, 153, 154,
    156, 190, 191, 192
Pite, Crystal vii, 129, 155, 168, 169, 170,
    171, 177, 192
Plunge 84, 85, 91, 107, 179
Present Tense 106, 179
Psychobabble (Ahmed Hassan) 59

R

Radius (originally *Ray De Us*) 44, 180
Randle, Chris vii, 11, 12, 45, 56, 70, 72, 77,
    90, 95, 97, 98, 99, 101, 104, 106, 108,
    110, 119, 134, 144, 145, 149, 158, 169,
    187, 191
Ray De Us (later *Radius*) 44, 45, 46, 53, 180
Reflect 44, 45, 180
Rehak, Gabriela 151, 155
Remember Me From Then 125, 128, 129, 130,
    131, 133, 143, 157, 160, 178
Revengers, The 111, 179
Ricketts, Kathryn 61
Ross, Paula 14, 17, 21, 32, 34, 36, 38, 41, 43,
    49, 66
Rubin, Linda vii, 13, 14, 15, 16, 17, 18, 19,
    20, 21, 22, 23, 25, 30, 35, 51, 67, 181,
    182
Run Raw: Theme and Deviation (*Run Raw*)
    47, 48, 49, 53, 69, 180, 184
Ryan, Peter vii, 21, 22, 25, 26, 29, 30, 34, 35,
    37, 39, 40, 41, 42, 43, 44, 46, 47, 53, 54,
    56, 57, 58, 60, 61, 62, 63, 64, 65, 66, 67,
    68, 69, 70, 72, 73, 78, 158, 163, 179,
    180, 182, 183, 184, 186

S

Samworth, Ron 75, 95, 96, 120, 124, 133,
    134, 135, 136, 147, 180, 191
See Me, Feel Me, Touch Me (Linda Rubin)
    16
Senez, Sylvain vii, 127, 128, 129, 190
Senseless 88, 179
Seymour, Lynn 15

Shadow of Myself, A 110, 111, 178

Smith, Nancy Stark vii, 25, 28, 34, 122, 123, 124, 157, 174, 177, 180, 189

Snelling, Lin 157, 177

Snipper, Chick vii, 71, 142, 161, 162, 168, 174, 175, 190, 192

Software (Linda Rubin) 18, 19

Spare Time Quartet 84, 85, 88, 91, 179

Stewart, Ron 151

Still Bound to Earth (I Refused) (*Still Bound to Earth*) (Jennifer Mascall) 60

Stroud, Tom vii, 151, 152, 153, 154, 155, 156, 177, 191

Stuck on You 66, 180

Sufrin, Gina vii, 91, 98, 100, 102, 117, 188, 189

Synergy 13, 17, 18, 20, 21, 22, 23, 24, 25, 28, 30, 35, 46, 67, 71, 75, 89, 118, 151, 171, 174, 182

T

Tell a Tale 88, 179

Teller of Visions 69, 70, 72, 73, 74, 79, 93, 97, 179

Terminal City Dance Research 34, 37, 40, 41, 44

Thirst 157, 158, 159, 169, 175, 177

Trudeau, Dawn 70, 76, 77

Tuning Effect, The 157, 158, 180

V

Vanishing Point 168, 169, 170, 171, 175, 177

Vesak, Norbert 13, 14, 15, 16, 17, 18, 181

Vuelta 151, 153, 154, 155, 156, 157, 177, 191

W

Walkley, Helen 157, 177

Walling, Savannah vii, 34, 37, 38, 40

Wang, Wen Wei vii, 127, 128, 129, 130, 155, 157, 158, 159, 160, 161, 168, 177, 190, 192

Wangarata Crawl 44, 45, 180

Western Dance Theatre 15, 16, 17, 18, 181

Western Front 19, 20, 21, 22, 29, 30, 32, 37, 40, 41, 43, 46, 48, 51, 52, 53, 59, 63, 66, 115, 122, 167, 171, 184

Wild, Dan 30, 151, 154, 155

woman walking (away) 143, 144, 145, 178

Wright, Chris 136

Wyman, Anna 14, 17, 32, 34, 57, 66

X

XYZ 56, 57, 60, 63, 180

Y

You Leave Me Breathless 105, 106, 179

Z

Zagar, Mirna 161

Zagoudakis, Jamie 18, 34

DANCE COLLECTION DANSE PRESS/PRESSE 1989-2008

Spotlight Newsletters 1951-1956 by Bernadette Carpenter, 1989 (e-publication)

Dancing for de Basil – Letters to her Parents from Rosemary Deveson edited by Leland Windreich, 1989 (e-publication)

Just Off Stage # 1, 2: Selected stories from Canadian dance history by multiple authors, 1990 (e-publication)

Encyclopedia of Theatre Dance in Canada by Jill Officer, 1990 (e-publication)

Did She Dance: Maud Allan in Performance by Felix Cherniavsky, 1991 (e-publication)

From the Point: National Ballet of Canada Newsletters 1950's -1970, 1991 (e-publication)

Jean-Pierre Perreault Choreographer edited by Aline Gélinas, 1992

Moon Magic: Gail Grant and the 1920's Dance in Regina by Karen Rennie, 1992

Judy Jarvis Dance Artist: A Portrait by Carol Anderson, 1993

Form Without Formula: A concise guide to the choreographic process by Patricia Beatty, 1994

Cecchetti: A Ballet Dynasty by Livia Brillarelli, 1995

Spotlight Newsletters, 1951-1956 by Bernadette Carpenter, 1995

Toronto Dance Teachers 1825-1925 by Mary Jane Warner, 1995

Dictionary of Dance: Words, Terms and Phrases edited by Susan Macpherson, 1996

Dancing for de Basil – Letters to her Parents from Rosemary Deveson edited by Leland Windreich, 1996

Guide to Career Training in the Dance Arts by Grant Strate, 1996

101 from the Encyclopedia of Theatre Dance in Canada edited by Susan Macpherson, 1997

China Dance Journal by Grant Strate, 1997

This Passion: for the love of dance compiled and edited by Carol Anderson, 1998

Dictionary of Classical Ballet Terms – Cecchetti by Rhonda Ryman, 1998

Dance Encounters: Leland Windreich Writing on Dance by Leland Windreich, 1998

Chasing the Tale of Contemporary Dance Parts 1 & 2 by Carol Anderson, 1999 & 2002

Maud Allan and Her Art by Felix Cherniavsky, 1999

June Roper: Ballet Starmaker by Leland Windreich, 1999

Encyclopedia of Theatre Dance in Canada/ Encyclopédie de la Danse Théâtrale au Canada edited by Susan Macpherson, 2000

Theatrical Dance in Vancouver, 1880's-1920's by Kaija Pepper, 2000

Express Dance: Educators' Resource for Teaching Dance – Grades 4-12 by Carol Oriold, Allen Kaeja and Karen Kaeja, 2000

Revealing Dance by Max Wyman, 2001

The Dance Teacher: A Biography of Kay Armstrong by Kaija Pepper, 2001

Estivale 2000: Canadian Dancing Bodies Then and Now/ Estivale 2000 : Les Corps dansants d'hier à aujourd'hui, edited by Iro Valaskakis Tembeck, 2002

Grant Strate: A Memoir by Grant Strate, 2002

An Instinct for Success: Arnold Spohr and the Royal Winnipeg Ballet by Michael Crabb, 2002

From Automatism to Modern Dance: Françoise Sullivan with Franziska Boas in New York by Allana Lindgren, 2003

DanceForms 1.0 Software for Visualizing and Chronicling Choreography: A Practical Guide by Rhonda Ryman with Lawrence Adams, 2003

Building Your Legacy: An Archiving Handbook for Dance by Lawrence Adams, 2004

Canadian Dance: Visions and Stories edited by Selma Landen Odom and Mary Jane Warner, 2004

David Earle: A Choreographic Biography by Michele Green, 2006

Coleman Lemieux & Compagnie Reconstructing/La reprise de Fifteen Heterosexual Duets by/de James Kudelka, 2006

Betty Oliphant: The Artistry of Teaching - A Series of Ballet Classes by Nadia Potts; DanceForms Illustrations by Rhonda Ryman, 2007

The Man Next Door Dances: The Art of Peter Bingham by Kaija Pepper, 2007

Unfold: A Portrait of Peggy Baker by Carol Anderson, 2008